Jungle
Janes

Jungle Janes

by peter burden

PUBLISHED BY TravellersEye

Jungle Janes

1st Edition

Published by TravellersEye Ltd, January 2001

Head Office:

    The Outbuildings

    Colemore Farm

    Colemore Green

    Bridgnorth

    Shropshire

    WV16 4ST

    tel:(0044) 1746 766447

    fax:(0044) 1746 766665

    website: www.travellerseye.com

    email: books@travellerseye.com

Set in Times

ISBN: 1903070058

Copyright 2001 Peter Burden

Photographs, Paul Berriff, Isobel Howells, Susanna Spicer

Printed and bound in Great Britain by Creative Print & Design Group.

Acknowledgements

This book is based on the television programme 'Jungle Janes', produced for Channel Four by Anglia Television Limited.

We would like to take this opportunity to thank everyone who has made it possible for this book to be published in the short amount of time available to us.

With special thanks to:

The 'Janes' for their co-operation and time and support. In particular Susanna and Izzy for their help with photographs.

Paul, Becky and Tim at Anglia Television for their thoughts and input and everyone else who hepled turn 'Jungle Janes' round in a fifth of the normal time it takes to produce a book!

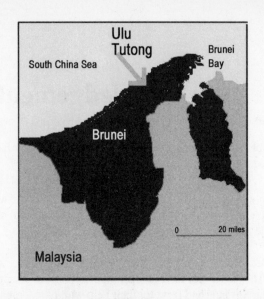

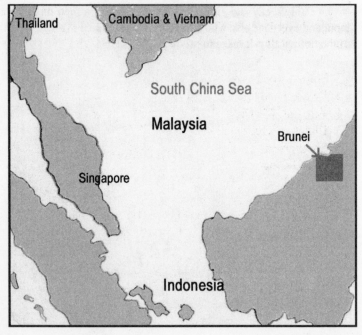

ULU TUTONG: THE 'JANES' VIRGIN JUNGLE.

Contents

Acknowledgements
Maps
Brunei Expedition: Statement of Intent

1. The Last Ridge	9
2. The Jungle Janes	16
3. A Baptism Of Water	42
4. The Alex Laughing Bird	57
5. Who Wants To Be A Raisinaire?	71
6. The Birthday Party	83
7. Generation Gap	92
8. Lazy Day	101
9. Dr. Wong Is Watching You	109
10. Is It Uphill All The Way?	120
11. Bliss	136
12. Follow My Leader	147
13. Empty Bladders	156
14. Tail-End Charley	166
15. Bleeding Trees	178
16. Shrangri-la	190
17. Star Gazing	206
18. Pig Fight	220
19. Come On Ladies	230
20. To The Limit	247
21. Home Sweet Home	264
22. So Near Yet So Far	271
23. Too Near By Far	276
24. The Bloated Leech	281
25. Out Of The Jungle But Still A Jane?	292
Appendices	305

Brunei Expedition
Statement of Intent

Dear 'Jane',

This document is designed to give you information that will help you prepare psychologically for the expedition. It is also a declaration of the training that you will have to complete and some extracts for you from my risk assessments. It is not intended to scare you or to sign you up to circus acts; it is intended more to allay your fears and put them in proper perspective.

You and your expedition are about to travel to a remote part of South East Asia and into one of the most demanding environments on this planet. The rainforests of Borneo are probably the most beautiful in the world and in the case of Brunei the most pristine. Like most jungles they are hot and humid and have their own inhabitants who bear little or no responsibilities for their actions when greeting newcomers. Finding your way around is difficult and requires patience and accuracy. Normal daily routine becomes the be all and end all of life and fresh water is gold dust. You are of course on a journey of discovery; your feet will tread paths that no other living person has ever trod and your eyes and ears will discover things that will make you see this world in a whole new perspective. It can be a place of misery and despair but it can also be a place of peace and serenity.

This is just not an observational exercise. The jungle is a place for the inner spirit. It can devour you pretty quickly and in its grasp you will initially feel exposed and wary. After a while, provided you follow instructions you can become harmonious with it and able to enjoy it. Do not attempt to fight it, for whatever reason – you will not win. The jungle is a great leveler and brings strong emotions to the fore; it will not be your physical prowess so much that pulls you through, rather your ability to tap into your mental reserves.

This expedition is both an opportunity and a necessity for measured thought and careful appreciation. The jungle will create exceptional pressures, both physical and mental and there can be a tendency to rush into situations and create more harm than good. Whatever action you take, give it an extra seconds thought and keep the log term consequences of you actions at the front of your mind. Learn the art of selflessness quickly, it creates an atmosphere of goodwill and collective purpose. Learn to share your anxieties, often you are not the only one fretting.

Expeditions are never straightforward and often plans have to be re-evaluated and changed. Weather and terrain can often curtail objectives and personal aspirations may go out of the window. Also remember there are no experts as such in this complex inter-personal process, we all have to evaluate things carefully and make decisions based on sound judgement. The bottom line is to be flexible and listen. Somebody else's rheto-ric is often a cry for help and an arm around the shoulder, rather than condemnation.

You are not yet a team and it is only fair to say that you have had limited time to sort out your differences. You must not form cliques from the outset, even if you have close friends on the expedition. This week-end you will be required to discuss the role of leader until you depart UK and divide administrative responsibilities between you. Please try to be punctual and eager to move on. Time is now of the essence and we must use what time we have constructively. When you have free time use it well to repack your equipment or make notes on the mass of infor-mation you receive. Events will move at quite a pace and you must be prepared for the unexpected - that said the weather forecast is good!

With only two weeks to go you will be feeling a bit nervous. Don't worry so am I! We will achieve everything we want to if we stick together and work together. Above all let us enjoy this experience - it will change your lives to some extent but I hope it is a path to fulfillment and reward.

You will find yourselves facing some unique challenges and not all of these will be easy. To give you an idea- if you imagine yourself on a selection course to be Mrs 007 (without a license to kill) you wont be far wrong. For peace of mind it is important to discuss risk and danger and possible outcomes. You will get the opportunity to discuss these things tonight. Other issues you may wish to discuss:

- Insurance and liabilities.
- Money.
- Itineraries.
- Equipment.
- Medical.
- Visas.
- Leadership.
- Packing.
- Fitness.
- Publicity.

You have all done fantastically well in getting yourselves prepared although I wonder sometimes if some of you are totally committed. An enormous amount of effort has gone on behind the scenes to make this happen and we must not forget those who are not in the limelight but helping us tirelessly. We draw a line under all our preparation soon and take whatever happens on the chin and improvise, adapt and overcome. No one said it was going to be easy!

Ken

chapter one

The Last Ridge

DAY 18 - Friday 21st July

It's 9.30 am. Four degrees north of the equator, the sun is already high and hammering down relentlessly on the jungle canopy. In the vastness beneath, amid the cathedral columns of the mighty tropical hardwoods, echoes a cacophony of whistling, shrieking, cackling and squealing – an orchestra of a million insects and birds that inhabit every square mile of the virgin jungle called Ulu Tutong. The birds and monkeys in the canopy live in their high-rise world, seldom venturing to the ground two hundred feet below where wild pigs and civet cats hide, snakes and scorpions slide and scuttle from the undisguised approach of human feet.

In the deep shade, the air is thick and soupy; the ground is cloaked in a vibrant tangle of clawing, grabbing, vigorous vegetation, green, green, green, broken bluntly here and there by a fallen branch or tree. Sometimes the booming crackle of deadfall overwhelms even the ceaseless jungle chorus as a mighty tree at the end of its life crashes between its neighbours to the ground, like a soldier fainting on parade.

From a ridge nine hundred feet above a gushing tributary of the Tutong River, twelve women work their way in a cautious file down its steep side. The night's rain has left the earth slippery and treacherous. The first woman picks her way with caution and newly acquired wariness. Her sandy-red hair is in neat rows of tiny plaits to keep her head cool, her face is pink with exertion and her wiry arm swings the *parang* in her hand with deft, labour saving strokes when the vegetation blocks the way she has chosen. Every few yards another checks their bearings, as the column of women follow numbly, brushing listlessly at the cloud of flies that buzz around their heads. Each carries a rucksack – a *bergen*, in army-speak – crammed with over fifty pounds of equipment. It would be a daunting weight for any human being – intolerable to most, here in the swelter of the tropical jungle. The women cling to the thought that this day, at last, will mark the end of their trek through the jungle.

But today there is no margin for error; they are already short of water.

The navigator has to find their position by dead-reckoning - counting their paces to measure distance covered on a fixed bearing. Her eyes flicker back and forth, to the map and compass dangling round her neck, trying to reconcile the contours. She knows they should be staying high, along the spine of the ridge. She knows they've got it wrong – she's got it wrong. And getting it wrong out here in the jagged jungle peaks of the Ulu Tutong with only two and a half litres of water each can mean the difference between finishing the day... or not.

The unremitting, overpowering humidity does the damage. There's nowhere to hide as it sucks the moisture from a human body as if it were designed for the purpose.

Besides, the women have been living on lightweight, jungle rations for the past three weeks, and yesterday was the toughest day yet, so tough it was hard to eat once they'd got their *bashas* up and their hammocks slung for the night. Although most of them started the journey as fit and ready as it was possible to be, some have lost dangerous amounts of flesh and every ounce of surplus fat; some have sustained injuries – twisted joints, a hernia, festering blisters and sores from their *bergen* straps – and three weeks' heat beneath fifty pound loads has extracted everything they had to offer.

They'd been told it would be tough. The men in special forces who trained in this same virgin jungle only stayed two weeks under *bashas*, and a significant proportion of those ended up injured or taken out by Cas-evac chopper.

But these are twelve women from England, who'd never been in any armed forces, or seen the jungle until three weeks before. Most of them are mothers, comfortably secure in their family lives, or their careers. Now they are asking themselves what on earth they're trying to prove?

Tensions are building; they have been for the past few days. The leader of the expedition is concerned; there were the beginnings of a mutiny yesterday. The women had got themselves lost and were forced to cross the grain of the land over a series of punishing troughs and ridges. After four hours of muscle-searing, sweat-soaked slog, they were confronted with a sheer rock wall. With a torrent of expletives, one of them tore her *bergen* from her back and hurled it to the ground. She'd had enough.

The navigators, also exhausted, looked at each, racked with guilt. What could be worth this pain – this constant nagging hunger and aching muscles?

What the hell are they doing here?

England, Autumn 1998

Like many great British adventures, the idea that a dozen, apparently sane women from Middle England, of broadly middle age and middle class, should fly into one of the world's few remaining, truly inhospitable tropical jungles was first aired at a country dinner party.

Gwenda Hames, fit and independent, was nudging forty, and that had been focussing her mind. Pretty enough to have starred in any TV soap, she'd had a varied career to date, and since becoming a mother in her early thirties, had had a string of unfulfilling office jobs, while moving around with the army. Now, in an effort to stretch herself, she'd become a student, aiming for a degree in tourism. But she was very conscious of the fact that her husband, Ken was still seeing the world.

Major Ken Hames was a career soldier. For years he'd been taking off for hostile shores with groups of men from special forces, to fight or to train – always stretching himself and the men he commanded, relishing the hardness and the sheer physical challenge of each trip he undertook.

In between, he would come home to Herefordshire, where Gwenda would be waiting with warm slippers, two children and a growing sense that she'd like some fun too, and if she didn't get it soon, she never would.

At a dinner party one Saturday evening in a quiet, unspoilt valley among the rolling red-soiled hills of North Herefordshire, someone broached the subject of army wives. Gwenda saw there were two other women at the table who would understand her restlessness.

She turned to Ken. 'It's all right for you; you can go off with your soldiers and play cowboys and Indians or whatever you do, then come back full of yourself and full of your sense of achievement. But I bet a lot of women could do it just as well.'

Ken laughed.

Alexandra James, who was giving the dinner party that evening, drew herself up indignantly. 'We bloody well could you know!' She probably believed herself; she'd been an actress with the RSC for four years and although she was no longer the wand-like waif she'd been when she played Margaret in *Much Ado* at Stratford, she still knew how to get into character. She would have been the first to admit that fifteen years of rural idyll with her quiet, circumspect husband, who farmed the thousand acres surrounding them had encouraged her to indulge a little more than perhaps she should – that, and producing three children. But Alex wasn't someone to allow a little temporary unfitness get in the way of such an outlandish proposition. 'Why don't you take some women with you next time? I'd come.'

Also at dinner were Alex and Mark's friends, Nic and Patsy Spicer, both doctors – he, an English baronet; she, the product of a strong line of New Zealand socialists. Patsy had been born with a big helping of Kiwi grit, and she didn't like to see it go to waste. Two kids and raft of rural patients weren't going to hold her back. She jumped in and gave the idea her backing.

Ken took the bait, and the rest of dinner became a game of 'Let's pretend'.

'Let's pretend' Ken is going to take a gang of women into the toughest piece of territory he's ever taken his soldiers – the virgin, tropical jungle of Brunei on the large, untamed oriental island of Borneo. 'Let's Pretend' that he'll train them, just like his soldiers, to live in jungle conditions, under their own temporary *bashas*, carrying forty to fifty pounds of equipment and rations on their backs as they hack their way through trackless rain forest. He'll teach them to navigate the sharp undulations and numerous rivers of Ulu Tutong, how to survive the intense heat and unbearable humidity; how to deal with scorpions, hornets, deadfall and flash floods; and how to live with and watch out for each other.

The women became excited. If the men were sceptical, they didn't let it show; they knew their wives. They understood; they almost approved.

Over the weeks that followed, the seed of the idea started slowly to grow roots.

Alex James recalls…
"It's amazing how casual words round the jolly atmosphere of a dinner table can stay in one's mind and grow into sentences that become paragraphs, that become ideas that eventually become real. That's how this whole idea of taking women on an expedition started.

13

I had known Ken before and had always held him in the highest regard. He has great integrity and feels a deep-rooted need to share the wonders of the world with anyone who is interested. The fact that they may be underprivileged or even overprivileged does not enter into the equation, but because he knows that wonderful feeling of achievement – he feels a need to share it with whoever shows the slightest interest. In this case, it was with me.

I jokingly tossed the idea of mothers at him, and asked how we were ever going to leave the family behind for however long – the family totally relies on the stability of *she* who must be obeyed – I led a life of fetching and carrying, trying to run a small business, never daring to put the cake in the oven for fear of never being able to take it out."

At first Ken Hames was doubtful that even a group of seriously fit female athletes could undertake what he was proposing. After all, his usual trainees were members of elite special forces, who had already proven their extreme and exceptional resilience to very strenuous activity in hostile conditions. But, a little to his surprise, the women didn't give up, and soon they'd been joined by others, friends of Gwenda's – a former colleague from British Airways, an opera-singing sister-in-law of Patsy's, a matron at the prep school which Alex James' children attend, Gwenda's hairdresser, a lecturer at her college.

Nobody selected them. They simply put themselves forward, volunteered in the real sense of the word, because, like Gwenda, Alex and Patsy, they felt it was time they gave themselves a real challenge and did something that 99.99% of women would never have done, even if they'd been offered the chance.

Ken was impressed that they meant it and that they were so determined. He found it hard not to get caught up in their enthusiasm. Besides – he'd be the first to admit – it represented a hell of a challenge to his own skills as an instructor and leader of expeditions. Soldiers, after all are trained to obey orders. This group of experienced wives and careerists were more in the habit of issuing their own.

Convinced now that this trip would be worth doing, and that it would be a unique experiment in female endurance in one of the world's harshest places, Ken started looking at ways of turning a crazy challenge raised at a weekend dinner party into a reality.

He was delighted that all the women who had so far shown an interest were keen enough to pay their way. Even so, he was already realising that to subsidise the trip, and, most important, to pay for the back-up safety which he knew he must provide, it would make sense if they could sell the idea to a television company. The women agreed, but they also felt, above all, that the trip shouldn't be hi-jacked into another of those fly-on-the-wall docu-soaps where producers effectively 'cast' the members of the team for maximum effect.

These women weren't going to be cast; they would pay the basics themselves, and receive no prizes or rewards. Above all, it was not to be an exercise in seeing who could be the nastiest, the most scheming or, for that matter, the most drearily self-obsessed.

So, the nucleus of the expedition was made up of independent-minded, educated, articulate women who knew how to look after themselves. It wasn't long before Ken's optimum number of twelve places had been filled. And although they had in common whatever it is that makes a normally sane middle-aged woman decide to risk her health and sanity trekking through the jungle for a month, they were in most respects a disparate group.

chapter two

The Jungle Janes

PATSY SPICER is forty-one and a native New Zealander, is the wife of an English baronet. She has two children aged seven and five and she works as a GP in a rural practice on the eastern boundary of Herefordshire.

"My extended family are intolerant and passionate socialists and pacifist intellectuals of moderate renown in New Zealand. I came to the UK eight years ago to buy a car and start on a Grand Tour of Europe but never made it. I met Nick at a dinner party and six months later we were married."

Nic Spicer, also a doctor, is an ex-chorister of St George's, Windsor and an Old Etonian. His step-grandfather, Sir Adrian Boult, was founder and conductor of the BBC Symphony Orchestra. From Sir Adrian, Nic inherited a crumbling Scottish shooting lodge and estate where they now hold legendary house parties.

"My husband doesn't say much about this expedition," Patsy said before she went. "I think it's something that will stretch me and have enough fear in it to make it something that I don't know I can really do. Obviously I don't want to get hurt or put in danger but I'm certainly more concerned about the dangers than he is. He thinks it's a bit of a lark. I don't want any harm to come to me because of my children. If I had no children I wouldn't give it a second thought, but I suppose it would be an irresponsible thing to do not to come back. If I die on this trip, my children will be more scarred by people telling them they will be scarred, than by my actual passing. I've not told them I'm going yet!"

As soon as you meet Patsy, you're aware that here is a woman who has little interest in trivia or gossip. If you were a fool, you feel, you would not be suffered gladly. With clear blue eyes, a good crop of healthy, sandy-red hair and a fresh, gleaming complexion, she has the air of a woman who knows how to look after herself. You just know she'd never get drunk, or pig out on burgers, or, heaven forbid, light up and draw lingeringly on a cigarette.

But soon you find that underlying this somewhat stern exterior, there is a woman who seems to understand the inevitabilities of human weakness, even considers it a weakness in herself that she does take a challenge too seriously.

Why did she agree to Ken Hames' proposition at dinner that night?

"Why not? I believe some of my greatest adventures have started with a whim. 'Why not' doesn't mean I don't care one way or the other or I think the question's unimportant. For me 'Why not' expresses a willingness to change track when an option is offered, and an openness to new ideas.

Some of the most inspiring moments in my life have been brought about by seeing someone overcome something that gives them great fear – when every voice in their head is saying 'Flee - safety's the other way!'

These may not seem great challenges to outsiders. It may be a matter of talking to a parent after a long period of deliberate silence, or saying a cheery 'Good morning' to the postman for somebody very shy. Every time we say to ourselves, 'Go for it!' in the face of the urge to flee, we become bigger than we were before.

I was invited to go on this trek – maybe because I'm a doctor. Whether that was the case or not, an invitation like this might never have come again in my lifetime, and there were only two possible answers – Yes or No.

And 'No' would mean sitting at home, wishing I'd gone.

So I said 'Yes'. Not because I need to prove anything to myself. I'm perfectly happy, life is great and there are no glaring gaps.

But I am very curious to see how I will cope, how we will all work together under stress."

SUSANNA SPICER is thirty-seven and Patsy's sister-in-law. Tall and statuesque, she is a full time classical mezzo-soprano who performs widely on the European concert circuit.

She was born, the youngest of four siblings, in Oxford, where her father worked at the OUP. After Oxford High, she did her A-levels at Marlborough, from where she got into Cambridge – a choral scholar at Trinity College. She read history and left with a 2/1.

After a stint at Christies in London, she decided to make music her career and went on a year's post-grad course at the Guildhall. She joined the Kent Opera, before going on to sing in the Glyndebourne chorus and Monteverdi choir as well as taking solo parts.

Now she also organises and manages several choral societies. She has travelled the world with choirs such as the Monteverdi and the English Concert and has sung oratorio solos in many cathedrals in Europe.

In 1982 she spent four months working for Mother Teresa in Calcutta.

She leads a frenetic life of work and travel, when weekends are often her busiest times. A few years ago she bought a cottage to escape to in rural Herefordshire, not far from her brother, Nic, and Patsy, who is a great friend. It was through them that she first met Ken Hames during the early planning stages of the Jungle Janes trip.

Susanna is a naturally strong woman, and normally fit; she's a regular walker and a fair-weather cyclist. When she heard Ken and Patsy discussing the expedition, she couldn't help becoming fascinated, and asking questions, to a point where Ken said, "You want to come too, don't you?"

Susanna, anxious not to tread on the toes of those already committed, hung back, until Ken had to ask, "Do you or do you not want to come?"

And she was committed.

Susanna is used to travelling and sleeping in a different hotel room every night. She can socialise when it's required. She also likes her own personal space, but she was undaunted by the prospect of spending a month in close company with twelve other women.

"This is going to be totally different from anything I've done before, a huge physical challenge and I'm not terribly fit. I've got plenty of fears and my lack of fitness is the one big thing I worry about which may become a drag and hold the other women back. I also worry about the physical dangers. You hear of people disappearing in that part of the world including the army. I'm a bit apprehensive."

DICKY (BENEDICTA) SEWELL is forty-five, married to a retired naval officer, with three children – twins of seventeen, and a twelve year old.

Born into a large catholic family in Worcestershire, she is one of four sisters and two brothers who were taught from an early age that the best amusements were those which you made for yourself, which demanded active input. She and her brothers spent many happy days and nights walking and camping on Bredon Hill, and all six children spent idyllic, carefree holidays with their ponies and dogs.

After a varied academic career at a convent in Worcester, Dicky joined the Royal Navy to train as an SRN. It was there that she met her husband, Douglas, on an orthopaedic ward.

"He was the first respectable man I'd been out with, whom I thought I could take home, and would get on with my Dad! Douglas doesn't approve of this trip at all and thinks I should be busy playing the good housewife at home – but then I don't take too much notice of what I'm told – I usually do the opposite! Our family motto is 'Viam Tritam Non Sequor' – 'We do not follow the ordinary way'. I take delight in living up to that. Douglas is frightfully organised and likes to make loads of plans for everything; even a trip to Tescos is planned with military precision with ETDs and ETAs, while I just dash around and take each day as it comes. He's not that keen on women anyway, and rudely refers to the female members of the Royal Navy as 'lumpy jumpers'. He thinks we're all batty doing this trip and has been muttering about it for ages. But as far as I'm concerned, it's too good a chance to miss, and he can jolly well peel the potatoes himself for once!

What I feel is that the two greatest gifts that parents can give their children are a secure nest and a strong pair of wings. I was very lucky to have a most secure nest in my childhood, to which I regularly return. And from an early age, I was given a huge amount of encouragement to try my wings. So when an opportunity like this Borneo expedition came along, it was obvious to me that it was no time to be hovering on the edge of the nest saying, 'I can't fly'."

Tall, lean, fit, fine-featured, with an unexpected, bright smile and a husky, naughty laugh, Dicky seems to be a bundle of contradictions. She is the boys' matron and a teacher at St Richard's, a Catholic prep school in Herefordshire with about seventy boarders and fifty day children. She's run the London marathon – quite respectably – and smokes like a power station. She's a devout Catholic, sings with the school choir (and her three sisters when she gets the chance) and loves a bottle (or two) of red wine. She has been a key figure in the school over the last ten years, providing a warm, secure background in which the children seem to flourish.

What made her decide to go on this crazy expedition?

"If someone asks if I would like to do something I've not done before, and it looks like fun, I say 'Yes, please'. A lot of us live a life of luxury - I've just read a book about a chap who walked to the South Pole. Until you read something like this you don't realise what sort of deprivation some people have endured, and you don't know how lucky you are. At the school I don't have to cook meals, clean out the bins or wash the lavatories, and I think it's good for all of us to break out of the comfort zone to see how we react when we're up against it. I also want to know how I will cope when I'm really frightened, really cold or really hot and sick and there's nowhere else to go. My fears are that something awful could happen and I might not come back. Having said that, I have a deep faith and don't fear death in itself – I know there is a greater world to come for eternity, but I so enjoy my children and my work that I don't really want to leave this life just yet. I also have an incredible fear of getting a snake up my trouser leg, though I'm not bothered about the lack of bathroom facilities."

For Dicky, going to Brunei meant missing the last few crucial weeks of the summer term, which would be the last ever at the school for some of the children she'd known for six years or more since they'd first come. Dicky isn't someone to opt out of her role at school on a mere whim. But everyone at St Richard's was urging her to go - the headmaster, the staff, the children, even the parents, and soon after the new Millennium had dawned, she started to prepare herself.

****

By the end of 1999, most of the arrangements had been made with the television company and Ken was confident he had the twelve women he wanted. He had turned down several others who had heard about the trip, either on the grounds that they simply didn't appreciate how hard it was going to be, or they were too young. An important element of the whole experiment was that the participants should be, for the most part, mature women who had already experienced careers or motherhood. But he had to encourage his team to get themselves as well prepared as they could possibly be to tackle the challenge the following summer.

"Before coming to Brunei the ladies were involved in quite an intensive training programme, which they started about eight months before we were due to leave and they really had to get themselves fit, which was a self-help thing, because I couldn't do it all. So a lot of them spent time walking the lanes of Herefordshire, walking up hill and down dale, and in the Brecon Beacons and some of them had to be content with trudging the streets of London."

As the Jungle Janes prepared themselves, Ken's plans were taking shape. Paul Beriff, an award-winning documentary maker had agreed to film the trip for production by Anglia Television and broadcast by Channel Four. Paul was as keen as Ken and the girls that no concessions should be made to the presence of the small DV camera he would be carrying. The television crew would consist only of him, and one female sound recordist, Lulu.

Ken was concerned that some of the women who had originally agreed to come would take a different view when they knew their struggles were going to be televised, and possibly goggled at by a large audience. Patsy Spicer in particular wasn't keen to become an object of scrutiny by a few million complete strangers. In the end, they all agreed that, provided it wasn't too intrusive, they would accept the presence of a single camera man.

They had their first experience of Paul back in January 2000, when all but three of the women met at Ken and Gwenda's place, a large, comfortable, gabled house in the village of Almley, in the heart of rural west Herefordshire, which Gwenda now operates as a B&B. It was here they discussed the finer points of the trip, and Paul was able to reassure them that their privacy would not be abused. No-one was seeking sensations, no-one was going to set up anything. The camera would be there simply and discretely to record how well they would cope and, he hoped, overcome the extraordinary pressures that the trip would present.

Paul came up to Herefordshire again in April to film Ken running the first of two training weekends he had planned. Appropriately, this was held on land farmed by Alex James' husband Mark, at Broadfield, where the dinner party that spawned the whole thing had taken place.

ALEXANDRA JAMES, at forty-two is full of fizz and an inspiration to her husband and three children, Sam, thirteen, Phoebe, ten and Jacob, eight. She was born and brought up in Pattingham, Shropshire, the eldest of three children. At the age of eleven she went away to school, Lawnside in Malvern, where she played in the hockey and netball teams, 'though I was never a star!' In class she was always good at English, and this manifested itself more strongly when she discovered Shakespeare. It was Lawnside, during the school holidays, that took her to Stratford, three or four times a year. And whenever she went, she would come back longing to see the next play. Where her school friends found the Bard a bore – a chore to be endured at school, Alex always loved the rhythms and cadences of his language, and a burning ambition to become a member of the RSC was born and burgeoned.

Over the next few years, while she was doing a diploma course at Webber Douglas School of Drama, followed by forty weeks' rep at the Chesterfield Civic Theatre (as ASM, just like Penelope Keith before her) and eighteen months touring with the New Vic in *The Canterbury Tales* and *Dracula*, she never stopped badgering the RSC. Until, one day, as she finished a West End run with the New Vic, she finally got the call, rushed to an audition at the Barbican Theatre, and was on a train two days later to start with the RSC in Newcastle. This soon led to inclusion in a tour with Derek Jacobi, all over Europe, and then in the States – LA, Broadway and Washington – with *Much Ado*, and *Cyrano de Bergerac*.

It was only then that Mark James, whom she'd known since nursery school, finally insisted that she stop acting, marry him, and become a farmer's wife in Herefordshire. And now she's one of the county's leading lights in viticulture, where her acting skills are deployed in lecturing the public on the virtues of English wines.

All the women would agree that she was the most extrovert of the group – a born performer and entertainer who doesn't know the meaning of the word retention or discretion. It is simply one of Alex's endearing traits to say exactly what she thinks, which, optimist that she was, is nearly always positive.

She was also one of the least fit at the start of the trip.

"But Ken's inspiration made me realise that no matter how many obstacles are thrown at you, there's always a way through," she said before she left. "It goes without saying that my husband, Mark, who has backed me all the way to 'get up those hills, pack on', day in day out, made me realise that my whole family really wanted me to do this.

But did I?

My parents are moving in during the holidays to care for our three children. I couldn't go without their help. My friends all stepped in to save the day while I was on the training courses, they've fed, fetched, washed, and ironed uniforms at a moment's notice, even delivered wine, because I just wasn't there.

And even after all this, I still ask myself, 'Why am I doing this?'.

I had no idea what the heck the training would be, for me at least. Our first weekend session was held up here at Broadfield. It was also the first time I'd met all the girls. I knew Gwenda, Patsy and Dicky before, but none of the others. I was thrilled to meet them – all smiling, certain that we were going to get on with each other."

GWENDA HAMES met Alex when she came to help out for a few months at the Broadfield Court Vineyard, which Alex runs with her a father-in-law. Gwenda is forty, married to Ken Hames and has two children, Katie who is nine and Harry who is seven. She was born and brought up in Uganda where her father had his own business. He was murdered by Idi Amin's troops. At the age of eleven she was sent to a boarding school in the UK but went back to Uganda every holiday.

"Uganda was wonderful though often quite frightening as we lived there during the time of Idi Amin. I left school at eighteen, not really sure what I was going to do (I'm still not sure!) worked in a pub for six months and then I joined the Metropolitan Police. I spent five years plodding the beat and driving my 'Panda' and then left to become a financial consultant for four months and hated every minute of it, so off I went to become a stewardess for British Airways.

I had a ball, saw the world and even met my husband between Bombay and Perth. I left BA when I was pregnant and then became a 'camp follower' as my husband was in the Army. I spent my time doing undemanding office jobs in between bringing up my children.

Nearing forty, I couldn't bear to do admin jobs for the next twenty-five years so I'm now an undergraduate doing a BA Hons in Travel and Tourism Management. I'm the oldest in the class and I really enjoy it but my brain has not improved with age. I'm determined to finish the course and I'm also determined to seek out adventure. This expedition will probably be one of the hardest things I will ever do, but if I get through it, I don't think I'll be frightened of doing anything again."

WENDY STUBBS is forty and lives with Alan, her partner of seven years in Hereford. She was lecturing at the local college on Tour

Management at the time Ken Hames was beginning to plan taking the Jungle Janes to Borneo. Gwenda was one of her students and knew that she'd spent a lot of her early career travelling and that she wasn't averse to a challenge.

Wendy has all the appearances of being a dependable, self-reliant but comfortable sort. She started life in Staffordshire, in Stoke-on-Trent, which she left when she went to college in Sheffield to learn how to teach PE. After that, with a taste for new horizons, she abandoned PE and travelled all over the world teaching EFL for the British Council and various independent language schools. On her travels she learned the art of self-containment, and the joys of discovery. And, true to her first vocation, she's always kept herself fit and obviously enjoys that. She has no children of her own, though she has a good relationship with her partner's two sons.

When Gwenda mentioned casually that they might be organising a group of women to trek across a tract of virgin tropical rain forest, Wendy put her name down at once and kept her fingers crossed for the next few months, hoping it would really happen.

What were her motives for responding to Gwenda's invitation?

"Among other things, the expedition is going to be an exercise in self analysis," she said. "Very challenging and very revealing, especially what I'm going to discover about myself and other people. My course at college is in practical Management Leadership; it's all about teamwork, and I'm going to look at that while I'm out there. How do these people work together, what are their conflicts? Are there any natural leaders? So I'm looking at the trip from many angles, both professional and personal. I'm fit; I did a PE degree, but I've never put myself through a test like this before. It's quite challenging as well as being quite frightening. My chief fear is that the others will be super fit and I will hold them back. I'm not fearful of being in a jungle environment, it's just the fear of the unknown. I come apart with creepy-crawlies especially the leeches. I think I have an advantage in how I'm going to perform with leadership. My partner Alan thinks it's extremely challenging but it's not going to be a jolly."

Six months before the trip, Wendy joined a new health club, worked out and swam regularly. She also took to tramping the streets of Hereford carrying a fifty pound *bergen* full of water bottles, accompanied by Alan who, sick of being stared at for being empty-shouldered, started carrying a pack too.

****

When all the women gathered at Broadfield for their first training session on a cold spring weekend, and Ken had a good look at them tackling the simple crossing of a small English brook, he wondered if he might have over-faced some of them. Of course, he wasn't going to let that show.

Alex remembers it vividly.....

"All the Jungle Janes turned up here, and Ken had put up a camp in one of our woods – some way from the house. It was a cold, wet April day, and the first thing he did was take us on a route march, straight down to the bottom of a valley and across a small river. I plunged in first, bravely, and fell straight on my backside, wet and miserable at once. Everyone was laughing at me, but I didn't mind at all. I knew they were just trying to overcome their own fears. The others were sitting on the bank, pulling off their socks and shoes! Little did they know how absurd that would seem in a few months time when we were wading through rivers up to our chins.

I was just thinking about going home and getting into a nice hot bath when Ken announced that we were off on a full-scale route march. By the time we got to the top of the hill on the other side of the valley, we were absolutely sweltering. We'd all put on far too much clothing. Ken let us peel off a few layers; I was wondering how the heck I was going to deal with blisters forming on my sodden feet when he said we were off again!

We went for miles. I thought it would never stop, and all the time I was thinking, "but home's only just over the hill, why can't I go back?" I told Ken I thought perhaps I wasn't going to be able to hack this trek.

He stopped and looked at me; his eyes didn't show a quiver of doubt. "Of course you can," he said, "and you're going to. You just don't know what reserves of strength you've got, because you've never had to dig for them."

I suppose I believed him; I certainly trusted him."

Back at the camp, we had stretched a tarpaulin across our campsite in an attempt to keep out most of the rain, but there seemed to be rather a lot of holes in it, and it leaked on us all night. We were lying in a row in our sleeping bags, like a lot of teenagers on our first sleep-over. But however tired I was, I didn't do a lot of sleeping. While I was really worried about the physical demands that would be made on this trek, I had been very heartened by the marvellous sense of camaraderie while we had sat around, eating and talking. I already felt that we were an unbreakable team, and it was that commitment to the other Jungle Janes that kept me going through the training sessions and, in the end, the trek itself.

The whole idea had brought together twelve very special but 'ordinary' women in our late thirties and forties. It was very apparent from the outset that we had become very close and the comradeship that developed after only one weekend just grew into something very special. I felt safe with my Janes. They made me feel special, which reminded me of what it might have been like in the trenches. You see, we all look after each other all the time. I was in need of feeling special. My life is a very rewarding one, with a husband I love and respect and three very special children, but in order to get better at what I do, I needed something in my spirit to be ignited. Indeed, to feel that sense of achievement all those admirable people feel when running the marathon, or climbing a mountain. The trouble was that I have never been a physically stretched person. I'm into books, poetry, literature, imagination and people. The strain of hiking has never turned me on, as my body had always shied away from physical exercise. As so many women will identify with – after having children and my rather sedate lifestyle (albeit rushing everywhere at breakneck speed) the weight piled on – everyone could see except me. So perhaps the major reasons for doing it are to get fit at forty-two, to sweat real sweat, to feel a muscle aching, to pass through that mental and physical pain barrier; to find pride in myself again."

Ken set up this first weekend to give the women a chance to get to know each other, to 'bond', as they say in the world of Outdoor Development Training. Undaunted by sexist propaganda about woman's natural lack of spatial skills, he taught them some map-reading and navigation techniques. Patsy, as the only doctor on the trip, lectured them all on how to deal with untimely periods, diarrhoea and other sicknesses. They played what Alex described as army-type games, designed to test co-operation and mutual patience. In a group of women composed almost inevitably of natural leaders, it was a useful exercise in personal restraint, particularly for the two junior members of the team.

The two wild cards in this unlikely pack of Jungle Janes were a pair of young women who had already thrown themselves hard at life, and have always come back smiling. They thrive on challenge and extremity. At thirty-two and thirty-five they weren't a lot younger than the rest, but in terms of feminine attitudes of self-determination, they were on the other side of a cultural watershed.

Neither came with any emotional baggage – no husbands, partners or children to consider. They'd known each other for a year or so, and their last two trips had been made together, running motorbike treks on Indian Enfields through extreme terrain in Tamil Nadu and the foothills of the Himalayas in Himachal Pradesh. Leading twenty very male bikers through unmade mountain roads at fourteen thousand feet with unprotected two thousand feet drops was not a doddle. They lost three bikes, but no punters.

They were both very fit, and good-looking, exuding confidence and experience. They were aware that making friends with the older women on the Ulu Tutong trip might present problems and require tact and a little holding back on their part.

FIONA SHAPCOTT at thirty-two was the youngest woman in the team. She was sort of educated at Worcester Girls Grammar School, where, she admits, she wasn't marked out as a girl to watch. She was already looking for more stimulating challenges. After blagging her way into Art College by submitting some 'borrowed' work, she only lasted two terms. After this, at a tiny college in Kent she enjoyed a course in restoring antiques but, despite the sharks in the business, she felt that life was still lacking the edge she needed. She went to Australia and worked on a sheep farm, then on a crayfish boat, before an impromptu tour of Thailand, Malaysia and Indonesia. Back in London, all options still open, she took the bizarre decision to train as a stunt woman but having spent all her money on kick-boxing, judo and advanced horse riding courses, she decided she needed a job that would make her some money. She became a bouncer at a London night club but decided it wasn't a serious career move and went on to be the Licensee of a club in Chelsea.

"This was a steep learning curve made slightly easier by the landlord of my local who kept his phone close at hand to answer all the questions I would throw in his direction. This job lasted two years."

After her motorcycle trips around India, Fiona was so impressed with how it went that she now specialises in Event Management.

"That trip changed my life," she told Ken in her application. "I've always been one of those people who likes to do something different. As a kid I always wanted to be an explorer, so this jungle expedition is like fulfilling a dream. I like adversity, especially when people turn round and say to me 'you can't do that'. Then you go out and prove that you can. It's having the chance to prove to myself that I can do things. So far, I've gone through life doubting my own abilities but I've found no matter how adverse it gets, if you come out of it and laugh about it you've achieved something. I suppose there'll be women on the trip I won't necessarily relate to and some I'll get on with."

IZZY HOWELLS, the second wild card, is thirty-five. You wouldn't think, looking at her neat little frame, innocent hazel-blue eyes and small freckled features, that she had the muscle or desire to do half the things she has. The middle of three daughters of a district nurse she was born and brought up in a sleepy corner of Devon. Her summers were spent messing around in boats and on the beach and working in local hotels and restaurants. She planned to become a nurse herself when she left school, but first, she went to Hong Kong to visit her father, who lived and worked there. Already of an independent frame of mind, she stayed for a year, working in restaurants and as an air courier, until the chance of working her passage to Australia on an antique yacht offered itself.

The wooden gaff-rigged ketch had just been refitted for the eccentric Australian businessman who owned it, and he was taking on a small crew, in return for passage, to sail it back to Australia with him and his wife. The trip was plagued with disasters, maritime and personal, and after nearly sinking on a reef off the southern Phillippines, Izzy couldn't wait to jump ship the moment they landed in Oz. On the way, though, they had dropped anchor off Bandar Seri Begawan, the capital of Brunei. Izzy went ashore, and looked around the mosque and floating villages, never dreaming she'd be back in seventeen years to trek through the rain forests of the interior.

In the end, she made it back to London and started at the age of nineteen to train as an SRN at King's College Hospital in Camberwell.

"London came as a shock, September '84 a student nurse, the lowest of the low, cold wet weather and no money! I managed to stick the first year and things improved. My first job as a qualified nurse was on the prestigious Liver Failure Unit, a job I loved.

I left the LFU to be a venturer with Raleigh International in Kenya, and embarked on a three month expedition working with other young people on community, scientific and adventure projects. I stayed on after the expedition and took a bus to Tanzania and climbed Kilamanjaro and then worked with a doctor friend from Kings at a dispensary he was running in Tanga. From there I met up with a girlfriend in Kilifi back in Kenya and we lived on the beach and learnt to dive. We then decided we needed a challenge so set off to climb and explore Mt Kenya. We had both been there with Raleigh but this was on our own and somehow more of an adventure.

Seven months later I came back to London and took a job back at Kings on a surgical ward. The ward was closed down after a year and I moved to Casualty. I loved A & E, the team work and not knowing what each day would bring, it also opened the door to more Raleigh expeditions.

I was accepted as a medic on an expedition to Botswana, a fantastic place with wildlife on the doorstep – sometimes a little too close! One of our canoes was attacked by hippo,

Elephants charged past our tents in the night, not to mention the lions staking out our camp. I stayed on after the expedition and drove one of the Landrovers to Chimanimani in Zimbabwe via the Okavango Delta, Caprivi Strip and Victoria Falls.

I picked up my old job in A & E but after six months I was finding the shifts hard to get back into. I was lucky enough to be offered a job as an event organiser by my sister's boss. I had worked at several Cannes Film Festivals while nursing which had meant I could spend time with my sister, earn some money and take a holiday. Now I was learning a whole new job. I worked in London but spent three or four months a year in Cannes or Monte Carlo at the TV, film and music festivals.

After three years I decided to move to South Africa to live with a boyfriend. It was a disaster and I quickly found myself back in London not sure what to do next. I freelanced, organising various one-off projects and launch parties in London and the European Pavilions at the Cannes Film Festival. Then, still restless, I took another Raleigh expedition to Zimbabwe where I was lucky enough to help organise a high profile cataract replacement programme. We screened patients in remote villages with the Zimbabwe Council for the Blind and SEE (Surgical Eye Expeditions) provided the materials, equipment and surgeons and operated on one hundred and thirty-four patients in four days."

A chance encounter two years ago brought Izzy into contact with Fiona, who didn't have to work hard to talk her into helping on the first of the two Indian motorbike trips they organised.

Fiona had worked with Ken Hames on an earlier project. Ken had already approached her about joining the JJs, and Fiona told Izzy. As soon as Ken met Izzy, he asked her if she'd like to be a reserve member of the team. She kept her fingers tightly crossed for the next few months until she knew the trip was happening, and she was in for sure.

Now, until the next extreme, crazy venture comes her way, Izzy's a marketing organiser based in London. As a trained SRN, she was chosen as one of the expedition medics.

"It's strange where events lead you, but I believe in grasping opportunities when they arise so it's with some trepidation but mostly excitement that I look forward to this latest adventure. Life should never be dull....

I enjoy a challenge. I find it interesting when a group of people are thrown together and fascinating to watch the relationships develop. You will see people setting off being polite but then the clashes develop before the team sorts itself out. With this being an all women team I think we will all start out on a level footing but then I suppose leaders will develop and others fall away. I think I will learn something about myself. What worries me most is letting other people down; I want to be part of the group. I will be the team medic so people will be coming to me all the time with their ailments. What can make life hell on this trip are the simple problems like sunburn, heat stroke and a twisted ankle."

CLAIRE ADEYEMI, is a purser with British Airways, where she once worked with Gwenda.

Slim, fit and striking, she was born in Westminster, and spent her early years in Primrose Hill. Her father, a Nigerian, and her mother from Guyana, met as students in London. From opposite sides of the Atlantic, their common language was English. Claire went to school in Islington and Lewisham before going to Nigeria for six months.

Back in England, she had vague ambitions to go into computers after she'd been at college, but another, longer trip to Nigeria to stay with family and friends intervened. She found herself flying out of Lagos, then Tripoli for a small airline, which gave her a taste for flying and the experience she needed to apply to British Airways, which in due course she did, joining them in 1984. Now she is a Customer Services Director in charge of cabin crews on long haul 747 flights.

She lives in Surrey, with her mother and her eleven-year old son, Nathaniel. She's ambitious and energetic, obviously a thorough perfectionist with very high standards who never wants to stop learning.

Besides her busy work schedule at BA, she is studying part-time for a degree in psychology at Birkbeck College, and she is setting up a childrens' nursery, Pippy Long Stocking, in Worcester Park.

She is also an active member of her church in Islington, and she took her bible with her to read in the jungle.

When Gwenda got in touch with her in early '99 to tell her about the possibility of the Jungle Janes trip, she jumped at it, and said "Yes" immediately.

She loved the idea of the peace and tranquillity she might be able to find in the jungle, and the chance to think and reflect, away from the hectic schedule of her life. She reckoned she was fundamentally fit for it. She swam regularly and spent time in the gym, doing aerobics.

Her bosses at BA took a lot longer to say "Yes", though they eventually did, about a month before she was due to leave for Brunei.

Claire met all the other Janes for the first time on the training session at Broadfield Court. She arrived a little late, and the others were already based up in the woods, but they all came down to greet her and help her with her bags.

By the end of the weekend, she felt totally integrated into the team.

On the second training weekend, she volunteered first to climb the telegraph pole, because it was something she could do to encourage the others.

Like most of the women, she found the climb up Cader Idris very daunting, especially as they weren't even carrying full packs. But she knew the trip would be gruelling and taxing, and she could cope with that.

CATHERINE KNIGHT, forty-three, is married to Lt. Col. Robert Knight, whom she met when they were both at university in Aberystwyth. After uni, she trained as a teacher, and took up her first post at St Ann's, Sanderstead. But before long, she was engaged to Robert. Once they were married and Catherine was an army wife, her work tended to be as a supply teacher, changing posts every few months, and frustratingly, never really getting a chance to see her students develop.

Before the Borneo trip she had been teaching in the American School in Bucharest, while her husband was on loan as an advisor to the Rumanian Army. She was also helping with the orphans and street kids who roam the Rumanian capital, many of whom turn to prostitution.

She has three children of her own, two of them, Lucy seventeen and Joseph fourteen, at boarding school in England, while the third, Jack ten, was at the American School in Bucharest.

"I've always wanted to do something like an adventure" she told Ken. "I've followed my husband for twenty years so I'm looking forward to this as something I've done. I want to go on this expedition because there are things that will frighten me. When you have been living in a family environment and you have all the support you need, you can get too comfortable. I want to do this on my own, it will be a challenge. Since living in the Falklands I've decided I like being on the edge of the world in terms of isolation and silence – though not forever! "

SALLY ROBINS, forty-four, slightly built with sparkly blue eyes and a soft thoughtful voice, is a solicitor in Ross-on-Wye, Herefordshire, where she was born and grew up. After school nearby at The Haberdashers', Monmouth, she went on to Aberystwyth University, where she read law, and met Catherine, with whom she has been friends ever since, wherever Catherine's been living.

Sally qualified as a solicitor in 1980, and was married in 1987. Her husband is a dentist in Hereford. She has a son of thirteen and a daughter of eleven, and made sure she took time off from her work to be with them. She hasn't worked as a solicitor since coming back from the trip, and isn't sure that she will again.

As a child, she had her ponies and played tennis, but she was never particularly keen on walking, or any of the things one might associate with trekking through jungles, but she'd reached a stage where she liked the idea of a challenge – of doing something outlandish. And she had always been interested in wild-life.

When she told people what she was considering, she was relieved that no one tried to stop her, and most gave encouragement. She was conscious, though, that she was not a strong woman, that she would be carrying a pack that was half her own body weight; and she'd always suffered from an acute fear of heights, and claustrophobia. It was from Catherine in September '99 that she first heard about the proposed Jungle Janes expedition. She pricked up her ears and said if there was a chance, she'd love to go too.

One morning, having woken with a strong feeling that something good was about to happen, Ken telephoned and told her that she was 'on'.

JULIE HALLAM, slim, forty-eight and single, runs a hairdressing salon in Hereford. The daughter of an SAS officer she was born in Somerset and brought up in Malaysia for the first nine years of her life while her father was posted in Brunei. When she was eight, she returned briefly to Hereford before being sent to a convent in Belgium for two and half years.

Back in Herefordhshire, she went to the grammar school in Bromyard, from where she went on to train as a hairdresser in Birmingham.

In the early seventies, she came back to Hereford where she worked for one of the better salons in the city, and met Mr Hallam, whom she married.

The marriage didn't last, and when it was over Julie went travelling for a year to let the situation simmer down.

In 1987, she started her own salon in Hereford, which went from strength to strength. Though she has a large staff, she still does a lot of cutting herself. She even took her scissors to the jungle, and was able to give Ken Hames a trim when he needed one.

How would she describe herself?

Julie rolls another cigarette and takes a thoughtful drag.

"I don't take myself too seriously. I'm loud, I like to laugh, but I'm pretty stoical too. And I like to think I'm loyal. I like people who are fun and spontaneous. Above all, I like them to be honest. Though I'm not particularly sporty or competitive, I'll try anything once. I've always been reasonably active and I knew I had strong legs.

I heard about the trek from Gwenda. I do her hair, and she was telling me all about it. 'Ooh, I love the jungle,' I said.

She came straight back. 'Are you up for it, then?'

And last November, I got the call confirming that I was going. I was really chuffed. Then once I was committed, I asked a few friends in the Regiment if they thought I was up to it. They reckoned I was; the challenge is more mental than physical. But I still started going to the gym three times a week after that.

I think it will be fun, a bit creepy but it doesn't worry me. Its what you make it. I'm more worried about mosquitoes than bathrooms but I smoke over twenty cigarettes a day so the smoke should keep the mosquitoes away"

****

In June, a couple of weeks before they were due to fly to Brunei, Ken Hames took the women off on another training session.

"The second training weekend was much harder, when I took them to the mountains of Wales and they did some quite exciting things - rowing out to sea, some high ropes at the Outward Bound School and culminating in the ascent of 2,800 foot mountain, Cader Idris. They all got to the top which was quite an achievement and I think that training paid off - they got to know each other well, they learned some basic skills but to be honest they were still on a steep learning curve and the jungle is a place where you've got to learn quickly or else you become immensely uncomfortable. I hope that the training stands them in good stead for the month in the jungle."

First Ken had them involved in exercises designed to test determination and team-work. The telegraph pole is a standard exercise in overcoming fear and self-doubt. Each of the women was required to clamber to the top of a twenty-five foot pole, always harnessed for safety, until they could stand on the tiny disc on top of it. From there they had to launch themselves onto a trapeze that was hanging tantalisingly just out of reach.

For Sally Robbins, this was a mind-numbing experience; with her powerful fear of heights, she'd always been careful not to expose herself to them in the past. But with the encouragement of the rest of the team, she clambered up – in a cold sweat – managed to reach the top and throw herself into space. This success gave her a great sense of triumph and boosted her self-esteem. It also showed her how she could do extraordinary things, with the right advice from people she could trust. The memory of this kept her going when the going in the jungle got tough.

Ken took the women out rowing in a dipping log cutter in Aberdovey Bay, another exercise in teamwork. But it was the next trek that really tested them.

It was hot when their minibus arrived at the lower slopes of Cader Idris, although the early stages are through woodland. But by the time they had reached a tarn half way up, Alex couldn't wait to leap in. It was freezing, and the next leg up the mountain looked like a sheer cliff face. Ken knew a less daunting path, but by now, Alex was almost wiped out. It was only with constant encouragement from the others that she made it to the top.

Coming down was worse - particularly on the lower slopes where the ground broke up into a series on grassy tussocks, designed to trip you up every few feet.

"I was desperate by then. I just knew I couldn't go on. I was wondering how on earth I was going to break it to Mark and the kids, and everyone else who'd rallied round. I felt such a fool and a failure to be giving up before we'd even started. But the thought of a month of this agony! I knew I'd never last.

It was only when we'd pitched camp lower down, and Ken came round telling us all how well we'd done, and that we wouldn't have any days as hard as that in the jungle, that I thought, 'Well, I've done today; I'm still alive,' and I decided to stay on the expedition."

Julie Hallam wasn't too happy either. 'I must admit I found climbing Cader very tough, and I was really cross with myself, because I knew I was already as fit as I could be, and I might end up letting the whole side down. It was bad enough on the first training weekend, with those tiny little hills. It's hilarious, looking back on it, falling into streams, and feeling that my lungs would burst from my chest, when you think what we had to deal with in Borneo.'

Gwenda also had reservations. "I was fairly worried that my left leg which had recently been operated on, wasn't going to make the downhill stretch, and because of this I was very grumpy with Ken for putting me in this position even though I knew I had to test it and it wasn't his fault. By using two sticks and setting the pace for the others, I made it, and the leg was brilliant the whole trip."

With hindsight, all the women agree, climbing Cader Idris in the conditions they encountered was as tough as anything they did in the jungle. Ken had known it would be, and he used it as a filtering process. He was reasonably confident that if they could make Cader, they could make the trek – barring accidents, of course.

That evening in camp, Ken announced an arrangement that would be a significant factor in the operation of the expedition. The twelve women would be split into two groups of six, and every woman would be paired with a 'buddy' for the whole trip.

The reason for this grouping was primarily to make administration easier. It is recognised in combat units beyond a certain size, that efficiency and effective communication suffer. And the pairing means that there is always one person specifically and mutually concerned with looking out for each individual. He tried to group the women in what he thought would be the most compatible units. He invited reactions to this arrangement from the women. He had a fairly firm idea of how it should be, and they saw no reason not to go along with it.

There were times, however, once they were in the jungle, that the divisions in the group became contentious and looked as if they would lead to serious ructions.

chapter three

A Baptism of Water

Claire flew via Kuala Lumpur to Brunei, arriving in Brunei at 11.15am on the thirtieth of June. She met up with the rest of the Jungle Janes when they arrived at 1.38pm on June thirty-first.

They were taken by minibus to a British Army camp near Tutong Village, currently unoccupied. With slatted walls, it was airy and cool. There were showers, clean loos and conventional beds.

The women spent the next three days, their last in civilisation for some time, acclimatising and preparing themselves for the jungle. They were lectured in helicopter evacuation, and general conditions. They met the Gurkha soldiers who were providing the safety back up team, without which they would not have been permitted to enter the jungle.

It also gave them a chance to sort out their rations, and in the case of one, to visit a hairdresser in the village to have her hair fully plaited to keep her head cool.

They swam in the sea, and took as much exercise as they could. They were also building up calories for the rigours ahead, by eating three cooked meals each day.

For Sally and Catherine, there was a rude introduction to the vast family of creepy-crawlies that they dreaded so much, which culminated in the undignified sight of two middle-aged English ladies, tearing across the compound of a British army camp, screaming their heads off in terror at some innocent and harmless insect.

All the Jungle Janes, naturally anxious to get on with each other, were being as accommodating as they could. The group scape-goats, the natural leaders, and any fundamental incompatibilities there might have been were still well under wraps. In the meantime Ken announced the teams. Team A was to be Gwenda, Alex, Izzy, Fiona, Julie and Susanna, while Patsy, Dicky, Sally, Catherine, Wendy and Claire made up team B.

DAY 1 - Tuesday 4th July

On Tuesday, July the fourth, the Jungle Janes leave the British army camp on the coast at Sittang. They know they won't see it again for at least twenty-three days but they're as excited as a bus-load of kids on a summer outing, although, of course, there are those who manage to maintain an outward appearance of dignified calm. The training sessions, Ken's talks, the helicopter training, the months of preparation and anticipation have got them geared up and ready for the real thing.

After breakfast, they clamber up into two army trucks that have come for them and set off on a two and a half hour ride to Landing Site 108, a quiet playing field by a school on the edge of the rain forest. Two choppers drop down to ferry them the last leg into the jungle proper. The women carry their packed *bergens* from the truck, across to the aircraft and fling them on board as they've been instructed, before getting in themselves.

They fly about twenty kilometres east, for about ten minutes, to landing site LS 230alpha, where they'll make camp for the next few days, until Ken thinks they've learned enough to start the trek proper.

Generally, their reaction is one of pure excitement. But Wendy has a cold; and Alex is feeling the heat.

The Jungle Janes have been asked to record their personal impressions of events each day, either on mini-discs, or in note books. Some are concise to the point of brusqueness; others more effusive.

CLAIRE (the purser)

Sittang Camp was a lot better than I expected, though I found eating three times a day extremely difficult. I'm used to being very much jet lagged and eating as and when I can when I'm at home, and even then, I'm rushing around. It's a very pleasant surprise – even a luxury – for me to be able to sit down and have three fantastic meals a day and, believe me, the chefs here are excellent. We were eating real Eastern food – spices, curries, rice, dhal. What can I say – I'm stacking up on proteins and carbohydrates and enjoying every minute of it, but although I'm trying to put on weight now, I've got to be careful that when I do get into the jungle, I burn it all off.

The beach is only a few hundred metres from here so I decided to have a dip in the sea before we leave; I've found it really cools me off in the mornings. But I'm ready to get on with it now and go into the rainforest at last. It's been a long, long haul from the outset of this whole thing. I think it really started to dawn on me when British Airways finally gave me the go-ahead which, would you believe, was on the day that Paul and Lulu came on the flight to film me.

I think that it's going to be quite tough going – however, we're only as strong as our weakest member, so that means we won't be going at the pace of the strongest.

Anyway here we go.

Gosh, this is really exciting – the helicopters are coming in now and it's just taking my breath away – it shouldn't really because it's the kind of thing that I should be used to – but these helicopters are just awesome.

One of the pilots has just stepped out and is walking towards us. Our team's off now – we're walking towards the helicopter – we're being shown right - three to the rear - left - that's me - three of us to the right. Stop! That's it, not to go any further. I've just been given orders by the pilot himself. Now his co-pilot is coming round opening up the helicopter doors and here we go – loading our packs in – one at a time. The best way to do it is to turn around - put the pack on the step, let the straps off, and then climb in. Now I may be able to put my rucksack in and help the others in one at a time. That's it – rucksack off, turn around, that's better, then I can put the rucksack back now. That's it, catch my hand everybody, right one at a time, in, and sit down. Gosh, fasten my seat belt – as ever – and give out orders.

Now off we go – my goodness look at this – it's magnificent!

We're lifting off! It's brilliant – I am so excited now we're finally getting on with it!

That's a wonderful sight – how often do I get a chance to look out of an aeroplane window? It's great here in the helicopter because you can just see so much – and at last I can see the forest as well. We're up above the second helicopter as it's loading the other group – that's Gwenda's group. We're circling now.

Gosh, it's beautiful here! It's phenomenal, it really is. It looks so dense down there. I wonder how high some of those trees are. There's a river winding it's way through the forest. It's all so amazing – and we're going to be there soon – we're going to be walking, trekking through it all – at last, what we've all been waiting for!

I must admit it is noisy in this helicopter; it's extremely noisy – you can hardly hear yourself think. No wonder they wanted us to wear ear plugs. I've got the headset on so I'm listening to the pilots chatting to one another. I told them there's a great difference from a 747/400, even a 777. It's amazing – so small, so compact.

My goodness! Is that where we're going to land?

You cannot believe this! It can't be more than 50 feet wide – no it's got to be more than that! Good grief! I've just said to the guys, honestly, the nose wheel of a jumbo wouldn't even be able to land there. Do you realise the wing span of a 747/400 is bigger than where we're actually landing. These guys are fantastic – they're so experienced. I do have to hand it to them – we are in good hands.

Gosh, we're just perched here, actually perched! We're not fully landed because the rotor blades are still going round and we have to step out. I just have to look back quickly and I'm amazed that these helicopters can perch on this extremely small space, then off they go.

We've landed finally in to the Tutong jungle, I can't believe it.

IZZY (the events organiser)

This morning, after a couple of hours' bumpy ride in a truck, we arrived at a kind of a football field. There was a little schoolyard beside it, and all the kids came out onto the balconies to wave at us. Once we'd taken off in the helicopters, it was only a short flight to 230alpha. I was in one of the side seats, and I could look out over the jungle. I could look out over the canopy and see toucans flying. It was amazing - it looked just like broccoli down below.

ALEX (the actress)

Well, we finally arrived in the jungle at about two o'clock. We had the most wonderful arrival, so exciting in the helicopter, but extremely hot. I've never been in heat like that before. How on earth these chaps landed a helicopter in the middle of the jungle is beyond me. It was just the tiniest little gap in this huge place with nothing but tree tops below. We landed and got out from the left hand side which is what we were supposed to do. We got our back-packs and then off we went. And now we're all alone here in the middle of the jungle!

We found our camp and it wasn't anything like I had expected. I'd visualised it by a river, on a flat bit. I thought there might be some nice flowers around but there aren't any. The trees are enormous – much taller than anything in England, and there are some very nasty leaves in here with great big hooks on them which sort of stab you when you're not looking.

We straight away tried to put up our *bashas*. It's extremely difficult to try and tie a hammock between two trees when there is only one of you, so we've been paired off into 'buddies', and Gwenda is my buddy. Anyway, we managed to get ours up in the end, but unfortunately it turned out we'd put them up in the wrong place. They were on a very steep slope. Mind you - this place seems to be full of steep slopes. There aren't any flat bits anywhere. But we were just putting up our *bashas* for the first time when suddenly the heavens opened and it started to pour with rain – rain like we never see in England – sort of metal rods shooting down at you, but we all stayed cheerful because it meant that at least we were cool. Usually, when it rains, English people just go and hide under cover, but here it's an absolute God send. The rain lasted for about half an hour – followed by the mud. Mud everywhere. It was while we were slipping and sliding all over the place that Ken came and told us we'd put our *bashas* in the wrong place, and we would have to start all over again somewhere flatter.

When I decided to embark on this trek, I felt what an immense privilege it was to be part of this team. Ever since we got to Brunei, I've upheld that belief. We were very lucky with the Sittang camp. It was just an ordinary Army base, completely empty apart from us, so it felt like it belonged to us, just us. It was very basic, but we had showers and clean loos and clean beds. It was very, very hot but we had a good couple of days to get ourselves together, and now I understand why.

I'm sitting under my *basha* in the rain. I'm covered in mud. I've got no idea how I'm going to get my boots off. I've got no idea how I'm going to get into my hammock; I can't find anything; my backpack is filthy and yet I know when I wake up tomorrow – if I go to sleep – all these things will be incidental. The fact that we will all be filthy dirty with black nails and filthy hair won't mean anything. We have one great thing between us and that is we are all very close and I hope we remain kind to each other because if we don't, I don't know how the heck I'm going to hack this. This is day one of twenty-three days. I've got to find something in me to cope and to give to the others when they can't. I've never done anything like this in my life. I've been mentally pushed before, but never physically; I just hope I can do it with these girls around me. I hope I can pull my weight and I hope I can go to the loo.

KEN'S LOG (The leader)

Some of the women seemed to be expecting something by the river, nice green grass and perhaps a few picnic tables. We're camped on the side of the hill above the river. I explained to them quite early on that there is a reason for camping a little bit away from the river, because of the possibility of flash floods. Even as I speak we've had quite a heavy thunderstorm and the river will have risen a few feet already. Anyway once we got into the camp the ladies started to shake it out into some sort of campsite.

It was interesting that straight away they got on with it, though it still seemed that some of them found it quite difficult to understand that they were being led; they couldn't accept that they should have gone where they were put. As a result, I had to move Gwenda and Alex because they were perched on the side of the hill and there was no way you could get any purchase underneath because of the wet ground. So pitching the *bashas* was the first taste of proper jungle life for the ladies and they did well, I must admit. I was very impressed with the way they got stuck in and managed to get their *bashas* up.

KH 04-07-00

48

CATHERINE (the teacher)

Okay, we're alive, so perhaps if I concentrate on that a little bit. It's been a true baptism of water here. It started absolutely pouring within an hour of us arriving. Today was the big day. I lay awake all last night – my third night of no sleep, but last night particularly because I had volunteered to be overall leader for the first three or four days I needn't have worried, though, because this morning at Sittang at six thirty, everybody got out of their beds in total silence, which is extremely unusual for this group.

For the next half hour, they washed, dressed took their mosquito nets down, packed up their bed linen and did all the things they were supposed to do – without a word from anybody. After breakfast I had to give a little talk about the sort of things we would have to carry with us at all times and then asked Izzy and Dicky to be leaders of the two groups. One of the things that worried me about being overall leader for the first few days was that we'd been told that darkness fell very suddenly in the forest. As we'd arrived about half past two and I thought it would take some time to set up camp, without the added burden of rain, I was constantly clock-watching to make sure that things were done before darkness came. I think it's incredible that twelve, basically suburban, middle-aged women have managed to put up twelve *bashas*, which are staying up, as far as I can see, in appalling conditions and all remain cheerful. I think it bodes well for the next few weeks.

DICKY (the school matron)

My very first impressions of the jungle were that it's – all the words anybody would use – unbelievable, amazing, extraordinary. But really, I felt as if I was in the middle of a fairy tale, like Alice in Wonderland or Gulliver's Travels, where suddenly you are so tiny in this land of giants, trees so high you can hardly see the top and everything seems to be magnified by about a thousand times. Everything is incredibly green and very steamy and it's really, really exciting. Despite the downpour that greeted us, somebody got the campfire going and we had a jolly good supper. Before that, Sally and I went off and started to dig this latrine, which we didn't do very well, but we got there in the end; we've even got a gripping bar.

I'm lying in my hammock now and I'm about eighteen inches off the ground. I think if it capsizes I might break my neck because there is a big log underneath. I haven't seen anything that slithers or slides yet or anything that buzzes. You can just hear the most amazing noise in the background – an absolute cacophony of sound. It sounds like an orchestra warming up, violins, trumpets and trombones all squeaking away, but nothing really frightening. It feels surprisingly comfortable and secure here in the jungle – I suppose a bit like a baby *in utero*. And now I'm just wishing that my children were here; they wouldn't believe it – it's a bit like a dream, except I know it's not because I can't quite reach my cigarettes and my hair is very wet.

Thank God there are no telephones here and I know I will say my prayers tonight – you feel very close to God here, in this wonderful part of his creation.

SALLY (the solicitor)

When I was coming in, sitting in the back of the truck, I felt as though I was being sucked in as the trees closed around us. I felt a tremendous thrill coming into the jungle proper, because the noise was terrific. It was awe-inspiring. Now we're here, it's raining, it's been raining for several hours, but we've got our little *bashas* up and we're relatively dry and it's just so exciting, I feel like squeaking.

We haven't seen much – I saw a little monkey on our drive in and apart from that, I saw a moth. The trees are very big and the roots show – they're sort of upright rather than spreading horizontal roots.

I'm not looking forward to getting into my hammock and taking my clothes off, so I'm putting it off. It's still early – not nine o'clock yet, although it's been dark for a couple of hours. It is quite cosy under the *basha*, and the rain has been very warm.

We've all been pretty busy with our jobs so I haven't really felt at all anxious or concerned about being here for a long time. It's almost still a game, like the beginning of term at school – all the excitement of meeting new friends, having new exercise books and so on. I'm absolutely loving it.

WENDY (the college lecturer)

(Wendy's partner, Alan had specially made for her a series of tiny laminated cards with a "Thought for the Day" for each day she was in the jungle. With great restraint, she read just one a day, in strict order, without peeking ahead.)

Thought for the Day:
Talk slowly; think quickly.

I woke up this morning with a raging sore throat so not really the best of days for me. We're feeling pretty miserable. I just wish it would stop raining so we could get into some dry clothes. I think the jungle's fantastic but obviously, not feeling a hundred percent, I'm not really getting involved.

The jungle itself isn't really what I expected. I thought it would be a lot darker, a lot denser with loads of insects buzzing around but there's been none of that yet. We went down to the river to get the water. It's very pretty, and I'm looking forward to a good dip in there tomorrow, that's if it stops raining.

SUSANNA (the mezzo-soprano)

I can't believe that we are here. The ride from Sittang Camp to the landing site where we were going to pick up the helicopters was incredibly long, over two hours, down the bumpiest road imaginable in army trucks, which don't have anything to sit on in the back except bare wooden benches, and my God we had to hang on for we were fairly tossed around and bumped about. But it was quite exciting as we began to get into the secondary jungle and get some idea of what we were about to go into. But we then arrived at our destination - I can't tell you the name of the place, but apparently it was near the largest longhouse in Brunei, which, rather frustratingly was only five minutes walk down the track, but because we were waiting for the helicopters we couldn't go down and see it.

We got chatting with one of the teachers at the school, whose little boy was with him - absolutely sweet! He was very interested in it all. So here we are in the jungle. There is thunder in the background which gives a bit of atmosphere! I can also hear the occasional bout of hysterical laughter from the other girls trying desperately to get into their *bashas*. I've had a bit of battle with mine it has to be said. They are very narrow, and the knack of getting them the right height off the ground in relation to a height which you can get into them at is crucial, along with hanging the mosquito net at the right height so that once you weigh down the hammock by lying in it, the sides of the net will still hang down far enough to tuck in, not to mention the angle of the tarpaulin, which is really a fine art.

My *basha* is also pitched on a slope, covered with dead leaves and general 'fall' that conceals mud which becomes extremely slippery very quickly. I've already 'gone for a burton' several times.

This afternoon, we constructed a latrine, which is a five star affair, but rather far from where we are based so we are either going to have to move us or it. Personally I think it should be us that moves, partly because my team (team A) are mostly on slopes and one or two were having real trouble earlier and had to move even before it got dark, so there is going to be some house moving tomorrow. Alex is finding it rather tough. On arrival she described it as the "worst hole on earth", but I think she will come round.

PATSY (the doctor)

The journey to the landing site from the camp took two and a half hours and was incredibly bumpy. As we got closer to the native village from where we would fly, the jungle got thicker and thicker until we arrived in an unexpected clearing of mown grass.

Like the others I found flying in on the helicopters an unforgettable experience. The place where we were going to land appeared as a tiny spot in the distance, surrounded by jungle canopy – a narrow saddle about twenty feet wide, with a hundred foot drop on one side.

In the jungle proper, under the canopy, it was dusky and cooler. My first impression was that it isn't unlike the New Zealand bush, though it's hotter and the insects are much noisier. Because the canopy is so high, it is quite airy and not at all claustrophobic. The noise though, is relentless.

I was surprised to find that we were supposed to pitch our camp on the side of a steep hill.

Our *bashas* consist of a hammock, suspended level between two trees, a mosquito net, and a small tarpaulin spread over them in an 'A' to keep the rain off. We soon learned that we have to get it just right. Even a tiny bit out can lead to a sleepless night. It's much easier to erect a *basha* in pairs, though I wanted to battle on and do my own.

To cut away any intruding bush we have been issued with *parangs*, which are very sharp, vicious-looking knives.

We had just got our *bashas* up when there was a rustle of leaves in the canopy, at which Ken and Sergeant-Major Bhuwani exchanged glances. Apparently this rush of wind always heralds rain. When it came a few minutes later, we got under our shelters and watched. It didn't worry me; I don't mind the rain, as long as it's warm.

We had to go down to the river at the bottom of the bank to collect water which we purified and carried back up in big plastic bladders. Looking at the river bank, I could see that it sometimes rises as much as twenty feet, which is why it was so important to camp well clear.

We were told there are crocodiles in the river too. The Gurkhas carry rifles specifically to deal with any that might appear.

I don't think the sleeping set-up is well designed. There are no pockets to keep anything, so we are constantly unpacking and re-packing bags. I have been very minimalist in what I am carrying, knowing I might resent unnecessary weight. I have also decided to eat my rations cold, so that I don't have to wait for hot water (for which there was always a big demand). They are designed to be eaten cold and I find they are delicious like that. I won't be drinking tea or coffee either, only water, though I have brought a few emergency extras: flavouring for when the water is a bit murky; lemon tea powder and a few boiled sweets.

Although the jungle nights last twelve hours, I didn't even want to carry extra batteries.

The noise is incredible – a day shift and a night shift. All the time the whole jungle heaves with insects. I also heard a lot of human snoring. And last night, I had an awful dream - one of my sons appeared, and looked at me accusingly for going away.

KEN'S LOG

The wildlife has already been around. There have been a lot of moths and spiders and most of the ladies have had their own visitors in their *basha*. This has been good experience for them; they've got to learn to live with these creatures. I must say, it's very different having your wife along with you. Gwenda's just up the bank, albeit about 40 metres away and I do feel I've rather dropped her in it, but she's a good team player and I think she'll do very well throughout the expedition.

However, I can see that Alexandra's having difficulties. She's clearly used to having her home comforts around her and is having a bit of an administrative nightmare at the moment. I hope in a few days she'll get that sorted out.

There is certainly quite a bit of friction in the top group - Izzy, Fiona, Gwenda, Julie, Susanna and Alexandra and they're perhaps not getting on as well as I would have hoped at this stage. I think it's the fact that Izzy and Fiona are younger, with more get up and go and more decisiveness. But they've got to sort out these differences as a team and come to terms with each other's strengths and weaknesses. They've got a lot of hard miles to get under their belt.

I had a long chat this evening with the Sergeant-Major Bhuwani, the senior of our Ghurkha back up team. I asked him what he thought. He said the ladies were all very brave to do this because life is an adventure and it's important that people should grasp these chances when they arise. But he also said that we shouldn't push them too hard, that we should treat every day as a different objective and if they make it through that day then they have achieved something. I think there is some wisdom in what he says; I'm not trying to break them. I want to give them an experience which is a growth experience - something which I hope will influence them to go on and do greater things.

KH 04-07-00

chapter four

The Alex
Laughing Bird

DAY 2 - Wednesday 5th July

Ken is planning to keep the Jungle Janes in static camp at 230alpha until he's sure they're ready for the rigours of a gruelling, self-navigated circular trip through the raw jungle. They need a stronger grip on camp-craft. The quality of their *bashas* will be crucial under the regular tropical downpours. They need more training in navigation by dead-reckoning if they aren't to get lost in the first few hundred metres each morning.

They need to learn some basics in tracking, at least so that they can re-trace their own steps if they have to. Above all, he doesn't want any of the small irritations that are already showing to fester and burst at the wrong moment. However determined and circumspect this eclectic group of self-contained women may be, no one can predict what might set off vicious and irreparable conflict.

He knows that no-one slept a lot the night before, even though this close to the equator every night provides a full twelve hours of darkness. In the morning he leaves them to sort out their hammocks and experiment with *basha* construction. They spend a couple of hours navigation training, and in the afternoon he sends them all down to the river to relax and swim.

Alex seems disorientated and Ken is already wondering if he should have encouraged her so strongly.

KEN'S LOG

Alex is sitting away on her own. I can see her looking blankly into space. This is a symptom of finding the whole thing a bit overpowering. To some extent, that's inevitable, but nobody else seems to have noticed. There were quite a few tears from Alex earlier, too, probably due to lack of sleep.

In the lower of the two camps we've made, Sally has been a bit on edge because she feels claustrophobic, but everybody feels a bit claustrophobic in the jungle for the first few days; it can feel very oppressive with all the trees closing in on you. Sally is deceptively mercurial; she can look totally calm, when she's nervous underneath, but when it builds up, she can flip.

Wendy is a little more vulnerable than I first thought.

Claire, on the other hand is very organised, very calm, and taking the whole thing in her stride.

KH 05-07-00

SUSANNA

Tonight is as hot as last night was cold, though it's been dry all day, astonishingly. I got rather wet last night because I haven't yet learnt the refinements of putting up a *basha*. My tarpaulin turned out to be upside down, which meant that I had created three lovely conduits to drop water through the roof, one at my head, one at my tummy and one at my feet. Also the rain drains on my hammock cords were upset when we had to re-build my hammock at one point and so it poured down the straps. So I was a wet bunny and really rather cold.

Some valiant early risers got up and did breakfast and managed to get the fire going, which took forever because, of course, the firewood was all terribly wet. We ate whatever we had decided on - I had opted for porridge which turned out to be a rather stodgy concoction because we put in far too much oatmeal for the amount of water we had. I felt very bloated by the time I had finished it, but with the addition of a few raisins and some dates it was reasonably palatable.

Several people moved house this morning and the Gurkhas showed us how to use our *parangs* to cut stakes to make little wood piles to put our packs on under our *bashas*, because one of the major problems is that this really is a very sloping site and most of us are having trouble with kit rolling down the hill.

We had a meeting after breakfast, chaired by Catherine who is our current leader, and doing a remarkable job, as she claims not to be organised, and not to really want to do any of this. I am having enough difficulty coping with my own bits and pieces and my own existence let alone organising everyone else, so I am heartily glad that I didn't volunteer to be leader. At the rate I am going I will have to think very carefully before I do.

On the practical front, I think Fiona is probably doing best. She has unbounded enthusiasm and energy, but maybe that is what seven years behind most of us gives you. Maybe I am getting old and it is time to realise it!

After lunch we went down with Sergeant-Major Bhuwani and Ken towards the river. This was for three purposes: to sort out pacing (which is going to be crucial), to talk about navigation and how to use the material on our maps to best effect. And all the other lessons that we have got to take on board - that the maps are not necessarily accurate, that rivers are not necessarily a good key to navigation (which is difficult as most of us would use a river as an unarguable source of information, but it obviously doesn't apply here). While down by the river Ken gave us a talk about rivers - how they behave, with storms and constant rain, and the pitfalls to watch out for when pitching camp near a river. I think we are getting a lot of practical experience around the camp but of course setting up a camp that is going to be used for nine days is a luxury we won't have again, and I think at the moment most of us are fearful of moving on because it's going to be much harder. On the way back from the river, we passed a couple of the Gurkha boys coming down to fish. Patsy and I tagged along with them. It was a lovely chance to sit and be a bit quiet by the river and for us to have a chat, because teams A and B into which we have been split operate fairly separately, except at mealtimes.

I am used to being in quite close touch with Patsy at home, usually on the telephone every other minute, so it was nice to be able to have the chance to catch up with her quietly, and it was lovely and peaceful by the river. We watched the two boys fishing, and the largest one they caught, which was about six inches long, was the only one that seemed edible, we duly cooked it for supper. I fear it was one of those extremely bony numbers, hard to compare with an English fish; not a particularly strong flavour, a dryish white flesh, and very bony. And not really the sort of bones, like kipper bones, that you can just chew and swallow. These really asked to be fished out ('scuse the pun) but we managed two or three mouthfuls each. It seems to be better near the tail than the head, but it was interesting to try something local. After supper, which was delicious (these boil in the bags really are excellent – I had chicken casserole tonight, beef and dumplings last night), everybody seems to be impressed by the food.

Now it's a relief to be lying in my hammock, smothered in foot powder and prickly heat powder - many of the girls are now riddled with prickly heat – I have it on my inner thighs but everywhere else seems to have escaped unscathed so far, thank God.

The only person who seems to be really struggling at the moment is Alex, who had a bit of a crisis first thing. I think she always knew that it would be hard but from what I can gather she has less experience of having to sit things out than most of us, which makes it particularly hard. But since she made all the effort to get here, and put in an enormous amount of work at the gym and everything, I'm surprised that her desire to make it all worthwhile hasn't kicked in.

DICKY

It's been the most extraordinary day. We woke up this morning at six o'clock; it was pouring. Everybody was very subdued, and poor old Alex was crying and feeling sick and in a very sombre mood.

But there was hot water boiling on the fire, so we had some disgusting concoction. Fiona was eating porridge oats mixed with Milo, which is some sort of chocolate stuff. I tried a mouthful, it was horrible – glutinous and gooey. I nearly threw up. Instead I had a cup of three-in-one coffee, which is also disgusting, because it has sugar in it, and a piece of soggy bread.

I'm feeling really fine now; I'm beginning to thoroughly enjoy this trip. I do hope it doesn't get any worse and there aren't any dramas. I think it's going to be the best three or four weeks of my life. The only thing is – I think I'm probably not drinking enough, and I haven't peed yet today. The latrine is absolutely splendid, but if you look down between the poles, there are all these filthy little black bugs burrowing away and fiddling around down there, which is quite disgusting. Catherine screams every time she sees something flying.

We've been down to the river, and washed our clothes, but already within three or four hours of getting back from the river, you know, you begin to smell tacky again, and everything is sort of sticky and smells indescribable, a warm, little boy's sweaty pee smell. It's quite grim. Luckily down at the river today we didn't see any leeches or any crocodiles; nobody got leeches up their bottoms and we all washed our hair and had a jolly good splash around –

great fun.

The contents of the silver bags we have for our supper are filthy. I had something tonight called chicken tsitsaka, which is like a chicken curry – whatever it is, it's certainly foul! But I was so hungry, I ate it all.

For the first time this evening, I've had a bit of peace and quiet. I've hung my rosary off the handle of my hammock and I said some prayers tonight. There's the usual racket playing in the jungle – a thing we call the Alex laughing bird, and crickets and bats, and all sorts.

So, today being Wednesday, I'm rather wondering what's been going on at school, and how the poetry competition went. I wish my children could be here to see all this because they would not believe what their ancient mother is doing, and they would have such fun being here as well. I wonder what Lucy's up to, and the people at home; I'm not missing them too much, I just wish they were here to share the experience.

Patsy is being quite extraordinary. She's very independent, striding around, doing her own thing, not saying very much. But Patsy is my buddy, and we shared some treacle pudding this evening, which was a step in the right direction. One of the Ghurkhas caught a fish in the river today and Patsy fried it. When she was eating it, a bone stuck in her teeth, which is quite a human thing to happen to Patsy. Alex on the other hand is very emotional, and either high as a kite, shrieking hysterically and having a wonderful time, or just sitting around rather sad and weeping if anybody is too nice to her. I think she's finding it all very hard.

ALEX

Last night in the pouring rain I couldn't find my boots. I couldn't find anything – everything was covered in mud and it was very depressing but I thought that I would wake up in the morning and everything would be incidental.

Well, ha ha! For the first time in my life I stayed awake the whole night. I couldn't get comfortable. My hammock was wobbling and I was hanging on for dear life at the top end, hoping I wouldn't fall down and crash into Patsy below. Because it gets dark quite early here – there's nothing really to do except go to bed so I was in bed by half past seven, and I knew I had to wait until six in the morning until we could all get up because it was pitch black all the way through. The noise is electrifying – if only I knew which animal made which sound. But we did hear the mating call of the hornbill tonight – two hornbills actually. I have never heard anything like it in my life. So there have been special moments but day two was a tricky one for me.

When I got out of my hammock I thanked God I was still alive – everything was wet, the rain had poured all night and I was frozen solid. I was lying here trying to decide what I would rather be – freezing cold or boiling hot. When I was freezing cold I longed to be hot, but now I've been so hot all day I long to be cold again. We seem to be in a very extreme place; it's all or nothing here.

I lost it a bit this morning. I found it all rather frightening and nerve-racking and when I get nervous, my tummy starts erupting. When I woke up this morning – I won't say woke up, when I got up, I was on water duty and boiling up the water to make everyone a brew. I started to feel very sick and shaky and wobbly – partly because I hadn't slept, partly because I didn't know how the blooming heck I was going to cope with another twenty-three days of this.

Twenty-three days!

It's nothing when you're at home - months fly past at ninety miles an hour. I get up in the morning and five minutes later I seem to be jumping into bed again. But here I've got nothing else to think about except myself and keeping myself going. The Janes are wonderful; everybody sort of realised that I was about to collapse yet again – I seem to be the ropy one, but they're all so good at noticing when you feel a bit rough.

We went to the river today – oh the heavenly river! The jungle at it's most beautiful. The tall trees that grow straight from the water's edge covered in the most glorious greenery. The river clean as a whistle, although brown in colour because of the sand at the bottom and the wonderful Sergeant-Major Bhuwani stood watching out for – wait for it – crocodiles!

I can't believe I'm swimming in a river with crocodiles and I didn't give a hoot! I was so desperate to get in that water. We all were. We suddenly turned into water babies all in the space of five minutes. Everyone came – utter bliss – splashing, screaming, shouting, laughing, cooling ourselves from the insides out. It was fantastic. The thought of having to come out was a nightmare because you had to climb up a bit of a hill to come home, and of course, when we got home, we were all hot again but at least we had washed our clothes and our bodies and we felt like queens.

We're surrounded by an incredible amount of life. Everywhere you look there's heaps of insects – enormous ants and things I've never seen before; they look rather like pterodactyls. We had a little lecture on navigating but I felt so wibbly wobbly and sick and hot, not able to eat anything, still trying to drink, I found it rather hard to take in. I shall think about it this evening, lying in my hammock and try and take it all in, because it's very important that we know what we're doing when it comes to navigating. But it's all terribly complicated. I hope my buddy next door knows a bit more than I do, but I think we might be tested and I don't want to get zero out of ten.

So now I'm going to shut my eyes and I'm going to go to sleep and I hope that tomorrow I'll feel like a new woman.

PATSY

It rained all night last night, though quite softly, as the canopy seems to act as a sort of filter.

In the morning I had a breakfast of rolled oats and Milo, which tastes all right and is packed with calories. Someone found an enormous cicada that must have been ten centimetres long. It rattled when I picked it up.

It started raining again in the afternoon, and some of the others started grumbling about the mud. But what do they expect?

Later I went down to the river and watched two of the Gurkhas fishing. They use bamboo rods and, for bait, they mash up army biscuits, make a paste with a drop of water and knead it into little balls that they put on the hook. They gave me one of the fish they had caught. I cooked it, frying it simply, but I was disappointed; it was very bony and not particularly tasty.

I am quite content, but beginning to see how just the business of survival can take all day.

CLAIRE

It's four thirty in the morning. I'm still awake! Dawn is trying to break. The jungle's getting louder and I think I'm feeling a little more relaxed – maybe I will get a little bit of a sleep now. My mind has been playing the most amazing tricks on me through the night. I was just rigid with fear. I can't think why. I don't remember feeling like that since I was really small and I can't remember why I felt so petrified then. But there it was again, last night, lying in my hammock, thinking things were crawling all over me and crawling around under my hammock – fear of the unknown.

Sergeant-Major Bhuwani and Ken gave us a full talk on navigational skills and pacing. It's very interesting – but would you believe I'm looking forward to this dip in the pool? I can't listen to what I know is the end of the talk, looking out there at the

65

river, longing to get undressed and get into it. After an extremely wet night and getting totally soaked and everything else that went on yesterday, I feel quite dirty and I just want to get into the water and swim, cool down and clean off. There's washing to be done, too. I think I'll tackle that first. Actually it is quite good fun here, it really is, a far cry from the washing machine and all the different spin cycles and all the luxury things of the West. This is fun; it's back to nature and its relaxing and I'm enjoying it.... I think I've finished with my washing now and it's time for a swim. I'm lying here in the water and it's heaven, it really is. Looking around and everyone is so relaxed and calm because it was quite a strange night – not disastrous, but quite muddlesome because of the rain and the rush to put up our hammocks and everything else.

Now it's great to be able to calm down and just relax. Some of the others are lounging, some are in bikinis, some are just swimming in their altogether and my goodness aren't we all enjoying it!

It's five thirty. We've got a really good fire going and have put pans on to boil. Night falls really early here, so it'll be dark very soon. By the fireside there's lots of chatter going on while the cooking is being done and as dusk falls we will be sitting around eating out of our boil in the bags. There's quite a variety of food in these – sausage casserole, sausage and beans, lamb, Lancashire hotpot, chicken kiev and many others. I think there are about twelve, all quite tasty, all very filling and nutritious apparently – real army food.

There's a variety of different characters and personalities among the twelve of us and it's become very apparent that there are those who are entertainers and show stealers, those that are thoughtful and team spirited, those that are independent and self-reliant.

FIONA

I can understand why, and I'm really glad that we took a day off today. I enjoy a break as much as anyone else, but I slept so well last night that now I want to get going. I would rather take more rest days and do a slightly shorter route, than split the group and send someone home. We're in an environment that could potentially kill if you got just one thing wrong – if you didn't drink enough, if you didn't eat enough, if you stayed too wet and didn't dry your feet, if you didn't watch out for the insects and the scorpions, and the spiders and the snakes, and the other caterpillars, that can do serious harm. Any one of these lapses could damage you to the point that you could be sent out, or die. And every day, we're getting one more skill under our belts. We're becoming aware without even thinking that we have to drink enough, that we have to check our feet, that we have to check our bits, we have to check our bodies for leeches. And I think we're doing remarkably well. It just shows the sheer determination of an individual, and how as a group, you can really help each other. Everyone has their lows, but everyone respects the fact that maybe you want to be on your own sometimes.

The Ghurkhas brought in this giant insect, about the size of my hand. Do you remember those teddy bears when you were a kid that growled when you turned them upside down? They had this beetle in their hand which made a noise when you flipped it over. Quite novel!

I got really pissed off today with the navigation because I'm so crap at it. It doesn't help when you're told that the map is over sixty years old, and they only mapped it from the canopy, not from down on the ground. You're told to look around, and it's incredible because there is just so much to see. And you find yourself looking for a knoll, or something else that you can see, and suddenly you find a bright orange piece of fungus or a bright butterfly goes by, and you're distracted again. When we came back from our walk today, the Gurhkas had made us a long seat that we could all sit on. There's so much pleasure to be derived from something as simple as that, it puts everything into perspective. At home, you have the most expensive things, but here it's all stripped away; everything is done because it has to be done. And you appreciate it so much more because someone has offered you a sundried tomato, or a piece of chew, or a prune, because it's theirs – they've had to carry it, but they're offering it to you to share.

I've got the joy of being the leader of my group, which to be honest is a piss easy task, because I've got a cracking good group. Everybody just gets on with what they've got to do because they can see – if there are no logs they get logs, if water needs getting they get it. The only time that we're ever going to have to delegate is for the joy of the latrines. Though I do have to say, I've mastered the art of peeing standing up, which is an attractive option when you think it's that or a leech up your arse - which has happened, and I certainly don't fancy anyone burning that one off.

I think the atmosphere tonight is like Butlins. There's lots of laughter, but it all boils down to the fact that we're a group again. This seat that the Ghurkhas made for us is just awesome and has brought us all together again. We're all eating together, and we all stayed up to a ripe old time of 8.30, playing games and talking, which brought us together, and that's important, because I think that the two groups could become quite separate with a bit of a competitive edge, which could easily become really unhealthy.

I'm listening to Alex James laughing in the dark. She's a nutter, she sounds like the birds that fly over here in the mornings.

IZZY

After a really stormy night, I was actually pretty comfortable. I'm nicely set up here now. I'm just looking out of my mozzy net, and I have my candle perched on the top of a stick at head height, so I can read at night without having to sit with my head torch on. I have a rucksack at my feet, which has got all the essentials that I might need in the middle of the night. I've got my book, my glasses, my water, toothbrush.

After our *basha* rebuilding this morning, we did a few other chores around the camp - collecting firewood and improving the pathways, which were becoming quite slippery.

We built a better fire, and that's kept going beautifully during the day. I went down to the river this morning with a few people, Fiona, Patsy, and Alex. It's lovely, with a sandy beach and sunken logs. We quietly filled our water bladders.

This afternoon we spent some time just getting used to orientating ourselves to where we are in the jungle. Ken and Bhuwani walked us down to the river. We set out some markers to check our pacing. Navigating in the jungle is not quite like anywhere else. The maps are quite old, and made using aerial photographs. So while they show the undulations of the canopy, they don't give you any strong idea of what's on the ground.

Ken gave us some pointers on what to look out for, to open our eyes to what we can see in the jungle. There is so much going on and you can be quite focussed on putting one foot in front of the other, and really miss it. It's about trying to focus beyond the next backpack, and taking some responsibility for our progress.

We also learned some scary stuff about all the things that can happen, like deadfall from trees, snakes, what not to do, where not to camp. It's quite a bit to take in, but a lot of it is common sense.

I did feel for Alex this morning. I think she just felt so overwhelmed by it all. I think there are times when we're all going to feel like that. But she's brilliant. She's such a lovely lady, and I'm sure, with everybody working together, she'll just come through with the rest of us.

WENDY

Thought for the Day:
In disagreements, fight fairly. No name calling.

When I woke up it was absolutely belting down and I thought 'Oh flipping heck!' I imagined the whole area to be flooded, and my rucksack three miles away downstream. I imagined getting up into an absolute quagmire, but it's not too bad. I'm feeling much better today – sore throat's gone, cold's still there, but it's not making me feel miserable. A couple of people are annoying me but I've just got to cut them out – not let them affect me. It's so early on. There are just two at the moment, and it's their problem not mine.

chapter five

Who Wants to be a Raisinaire?

DAY 3 - Thursday July 6th

Ken knows the Jungle Janes still have a lot more to learn before they can be trusted to navigate their way through the jungle. He gives them more training and sends them out on a short ridge walk with Sgt-Major Bhuwani.

On the way, Bhuwani shows them how to pick a palm heart. He also introduces them to the deceptively named 'Wait-a-While' tree.

They spend the afternoon in Club 18-30 mode, down at the river beach, and top off the day with an evening of fun and party games.

KEN'S LOG

I'm sitting here in the middle of the rain forest at 9.20 pm on day 3. All I can see are little candle lights all over the place and one of the Gurkhas sitting looking at the fire. My first impression of today's activity has been that the camp has a holiday air about it. There has been lots of laughing and joking. Okay, so the ladies aren't soldiers and they haven't been under the sort of military pressure that soldiers experience in the jungle. Nevertheless after what they have been doing today, spirits are high. The danger is of course that they are being led into a false sense of security, and part of me wants to tell them, "Right, it's now 9.30. I want you to pick up all your kit and sit on your pack because we are moving at six, as soon as it gets light in the morning and we are going to walk 15 km." Then they won't forget that in a few days' time they are going to have to walk out of this place, carrying all their kit on their backs, and navigate their way through some fairly harsh terrain. And on that journey they are going to meet difficult obstacles. They're going to meet deadfall, river crossings, steep ground. They are going to get tired and they are going to get pissed off. And also they are going to see all the insects that they have met already - leeches and tarantulas. They haven't seen a snake yet, though they're about of course.

On the whole it has been a successful day. The ladies went for a walk - quite a long way -to the top of the ridge and back. They had a chance to know what it is like to march through the forest and follow a ridgeline track and they came all the way back without too many mishaps. Meanwhile I was busy setting a tracking lane for them tomorrow. They have had quite a relaxing afternoon in the river again getting washed, which is a real morale booster. The edge will come when they get on the move and don't have a river to go to at the end of each day. They'll be hanging around in sweaty kit feeling really manky. They'll all stink. We'll see how they cope when there's no river to wash their clothes in and freshen up.

It's difficult for me to make them realise what they are going to undertake in a few days. I think some of them are still bluffing themselves that they're going to stay here, but they're not. As a group they're doing all right. Some of the tasks people are allocated they don't do, of course, and it seems to be the same people who are cooking, the same people who are saying 'Come on let's put some water on.' You notice it when you stand back. The same people stoke the fire, the same people gather the fire wood. I gave Alex a bit of a kick this morning because although she was first up stoking the fire that was her main effort for the day. She was in charge of cooking, she didn't seem to do an awful lot.

My wife, Gwenda just chugs on. I can see her from here, reading a book. She's a very solid character. She still moans a lot, although she promised me that she wouldn't be my wife on this trip; she would just be one of the other expedition members.

[Gwenda, in the distance: You'd better wipe that off!]

Gwenda still won't share her cigarettes with me; she's really tight in that department and Alex won't do any rollies at all. Alex has been smoking like a chimney ever since she got here. She even smokes when she's on the move, which surprises me.

KH 06-07-00

SUSANNA

It's quarter to five, early evening by jungle standards, and I'm having a little quiet time to myself, which I badly need right now. All the other girls have gone down to the river, but I need to dry my clothes, and dry my boots. Getting them all wet again is not something I need right now. Perhaps I will go again tomorrow when I am a bit more under control. I think my main problem at the moment is lack of sleep. Last night was so hot to start with that I sweated into my sarong and made it all damp and yukky, so that is also something that has got to be dried out today. But at least my *basha* is drier and if not yet entirely waterproof, it's getting there. I have started using my silk liner which is a help, with the

73

sarong on top and a dry shirt to hand. I think I am going to get the hang of this eventually. Things otherwise are going well. This morning we had another meeting and Catherine put us all to rights, which again she did extremely well. I'm very impressed by her; she's a very nice girl. In fact I am impressed by a lot of people. I think I have now just about sorted out who will remain on my Christmas card list and who might not...On the whole everyone seems to be tolerating each other very well, but there is the occasional loss of temper, which isn't surprising.

ALEX

When I woke up this morning, I suddenly remembered – "Oh blast! I'm on duty for stoking up the fire." Of course, it was pouring with rain again but it didn't matter because I felt full of beans. I bounced out of my hammock and put on my boots and forgot to check if there were any scorpions; luckily there weren't. I bounded up to the fire which is just above where I am sleeping and stoked it up in the pouring rain. Slowly everybody started to stir and get up and I felt very chuffed with myself. Usually, it isn't me that does those sort of jobs. There are a couple of girls here who are very good at getting up early and getting cracking with life. I just sort of saunter in later, but it was my turn and I hope I did it properly.

Bhuwani taught us some navigation today. It's imperative that we learn this – it has to be taken very seriously. My dear friend Kevin at home had helped me a lot with navigation. He was an SAS training officer out here about six or seven years ago – he knows the Borneo jungle and his love of the place certainly inspired me to learn more and I thank him a lot for all the encouragement he gave me to come here. In fact I wear his compass around my neck for good luck.

We walked for about eight hundred and fifty metres north east and climbed two knolls. It was very beautiful - the Jungle at it's best. Gwenda saw a pig. I didn't. I was too busy checking my feet for snakes and those ghastly leeches. We saw quite a few of them although luckily none of them attached themselves to me. It was quite a hard walk, it was very hot. We only had our water bottles on our backs and our little day sacks. I kept trying to picture what it would be like with our great big monsters on our backs when we go on Monday. Heaven help us!

As we turned round to come home again, Bhuwani told us some secrets of the forest and one of the greatest secrets was this wonderful Palm tree – a tall, tall Palm tree which the *Iban* warriors pinch a lot of because it is a very good food in the centre of the top of the trunk. In fact, the *Ibans* have been chopping down these trees for many years to store – or to sell the sacred juices and the gorgeous heart in the middle. Naturally, we were all desperate to taste it ourselves.

Bhuwani chopped and chopped away with his *parang* – and I think he found it a bit tougher than he'd expected. The tree stood about one hundred feet tall and ten inches thick. He hacked and hacked at it in this heat, then with a thunderous almighty crash it came to the ground and he had to race to the other end of it to get the palm heart just for us to taste. It was delicious.

We found Ken back at the camp; he had been scooting down the river in the opposite direction and had found an *Iban* camp, either warriors or poachers. We were very hot and bothered, completely wringing wet with sweat. It's a funny thing I have never felt so wet with sweat before. We all took a look at each other and said, "Come on, let's go down to that river!"

We stripped off; none of us gave a damn what we looked like, we were all so desperate to get into the water. One of us had to do crocodile duty – can you believe that? – one of us has to stand on this little stump and check for crocodiles. It doesn't bear thinking about!

Ken and the other men turned up while we were all dipping with nothing on. It's funny that none of us give a hoot anymore – modesty is slowly flying out of the jungle.

Oh, yes! Something very exciting happened today when Dicky was putting on one of her designer scarves. Dicky has got loads of little knick-knacks we are all jealous of. Everything she has got is something no one else has heard of, everything is up to date and she is amazingly clean. She is wearing a white shirt and she looks immaculate – she never sweats, she is always starving hungry. But you know Dicky is always full of beans and she is always smiling and a real joy to be with. Anyway, she put on her scarf this morning, her designer scarf, and at the bottom of it was hanging this huge black scorpion. And in the usual Dicky fashion she did not panic. If it had been me, I would probably have swallowed it in horror, but it was the first time I had seen a scorpion in the wild. It was black and it was very big, and it was very angry and Ken called us all down and we sat and looked and hoped we never came across one because it was very vicious, and although scorpion sting can be rectified by an injection it is not a very pleasant thing to happen.

There are two camps now. I'm in the upper half and all the girls are trying to slide past me in utter hysteria. There is no alcohol in this camp and it just proves to me that you do not need it to have fun. We have laughed and laughed this evening with the simplest of knick-knacks to laugh with and everyone took the mickey out of me tonight because I was the chief cook and it is not very nice being the cook because all you have to do is stoke the fire and put the two pans on with the water and then you have to boil up everybody's silver package and everyone is starving and they want to hurry up and eat. It is sort of the highlight of the day to swim and eat and you can only get two bags into each pan. I had to have baked beans again with my Lancashire hot pot; still, mustn't complain.

CLAIRE

I have woken to a very soggy campsite. Goodness, I slept ever so well. I think that what helped me last night was the walkman. I was listening to a fabulous soul tape that my brother made up for me.

Well, I'm lying here at six thirty in the morning, and I'm thinking I don't want to get up. I could quite easily roll over in my hammock and have at least another two or three hours. However, one has duties to perform and my duties this week are catering, so I'm going to prise myself out of this lovely comfortable hammock and into the rain.

I need to get up there and get the fire stoked and get the pans on and ready, with lots of hot water for tea, coffee and breakfast.

Wow! Here I am, stoking the fire – pans are on, bubbling away. Lots and lots of hot water because when you wake up in the morning, it's nice to have a hot drink out here in the forest. It's all a far cry from 747 catering. Here in the Tutong it's slightly different.

It's two o'clock in the afternoon and I've just volunteered to become the new team leader. I'm looking forward to being in charge.

For group leaders I have the wonderful Sally – a person from the legal profession – and I've got the lovely Fiona – very young, very enthusiastic with an extremely bubbly personality.

There is lots of frivolity and we are having a fabulous time by the campfire. We are staying up a little bit later this evening, though a few people have decided to leave the group because they were obviously more tired. Patsy had a bit of a headache, and it looks like Catherine's gone as well. Everyone else seems to be here and we are having a really enjoyable time – lots of fun, lots of entertainment.

PATSY

On navigation training, we walked back past the landing site, and again I found the view breathtaking. We also had our first leech. Nobody likes the idea of leeches, but they don't hurt, and they don't carry disease.

When the Gurkhas chopped down an edible palm, they expended almost as many calories getting the heart out as they gained from eating it.

We saw very little wildlife and few birds. But we did hear the unmelodic call of the hornbills and the impressive sound of their beating wings, but we are living on the forest floor with the insects. I am getting used to the overwhelming greenness of the jungle. The others seem disappointed, although there were some wonderful leaf shapes.

We discovered a tree called 'Wait-a-While', which is a very pretty name, but it has hooks on it, ready to catch people as they walk along, so they can't go forwards or backwards, and have to wait a while for someone else to unhook them. There was also a tree with thorns that grew right beside the path, waiting for people to grab hold as they walked by.

This afternoon I had a headache and felt slightly sick, probably through lack of sleep.

We have realised that animals go through the camp at night, boar, probably, and I have also heard a barking deer. Apparently there are seventy thousand types of insect of which only half have been described; I reckon I have heard all of them.

Some sound like dentists' drills, some like mobile phones, hammers, or depth sounders.

My nausea and headache eventually turned into a migraine, so I went to my hammock. I desperately hope it won't come again. I lay and listened to the mirth and silliness around the fire which went on until late. I fell asleep wondering if the felling of the jungle in neighbouring Sarawak is causing more rainfall.

DICKY

We woke up this morning, and it was absolutely pouring with rain; we slid out of our hammocks and went up to the top where somebody was very kindly boiling a pan of water. I gave up on the porridge and just had a cup of three-in-one tea this morning, that was almost as bad as the coffee, but not quite. We were told that we were going to have a go at navigating with Sergeant Bhuwani, who was taking us on a long walk. My feet were fine so I was quite looking forward to it. I went to put my scarf on, just before we set off. I was about to run my hands down it, when I saw the most massive scorpion clinging to it! And the awful thing was, the scarf had been hanging on my hammock ties, so if it had crawled up along them, it would have come into my bed instead of sitting on the scarf! Anyway, I was quite calm. I flicked it to the floor, and called everybody. Ken got frightfully excited, and Paul got frightfully excited, and everybody photographed it, and it jumped around a bit, and flipped its tail. I suppose, if one was being truthful, it was about six inches long, but it was absolutely disgusting. Sergeant Buwhani picked it up between two sticks and took it off into the bush.

We had our first walk in the jungle. I have not got the hang of this compass business. We were supposed to be walking up this ridge from the landing strip, which looks like a little sausage, then we had to walk along three contour lines close together, which means a ridge, to another little blob. If you walk on a ridge, it means you've got land dropping away on both sides of you. Actually it was quite beautiful, and you're supposed to be doing this pacing business, which means you're counting your steps. I walk about ten steps every ten metres. So you know then that when you've walked a hundred metres, that's a hundred double steps, like you count every right step, or every left step. But obviously it's a few more if you're going uphill or downhill. Anyway, approximately every hundred metres, we stopped and checked our position. Fortunately, quite a few people seem to know what they're doing, so we got to where we were supposed to be going.

Sally and Catherine are very good fun. We've christened them 'The Dangerous Sisters'! Catherine screams loudly every time she sees an insect or an ant. She screamed so loudly this evening, just as I got into my bunk, that the cigarette dropped out of my mouth, and burned my bosom. I brushed it off and it landed on my sleeping bag, and burned a hole in that. So that was quite funny. This evening, for the first time, I quite miss my mum. I wonder very much how she is I'm also thinking about my brothers and sisters, John, Veronica, Mark and Kathy, wondering what they're all doing.

I hope there aren't any scorpions around tomorrow, because that really put the heebie-jeebies up me. Ken says if a scorpion stung you, you would be quite ill, and they wouldn't hesitate, they'd just evacuate you out, and that would be it. Thank God that didn't happen to me today, because that would have been the end of my adventure. I'm still at the beginning, still looking forward to it. I haven't lost any weight yet. But feeling very privileged to be here.

GWENDA

It's 9 pm, which is the latest any of us have been to bed. We've been sitting round the fire, playing 'Who wants to be a Raisinaire?' which is the same format as Who wants to be a Millionaire,' except you don't win money, you win raisins. That was quite a giggle. And then we played Capital Cities, Countries of the World, you name it, but we've all had a good giggle and a laugh. The camp is looking great now, with the Ghurkhas' bench.

We did a bit of navigation today, which I'm hopeless at, absolutely hopeless. Looking at the map, I don't know if we're going uphill or downhill, even when the contours are close together. I just haven't a clue. But hopefully, by the end of this week here, I'll have some idea. I won't be completely useless.

We also saw a fantastic scorpion today on Dicky's scarf. Luckily it didn't bite her. I saw a pig, too, running through the wood. And nobody else did because by the time I shouted 'Pig!', it had disappeared. We went for a swim today, and people are no longer shy about washing anything. And I was swimming with nothing on at all, in front of the men, I don't know what Paul must think of it all, but people are no longer at all self conscious. And at last my clothes are beginning to dry, which makes such a difference.

IZZY

We're going to continue to do day trips out and have a look around here, and pick up some new skills from Ken. We'll make some more improvements to our camp, and general camp craft. Everybody seems quite well at the moment. I don't think anybody has any major problems. I'm sure a few people are a bit nervous about going out and trekking on a daily basis, it seems like a lot of time we're going to spend on the move. But I think it's just best to take a day at a time. And doing that, you can enjoy the highs of each day, and move on if you're having a bad day. Fi's got a bit of wildlife in her *basha* tonight. She got spiders in her boots earlier. We got leeched today for the first time. We found the little critters, but nobody has been sucked yet, though I'm sure it won't be too long. I'm not very happy to hear that the socks I've got aren't much of a barrier to them. My tops don't tuck into my trousers very well either. So no doubt I'll be a meal just waiting for the little bastards to get at.

WENDY

Thought for the Day:

Remember that everyone you meet is afraid of something, loves something, and has lost something.

Apparently the Gurkhas think we won't even manage a kilometre a day and we'll give up after about seven days - they don't see us lasting the course – so we've got something more to prove now.

I saw my first leech today. Fortunately, I didn't have any on my clothes, though quite a few of the girls got them around boots and socks and things. It was much smaller than I had imagined and it walked like a spring – sort of jumped/crawled like a slinky, Fiona said. I think they must be very much bigger when they're on you. They're really small little tinkers – have to watch out for those.

Apparently we're not moving out of here until Tuesday which is a bit disappointing. We were supposed to leave Monday and we're all itching to go. I know we've got a lot to learn before they can trust us, but we are getting a bit restless.

chapter six

The Birthday Party

DAY 4 - Friday July 7th

The Jungle Janes are taught the vital art of floating their kit across a river, without getting it wet.

In the evening, they have a bit of a party for Paul Beriff, the cameraman, whose birthday it is.

GWENDA

We did our first river crossing today. Ken showed us how to wrap our rucksacks up in our tarpaulins, and how to cross the river. Alex went straight in, good girl. I think she felt very confident doing the swimming, because she's a good swimmer. She's so funny, she makes me laugh so much. She's a good bunny. When we sat waiting this morning, I was chatting to the others about the type of people we were and how we thought this expedition would change us. And if it did change us, in what ways. And would it only change us if we allowed it to. Ken seems okay. I think he finds it a bit lonely at times. He's got to keep separate from the girls in a way. But he's doing really well. The girls have taken to calling him 'The Hairy Bear', or 'The Grizzly Bear', one or the other, depending on his mood.

SUSANNA

Alas, I did not get much sleep last night - about three and a half hours. It's not enough and today has been one of brinkmanship. I am permanently behind, and always seem to be rushing to keep up, but now Ken has had a look at my *basha* and straightened it up so that it's flatter and I shouldn't slide up and down so much. However, it was quite funny that when we tested it the second time this morning I 'went for a burton' because one of the D-rings snapped. I was very glad it happened then, when everyone was there, rather than in the middle of the night. Last night after supper there was considerable campfire activity which sounded great fun, but I decided to turn in, because I just needed to lie still and cool off and dry a bit. It didn't rain at all during the night which meant that it remained very hot and humid. This morning we did a bit of tracking and trapping - not much trapping because apparently you need a lot of *rattan*, which is a type of coarse grass, and the *Ibans* have used most of the *rattan* in the area already so not many traps were able to be set. But those we were shown were remarkably effective - there was one extraordinary man-trap that looked rather like a larger version of a mine you would use at sea, floating, with great spikes of wood sticking out of it. They rig it up on a string with a trigger so that as the prey is walking along it is released to come swinging down. Unfortunately, one of the Gurkhas let it go and it hit the Sergeant Major who was teaching us on the chest. This evening he was able to show us the marks of its impact on his chest, so it shows how effective it can be. The other trap was for trapping animals, based on a catapult system with a pulled back string which is released by a trip to produce a noose round the animal concerned. It was very ingenious.

Tracking with Ken was fascinating. You can see so much when you know what to look for and how to interpret it. There was quite a big break that we were able to spend by the river. There were some very lovely butterflies about but they didn't seem to settle, and if they did they certainly didn't open which was frustrating, photographically speaking.

This afternoon we did an exercise in how to transport our *bergens* and *bashas* across the river. Again it was all very ingenious: parcelling our packs in the tarps, reminded me of the presents that Squirrel Nutkin and his friends gave to Old Brown wrapped in leaves. We swam across and presented our parcels to the opposite bank. It was blissful to get into the river. I was beginning to reek like nobody's business, just from one day of not having been to the river, so that was a lesson learnt - that I ought to try and get down there once a day, but there just aren't enough hours. I'm praying hard for a good nights sleep tonight. My main impatience has been with myself over the last twenty-four hours. Catherine has ceased to be our leader and we now have Claire who seems very efficient. Alex is now on cracking form.

This evening we had a terrific time because we went to the Gurkha camp which is only about twenty metres from ours, but is just the other side of a little bulge which stops them hearing us and us them, although they do hear Alex's laugh as did I until rather later than I would have liked last night, so we have agreed a 10pm curfew tonight which I think will be a good move overall. But we had terrific fun round their fire because it was Paul's birthday, and the Gurkhas had made a magnificent throne, complete with little notice saying 'Director's Chair' on the back. They had covered it in round palm fronds which looked fantastic. He sat in it in great state, and the Gurkhas cooked a magnificent chicken curry and some more of the fish they'd caught. We discovered that if you deep-fry them long enough the bones become almost crunchable. They were certainly more palatable that way than when Patsy had just fried them. Then the entertainment began. It took a long time to get the Gurkhas going but once they did it was quite hard to stop them, and they were terrific. We went through the old campfire routines of singing repetitive songs and Ken has got a pretty good repertoire and a good voice when coaxed into it. I just about remembered 'Tit Willow' and attempted 'Stately as a Galleon' but after a couple of verses had a complete default. My brain is simply not here at the moment. But it was great fun, with candles and those coloured light sticks which were very jolly. Then it was time to come back and get sorted because we've got a long day tomorrow. Ken is beginning to warm us up for the big one and so we've got a walk with half-filled packs which will get us in the mood. We've got to make an early start. So please may I get some sleep.

CATHERINE

We set off in two groups one to do tracking, and one to do trapping. And of course trapping is something that I have always wanted to do! But seriously, I found it very exciting, and enjoyed it very much. And in a way it's like being transported into a different world, a second childhood – all those things you really wanted to do when you were a child, but never had the opportunity to. And of course, my children are probably now too old to learn those particular skills. Or rather, not too old, but just at the wrong age. It's fascinating when you're tracking because obviously you have to be very observant. But it's the sheer concentration that's required that's so astonishing. And apparently you'd only do it, if you were doing it properly, for about forty minutes at a time. That's something I can understand, having tried it today.

In the afternoon, when we went down to learn about river crossing, everybody was dying to get into the river on any pretext. So learning how to cross it was as good as any. At one point it became quite hysterical as various members became very vociferous, and were told that they would have to take off their clothes in order to keep them dry, of course. Several had failed to put on any underwear – a normal occurrence in this place, because it is just so hot that sometimes you're quite desperate to find ways of keeping cool. On the positive side, I've now learned how to keep my clothes dry and to cross a river safely – a vital skill in the middle of Brunei, but not much use in the shires of England. But then again, that's exactly why I'm doing this crazy thing.

Ken has also told us about incredible flash floods that can occur, and last night I heard a very deep rumbling - low, quite threatening, at first I thought it was an aeroplane, but it was the wrong time of night, and I haven't heard a plane crossing over here before. Then I realised it was probably this sort of tidal wave that comes down from the hills. In isolation, it's nothing, but when you think what it means, it becomes quite terrifying. I'm very glad to be here with someone who knows what's he's doing.

PATSY

The daily act of courage we have to perform is the donning of wet clothes, which never seem to dry because of the humidity. Our clothes dry on us, then get wet again, but we all keep one set of clothes completely dry, come what may, to sleep in.

We are all completely fascinated by dung beetles. They never stop working. We have spent hours watching them. There are also iridescent blue dragonflies that are very beautiful.

We have learned how to build vicious traps from practically nothing, and have seen a few realities of jungle warfare, which were nasty. Tracking training has taught us to be observant and aware of what we are seeing around us, which will help with navigation.

There was singing around the fire last night. Once the Gurkhas were persuaded to join in, they wouldn't stop for quite some time, with much grinning and dancing. They're very proud of their British military tradition, and some of their songs go back to World War I. I did the beginning of a 'Hakka' and 'Pokarikariana' with Alex, who's half Kiwi.

CLAIRE

I found the tracking that we did today absolutely fascinating. Ken described it perfectly though I must admit, initially I thought I wouldn't be able to see anything. I was so pleased when it came to my turn. They said I did very well and I noticed all of the tracking markers i.e. signs that were in the section. Gold star for Claire!

What you have to look for are signs as you are going along what you believe to be the trail of the person that you're tracking. Sometimes you're stumped between two or maybe three trails but you look out for signs – such as an indication of somebody having stepped on a leaf or a few leaves that look very flat – or maybe even an indentation or a footprint, especially if it's softer ground. You also look out for signs like leaves that have been turned over – sometimes people leave tracking marks because they're wanting someone to follow or they expect to turn around and return along that self same track. It was really good – something I will be doing when I get home one day – in the forests out in Surrey with Nathaniel.

Here I am at the river at the end of a swim and a washing period – not a lot of people have done washing today because it's been such a dry day that we're all glad the things we did wash yesterday have dried! 'Big Bear' Ken is sitting up on the bank – I think he's doing 'croc watch'; he's got a face as grim and stern as can be. I know sometimes we do wind him up. Imagine taking twelve women trekking in the rain forest jungle – you've got to be very tolerant, and you've got to like women an awful lot. Well he knows us all so obviously he can tolerate us all but my goodness we do give him a hard time.

As it's Paul's birthday, we've had a bit of a party. It was full of frivolity, lots and lots of singing and dancing going on. We can see that there are some fantastic singers amongst us and there are people who really enjoy doing their party pieces. It's lovely to see that Susanna, who is a wonderful opera singer, and I've heard will not generally sing along when others are singing, got up on centre stage and did a rendition for us, so we are very much honoured.

She is getting into the spirit of things. I'm really pleased about that. My buddy Wendy and I had noticed there was an awful lot of noise going on late last night and we felt, particularly because Patsy and Susanna had gone to bed quite early, that it was quite thoughtless of others. So I got together with her and asked if there was anything that was bothering her.

FIONA

We've already been here a week, and it's gone so fast. Today has been the best day for me. We swam across the river, which was great when you're not wearing any knickers, bottom bobbing, but I was determined to keep my hat on.

We were invited to dinner by the Ghurkas, for Paul's birthday - our first chance to put on some make-up, mud being the main feature, and powder coming a close second. A little bit of leaf jewellery and leaves in various people's hats. Being girls, we were fashionably late, and we accompanied the birthday boy in his kilt, complete with a leafy sporran. They fried us some fish, which was incredible, and passed round this jerky which everyone turned their noses up at, and they cooked us a curry, which was just delicious. We then presented the birthday boy with his chair and it turned out to be possibly one of the best evenings I've ever had. It was one of those evenings that money just can't buy. Twelve girls, sitting around a little fire, all with the Ghurkhas. We sang, then they sang, and they danced, and it was wonderful just seeing their faces, and how relaxed they are with us. You see these guys could, at the drop of a hat just blend away into this jungle and survive. I just feel kind of honoured to be a part of this evening. You really can't create something like this, and this is just a week in. It amazes me how far we've come in such a short time.

I'm sporting a rather attractive rash, though my feet are fine. My toe rings are still intact. I have no intention of removing those little babies. It's good, I really like it here. I don't think I could stay for eternity, but each day I'm beginning to appreciate more and I'm seeing more. I'm becoming aware of the people around me, and I'm learning about them. There's always more to people than meets the eye, and you don't often have the opportunity to get to know them properly.

One thing I'm really learning to do is conquer my fear of spiders. I'm not saying I'm ready to sit in a bath with one, but before, whenever I walked into a bathroom or a room in my house, I could just about bear dealing with a spider, to the extent that, as a last resort, I would stand as far away as I could and shove a box over it and get rid of it half way down the road for fear it might return. Whereas here, I'm sitting on my own in my *basha*, and on my rucksack there's a spider, not unusually big, but, thumb and forefinger, and I'm just like, shoo, go on, get away. Not a second thought, which is unreal, a real breakthrough for me.

Today is the first day that I've felt really emotional, just because it's so incredible. It's Friday evening and back home I'd be getting ready to go out, having a bath, shaving my legs, putting on a nice dress and my shoes to have a few drinks and go dancing. I did everything tonight, I did the shoes, my boots, I got dressed up, put on a dry pair of trousers, I did my make-up, removed a bit of mud from my face, wiped a bit of sweat off. Put my jewellery on, tied a nice green necklace around my neck. Went off partying down to the Ghurkhas. I sang, I drank, I ate. I did everything I do normally every Friday, but in the middle of the jungle.

WENDY

Thought for the Day:

Remember the three R's: Respect for self. Respect for others, Responsibility for your actions.

I was getting the water bladders ready to go down to the river and a wasp went into my shirt. I felt something. I wasn't quite sure so I sort of pressed my finger against my arm and the wasp stung me which was a major panic. I had to take my rucksack off and the girls – Gwenda and Patsy – quickly took off my shirt, by which time the wasp had gone away but left a quite nasty sting. Fortunately, I found that I don't get a shock from wasp stings. I'd never been stung before so I didn't know how I was going to react. It seems to be okay. The swelling has gone down, it's just very red. We did a bit of tracking with Ken for an hour or so, which I thoroughly enjoyed. It was quite difficult and took a lot of concentration, but I would love to be able to go into the woods with Sam and Chris and do a track for them - I think they'd like that.

chapter seven

Generation Gap

DAY 5 - Saturday July 8th

This is the first day Ken asks the Janes to cover a substantial distance through the jungle. He doesn't want to over face them, and tells them that if they can hack their way through one and a half to two kilometres, that will be an achievement. They are to carry around twenty five pounds - about half the weight they will carry when they move off for real.

They were three and a half hours late getting back, but they had covered four kilometres.

ALEX

Still in a strange world. None of us really yet knows what we're in for, I find myself counting the days, twenty one days in this funny old place.

I seem to be rather unsure of myself. The nerves in my stomach are playing up. I do wonder to myself whether or not I'm going to be able to cope with this. At least we've got a nice bit of river here. It has a little beach attached to it, where we can all sit comfortably. That's another thing here, you can't sit down anywhere comfortably, though I suppose when we start our big trek, we'll be lucky if we find another place like this.

It poured with rain this evening. It's terribly depressing because we can't all get together, we all sit like little bees in our hives, on our own. Stuck in my little hut, I can feel a little madness in my mind - if anybody pinches my spoon, I'll get them! I can see that happening. We did have a little bit of a lift today when Ken swam nude in the river. That was a laugh.

CLAIRE

Our fifth day in the rainforest, today will be my first full day as leader of the twelve. Last night Ken had a discussion with me. He said that we were going on a full trek through the jungle, until approximately 1.30pm, so he wants us to be moving out at eight o'clock sharp in the morning. So as the evening after Paul's party was rounding up, I decided to notify everyone of our requirements for the following day i.e.: the equipment that was to be taken. We needed our rucksacks to be packed with approximately twenty pounds of weight in them; we also needed to have our maps, compasses and penknives, pen and paper and walking sticks, water bladders, totally full, the two water carriers that we have, as well as our own individual water bottles.

I recall Ken saying that he expects us to complete possibly one maybe one and a half kilometres a day so that's my goal. If I am honest, my goal is beyond that. Obviously Ken has the expertise, but let's see how things go. I know what we are aiming for and if we achieve more than that I will be very pleased. Gwenda is doing my timekeeping for me and she is very good at that. She automatically seems to know what needs to be done and suggests things to us. She is an extremely good team player and a good leader as well. She has taken it upon herself previously, on the training weekends, to do the timekeeping so I decided to delegate that out to her on this trip.

Ken also asked me to choose someone to be in front with me. I chose Patsy because I saw that when people put their hands up to volunteer there was Patsy, and also Alex and Dicky. I wanted

Patsy specifically because as the doctor I felt that it was good to have her in front and then Alex with us, either behind me or preferably behind Patsy. Because of Alex's size, we have to keep an eye on her at all times and she has to be at the front with the person that is setting the pace. I found out for myself, being at the back climbing Cader Idris on the second training weekend, you tend to lag behind, you're focusing on being the person at the back and that can be very demoralising.

Another thing I noticed on that training weekend was that Fiona who has got lots of energy and is young, came to the back to help those of us who needed geeing up. She has this amazing quality of always being bubbly and full of life, no matter what. She has strength in her body, strength in her character and boundless energy.

I felt it was a successful day. Even though at one point we came to a halt, where I was thinking, my God, we're lost - after all the hard work that we've done. But we weren't lost and I'm so pleased that at the end of it all we did about four and a half kilometres. I knew we could do it, I knew we could do one and a half, but, my gosh, four and a half totally exceeded my expectations.

Apparently, through the grapevine, I heard that the Ghurkhas feel that we've done exceptionally well. They did not expect us to even last a week, so there we go! I really am very pleased.

SUSANNA

Needless to say I didn't get much sleep last night. However, today's trek was very interesting, the jungle was looking fabulous and I am getting more and more inspired by it. We are in an astonishing environment, though most of us are taking a while to realise that we have to look for the minutiae and appreciate things like the tiny insects camouflaged as bits of lichen, insects attached to trees that look like leaves and only when they move does one realise they are there. And the height of these really old trees - they have huge buttress roots, looking like rockets, - towering into the sky for two to three hundred feet!

Alex struggled a bit, walking with a lot of grunts and groans which, it emerged in conversations later, are beginning to grate on a few peoples' nerves. They feel that as a result, she gets more attention than those who complain less. There is also a bit of jealousy about the camera in the sense that people feel it is turning into a show with two or three stars as opposed to twelve equal players. I personally feel that it is a bit early to judge and I think we have got to trust Paul, who all along has said that he wants it to have twelve equal parts. I think he is understandably wary of one or two, and one or two have also stated quite specifically that they are not interested, so he may be taking that into account as well.

PATSY

Ken took us on a route march today, as a reality check against the tendency of some of the group to turn the whole expedition into a party, and to prepare us for what is to come. He said he didn't enjoy that role.

We climbed and climbed. Everything in the jungle is steep but it was hard – even though we were only carrying half kit, plus sixteen pound water bladders which we shared between us. We had lunch at the top of a hill, and on the way back, all struggling we got lost frequently, which was alarming. We found our way home, three and a half hours late, after walking for eight hours – and four kilometres.

When we got back, there was a torrential downpour, which made it difficult to light the fire, but luckily on the trek we had found something called *demmar* – the solidified resin of a tree – which Ken told us could be used for lighting fires. Some of the girls had picked some up, as souvenirs. They saved the day. We found that if we scraped some onto the fire, it ignited.

I am beginning to think that the reason I am organised and on time, is because I have surrendered to the mess, mud and water, and don't waste time trying to fight it.

I don't think that Alex should ever carry water on top of her full kit. I don't know what the others will think; some have already told me they would begrudge carrying Alex's load on top of their own.

As we were collecting water from the river, I noticed it was changing colour, owing to silt coming down – a sure warning of a flash flood as a result of rain further up the hills.

SALLY

I enjoyed today. It was nice to get back and to feel a sense of achievement at having completed a long walk, which was probably about half an hour too much for me, but I suppose that's what training is – doing a bit more than you wanted to. A couple of things happened on the walk. A baby bamboo snake slid across Alex's foot, and was caught by Bhuwani, so we all had a good look at that. And although I'm frightened of snakes, I'm also fascinated by them. So I'm pleased to have seen one, even though it was being held up at the time, as an exhibit. I wish I'd seen it on the forest floor. The other interesting thing was that we appeared to get lost, and there was a variety of reactions to that, because we were fairly near the end of the walk, and for some it was demoralising, while others managed to summon up some Dunkirk spirit to carry us through.

DICKY

Well, well, well. Oh, bummer. Well, oh crikey. This is Dicky, Bloody hell, today is, crikey, Saturday, the... I don't know what... of July. Must be about the eighth or ninth. And we were woken up this morning by the siren bird that sounds exactly like a police car, going dee da, dee da. Anyway, we were supposed to be up and ready by quarter past eight to start our practice walk.

This turned out to be quite heavy going, and on one of the first slopes we came to, I slipped down, distended my leg really badly and pulled my top thigh muscle, which was really painful. Fortunately we stopped soon after that at the bottom of the slope by a river. People were busy filling up the water bladders so I sat very still, for about five minutes, feeling sick, sweaty, and very faint. But nobody asked me to carry a water bladder, and I didn't offer to, so that was fine. I took two Nurofen straight away, and off we went again. The pain eased after about an hour, but it's really been quite bad all day. What's interesting is to realise how vulnerable any single one of us is.

We finally stopped at the top of some ridge at about one o'clock, and got out our *hexi-burners*, very efficiently, and cut up our blocks of whatever it was, looked like Kendal mint cake, boiled up some water, and had a lovely cup of corn soup. Actually I'm lying, because corn soup is absolutely disgusting. Anyway, the rest seemed to do my leg a lot of good, and it wasn't quite so painful. Still painful going downhill, but fortunately not uphill. We continued going uphill for quite some time, when there was a huge scream from Alex, who incidentally is an enormous drama queen. She screams and grunts and goes on as if she's going to give birth any minute. Aah, ooh, aah, ooh. All these dreadful noises from her, but this was a genuine scream; she had seen a snake, which Buwhani then caught. It was a bright, lime green, about eighteen inches long. Bhuwani was holding it with its mouth wide open. He told us that if it bit any of us it would be fatal, and we'd have to be flown straight out, so it's pretty poisonous.

When we stopped for lunch, Sergeant Bhuwani said, 'Oh Dicky, you've been bitten by a leech!' I looked under my arm, and there was blood all over my white shirt. And so I had to take it off, and find where the leech had been. There was a puncture mark, just under my left arm and a lot of blood. Funnily enough, I hadn't felt a thing, so what they say is quite right – you just don't feel them. Where it had gone to when it had had enough, I dread to think. It's probably down my trousers. Having had the first scorpion, and seen a snake now, really the leeches are not too bad. They look like little thread worms, and they do sort of summersaults, head over heels. Apparently if you cut them in half, the head end grows a bottom and the bottom end grows a head, so you might as well not bother. Ken had originally said we'd be back by about two o'clock, but we still weren't. The jungle we were walking through had deteriorated fairly rapidly into a lot of bamboo shoots and things and we couldn't go any further. We thought we had got well and truly lost, so we all sat down and contemplated spending the night in the jungle, because by this time it was half past four, and it suddenly gets dark between half past five and six.

Eventually at about five o'clock, we staggered back into camp. I think everybody had pretty well had enough. We'd been on the go from half past eight , with packs on our backs, walking fairly steadily. Every half an hour we had stopped, and had a quick sort of five minutes rest, and probably every hour and a half we had had a ten minute break, with back packs off, and water. But it was very heavy going. I think we covered about four kilometres - which was the buzz going round. It doesn't sound a lot, if you consider it took us from half past eight to half past four, but it's just so different walking in these conditions.

I came to at about six o'clock. People had got our campfire

going, and we had our army issue silver boil in the bags. Tonight I had sausage casserole, which was very nice. And just when I thought I'd got to my last sausage, I found another underneath that one. It was a real bonus; it felt like Christmas. It's quite extraordinary how one can get worked up about an extra little sausage in a silver bag. Anyway that was jolly good, and then we had some hot Milo, which is rather nice chocolate for drinking afterwards. Everybody seemed to come back to life, and Alex' spirits were soon restored. As soon as you've had a hot meal, even though it's still pouring with rain, it's fine.

But I'm still going to have my usual fantasies about digestive biscuits. I was thinking about Ritz biscuits today. Ritz biscuits with some butter, real butter, and some Stilton cheese. And an ice cool, gin and tonic, I would die for, just die for.

And I must admit, I did take a bag of lemon tea out of our communal sack and put it in my left pocket. I'm having a bit of conscience about it, so I may put it back in the morning, but on the other hand I may not. As somebody said to me back at school, I think it was my cleaner who is a great friend of mine, she said, 'Dicky, look after yourself; sod the others.' Which doesn't go down very well for a Catholic girl, but the temptation is very strong to grab for yourself and not worry too much about the others. I'm fighting against it, but I tell you what, if I had a bar of chocolate here now, I wouldn't share it.

So, it's been an exciting walk today – far more than any of us could really manage. And far more than we'll ever have to do again. But we survived.

Alex cheers up the minute we get back to camp. She does an awful lot of whimpering on the trail, but really, she's a very jolly person to have around, and I think incredibly brave, because she's carrying around a fair amount of excess weight.

Claire's being a very good leader, terribly sensible and

positive. I should imagine she makes a very good air hostess. Wendy is being a little bit quiet tonight. I think she sets herself rather high standards, and she's a little bit disappointed that she feels tired, and wet and miserable, like all the rest of us. Sally and Catherine have been having great giggles, and they're absolutely fine. Catherine and I have decided we're going to say Mass tomorrow, as it's Sunday.

IZZY

What made today tough was that we had to carry our day's supply of water with us. We were carrying an extra sixty odd litres of fluid between us. After we stopped for lunch, we tried swapping the bladders round, but I don't think we swapped enough. There were some people who took a lot more responsibility for carrying the water than others, and I think that's our own fault. What we've got to do is share the jobs out, and not let the same people take the responsibility for the rest of the group.

We saw our first snake today when it ran across Alex's boot. She probably wasn't the best person for this; she jumped out of her skin. I think Alex found the trek quite hard, but I really admire some of these ladies, in fact I admire all of them. I don't have it very hard, I'm reasonably fit, and I don't have any responsibilities at home. I do exactly as I like, really. But for them, it's a lot more difficult. If you've got family you've left behind, children and husbands, I admire them for putting themselves in this position.

chapter eight

Lazy Day

DAY 6 - Sunday 9ᵀᴴ July

Ken gives the Jungle Janes a day off.

The day before took a lot out of them, especially the less hardy and, provided there are no last minute hitches, he plans to leave their static camp at 230alpha the following morning and set off on a full circular trek.

He has arranged for a helicopter to come in that morning to the landing site on the top of the ridge behind them, where they landed at the beginning of the week.

Some of the women are nervous and apprehensive about finally heading off into the real unknown. And there are signs of cracks appearing in the seemingly indestructible relationship the women have formed since the training weekends in Britain.

SUSANNA

A day off, but an early start as the helicopter with the re-supply was due at about eight am. In fact it didn't turn up until an hour later so we spent the time sitting about on the landing site which was lovely. Good view and all very splendid.

I had a very interesting chat with Claire up at the landing site where we have constructed a washing line to dry our clothes. She is a very nice girl and I've got a lot of respect for her. She talked quite a bit about her team and her frustrations and there is obviously a lot of camera jealousy going on in team B that I don't think many of us were aware of. More people seem to be fussed about the cameras than I would have guessed.

In the afternoon I did some photography, but it was frustrating, as I couldn't find very much on the two paths that I am allowed to go down on my own. They are too well 'man trodden'. Yiso, one of the Gurkhas, turns out to be a very keen photographer and came and had a long chat with me, leaving me feeling very inadequate as he clearly thinks I am a much better photographer than I am! We have had an early night and the bliss of dry, clean clothes, probably the last ones we'll have for a while.

SALLY

For our last day in base camp, we had a relaxing day.

It was wonderful to get out onto the landing strip where everything was just huge in front of you after being down in the trees, with only glimpses of sky.

The sky was a vivid blue; it looked almost like a child's painting. There was one tree, which I think was dead, that stood out against the blue sky, and it was incredibly definite in its outline. I loved being in the open, and so it was a treat that the helicopter was late.

We all did our washing in the river, and hung it up on the landing strip. And there was quite feverish excitement at the prospect of nice clothes to wear. I feel very happy tonight and not really apprehensive about tomorrow. Whilst it's going to be hard, this is what we've come here for, and though I'm not as physically strong as some of the others, I'm going to have a jolly good crack at it. That's what's in my mind at the moment.

I do miss the family but really, I'm not longing to be at home.

ALEX

Day off, oh, what a relief! We've been put into two groups of women here. Our group is Susanna, and Jules, Fi, Izzy, Gwenda and me. We all get on extremely well together. We laugh and laugh and laugh. We care for each other. Nobody does anything on their own, automatically we look out, to check if anybody needs any help.

The other group is Catherine, Sally, Dicky, Wendy, Claire, and Patsy, our doctor.

To be quite honest, there's quite a difference between the personalities in the two groups. We're the sort of mad, 'hooly booly' ones.

But Dicky is such a laugh. Every time she opens her mouth and says something about Douglas, her husband, and we all fall flat on our faces, and think that it can't be true, this relationship. But I happen to know that it is, because I know Dicky and Douglas. And everything she says is quite true. Poor chap, he's getting a bit of stick but he knows that it's all done in jest. But, I've noticed that the two groups are separating from each other. I suppose twelve is quite a big number really to keep together, so perhaps it was sensible to split us up.

The other group is at the bottom of the hill, and we're at the top. And when it rains, there's mud everywhere so when you try to climb to the top of the hill to the fire, it's muddy and slippery and dark and dreary, so I don't blame them for having their own fire at the bottom, but it's separated us, and it's not a good thing. We're all having to try and get used to each other. You assume that everybody is going to be like you, but of course, they're not. You assume that you're the uncomplicated one, and then you find that you're the complicated one.

For me, as an actress, it's fascinating to sit and watch how everybody works. I've spent my entire life trying to get inside other people's minds and create them on stage. It's a wonderful exercise for me to watch how we're all developing together, and a very strange exercise, too, because for the first time in my life, I'm doing something where I am being *me*, not a character that I've studied, or had to learn the lines for. I am *me*, stripped naked of all personalities and I have to find my own. That's a huge lesson for me to learn, but a fascinating one.

All of us are trying to get to grips with the idea of the trek. I'm nervous as hell. I'm terrified of what might go on. I mean, we've had all this 'gen' on rescue and all this worry about what happens if somebody is sick or ill, and if their ankle's twisted. Everything has to come to a complete halt. Then what do we do? The whole thing comes to an end. I think that's why I'm frightened. I'm very anxious about all these things that might happen. I find myself thinking, 'God, I've got all these responsibilities at home. I must get back safe.'

CATHERINE

Today is Sunday. It's a day I normally go to M ass.

But we're in the middle of the jungle, so that's an impossibility. I love the sound of the forest; I'm beginning to be able to distinguish the various noises. But I'm very frustrated by not knowing the names of things.

I'm beginning to get used to the insect life, particularly the buzzing and flying variety. I'm coping quite well with the forest floor, but I'm still in screeching mode.

Today was also washing day, a scrubbing washing day, which was sheer bliss. I loved it, a simple pleasure became very important. I nearly had a fit when I thought I'd lost my blue mug, which meant I wouldn't be able to have a cup of tea. Tea is very important anywhere, especially here!

CLAIRE

It's going to be a much calmer day. How wonderful! I believe we deserve it. And guess what, at eight o'clock we're having our first drop. A few of us are going up to meet the helicopter, and boy am I looking forward to it.

Ken has organised a meeting at five o'clock, and that is when I hand over to the new leader. And I wish them the best of luck. I hope they get as much out of it as I did.

PATSY

I haven't been hungry at all, and am only eating because I have to.

It was a rest day today and everyone was busy hanging out washing on a line we have put up at the landing site, which is right in the sun.

I had a leech, and I realised that I haven't looked into a mirror since we arrived here, but Dicky, my buddy, has promised to tell me if there is any mud on my face. Although I won't compromise in cleaning teeth.

The threats we must look out for are:

Hornet stings. (Alex is allergic to bees and wasps, and a hornet sting could provoke a life-threatening condition, so I'm was carrying adrenaline and auto-injectors.)

Deadfall. (Because this isn't a managed forest, dead trees simply collapse and crash down as they die.)

Flash floods. Also precipitous drops, and trauma.

I have been getting nervous seeing so many wasps around Alex. I am even beginning to think that I should have discouraged her from coming.

I am surprised at the narrowness and steepness of the ridges, with huge drops on either side. I suppose that the forest itself has protected them from erosion.

IZZY

A nice peaceful night.

People keep hearing civet cats and pigs around their *bashas*, but unfortunately I'm either sound asleep, or just not paying enough attention.

We've just had a really lazy day, washing clothes, setting up washing lines and chatting. We've really got to get all our gear together this afternoon, ready for setting off early tomorrow morning. I think it's going to be quite sad to leave here; it's become quite homely. I'm very happy with my *basha*, it doesn't leak, and I know where everything is.

At the same time, it will be really good to be on the move.

I think there's a bit of polarity between the two groups. Partly because of situation, and partly because of the way we've shared the food. But I'm trying to keep in touch with people in the other group, camping below us. It will be a bit easier once we get out of this static camp.

I think the sooner we get going, the better.

FIONA

I have an incredibly good group. It's self-sufficient, everybody looks out for each other. The other group are very regimented – two people do the water, two people do latrines, two people do the cooking. Whereas in this group, the person that does the latrines will help the cook, the person that does the cooking helps the person that does the latrines, and so on. The same with the *bashas*, the packs, everything. It's never, 'This is mine,' or 'This is half full, yours is a quarter full, I'm going to take yours.' The people in this group are prepared to give all they've got, because they know that if the shoe were on the other foot it would be the same.

My role as group leader came to an end, but as I said, with a group like this, it's not hard. Alex has been nominated as our new group leader. Julie has taken over from Claire, who did a really good job of being the main leader, although I did have to ask her to call me Fi, not Fiona, because Fiona, makes me feel like I'm being told off by my mother.

I know Julie will do a really brilliant job. I'm sure she'll have a really different approach to everybody, but she's got a real sense of humour.

While I'm lying here, talking into this machine, I'm being accused of sleeping with my legs open. Ha ha. It's a bit hard, in this cocoon. Today we had a chance to sort out our packs and our *bashas*. Mine's been up and down more times than I care to remember. Last night I slept at a decidedly odd angle, and I spent half the night clinging on to one side, so I didn't hit the mud or the various creepy crawlies with a big thud.

Today the flies annoyed me, they were constantly buzzing around on my food. And they don't fly away when you get near them; they just crawl up your leg a bit faster.

I had a leech, too. Somehow the bugger got to my, oops, I shouldn't swear, somehow the leech attached itself to my thigh, fell from there to my ankle, where it was feeding quite nicely. It was covered in micel foot powder, which had as much effect as an ice cube in the Antartic. So Gwenda approached with a lit cigarette and zapped the little thing. Izzy flicked it off, and I've now been blooded - I'm an official member of the leech club, of which I think there are about six of us.

The leeches are possibly the least harmful creatures here. Although they are fat as they blow themselves up with your blood and they're pretty offensive to look at, they do no harm at all. They are amazing to watch when they pop their heads out, like little probes, like the eyes of snails, when they go up and start looking around.

I know tomorrow morning this *bergen* is going to weigh a ton, and I don't know why; I really can't throw out any more things. I didn't sleep well last night, and I'm really wet. Oh god, I'm still very precarious tonight, but, that's it, tomorrow morning, we have a six o'clock start, breakfast, then we're off!

chapter nine

Dr Wong is Watching You

DAY 7 - Monday 10th July

Ken leads the Jungle Janes out of 230alpha. They don't expect to return for about two weeks. They have jettisoned any surplus baggage in their attempts to keep their load down. Even so, most of them are carrying forty-five to fifty pounds. They are grateful they will be passing several rivers, and they don't have to cart another ten pounds each in water.

KEN's LOG

There was a very significant start to Day 7 when we departed from the base camp. It was a quantum leap for the ladies, as they were carrying their full packs for the first time.

They got off to quite a good step, although right from the start Alex has been holding the group up as she can only go very slowly. I think as time goes on this is going to cause some frustrations, particularly as other people will want to complete the expedition.

Catherine and Sally go through this incredible daily ritual of looking for creepy-crawlies and bugs. They haven't accepted that they've just got to become part of the jungle. Also some of the others tend to withdraw into themselves and become almost morose during the day - sort of immersed in their own personal anxieties. Somehow I've got to try and get them to break out of that.

Today was pretty hard, following some difficult terrain along the river. This we call cross-graining – turning away from the natural linear features, such as ridge lines and crossing the small rivers and ditches and the bottoms of the ridges. It's perhaps the hardest way to travel in the jungle, though soldiers cross-grain a lot because, clearly, it's dangerous to follow a ridgeline track. But the ladies coped pretty well.

Right from the outset, this expedition has belonged to the women themselves. Although I'm the expedition leader and am responsible from a titular point of view, they are here as a team to get through this expedition using their own initiative and teamwork.

When they got themselves together at the start it became obvious that there were going to be weak links - not necessarily from a mental point of view but from a physical point of view.

They had the opportunity on the training weekends to voice their opinion as to whether Alex should come on the expedition, whether she was going to hold them up. But I think their perceptions are influenced by an underlying wish to be a unit and not to be broken up in any way, so there seems to be general acceptance that she's going to be the slowest and she's going to have to be helped.

Certainly Alex, and most of the other women seem to have this remarkable ability to bounce back at the end of the day and that's the strength of the team. I think they can be very strong in adversity; they'll sit and moan about it, but once the rain's stopped, they'll get themselves sorted out and quickly bubble back to life.

Gwenda and I are getting on fine. We've sort of drawn our lines of contact and I just let her get on with it. I must admit I'm full of admiration because she's not really a great outdoors person. She's been good with the way that she's supported Alex, not in a totally sympathetic way, more in a fair but firm way, saying, 'Come on Alex - get a grip on yourself.'

Fortunately, she knows her well enough to do that. Gwen's a very strong character. In many ways, she's very tough. I think her African upbringing is part of that. And she's quite used to the bush. I don't think the jungle fazes her at all. It's strange in another way because we're both parents away together and that is a risk. I think she feels that, but she's given me tremendous support to make this thing happen, with all the trials and tribulations and egos and doubts involved.

One group thinks the other is terribly dysfunctional and disadvantaged all the time because the others get their water first or they get their fire going first or get their food first.

There's a certain amount of inevitability to that. I think the base camp didn't help in a way because you had one group on the bottom who had to come to the top to eat and they had to bring all their bits and bobs with them so that always caused a bit of friction because they were always late. But I think that Fiona, Izzy and Gwenda's group is much better organised in a way - they take much less time to get themselves administered. Later on when they're more in charge that could cause some friction if, for instance, they were waiting to move off and people weren't ready.

With regard to the rain - this is a tropical rainforest. I don't know what they were expecting because they were all saying to me 'When's it going to stop? When's it going to stop?'

I told them it might go on all night, as it can, and it's usual in a tropical rainforest for it to rain every day. Although we're in the so-called dry season, we're still going to get local thunderstorms dumping on us and that's what we had this afternoon. I told them the good thing about it is that it gives us water - it fills the river and water is an absolute necessity.

KH 10-07-00

SUSANNA

Today we started the big one. We had to get up at sixish, to strike camp. I filled in the latrine. We took down our *bashas* and set off at eight thirty on the same route we'd taken with Ken on the training walk, but then we struck down towards the river, rather than turning up a ridge. This meant there was a lot of cross-graining, which is hard - slithering down and scrambling up ditches with our packs on, which are undeniably very heavy. I would say that mine is a good fifty pounds if not more.

But the pace was very slow and we do manage perfectly well.

There have been one or two moments when I have wanted to strangle people today. I get very tired of having every move I make criticised. This morning I was even stopped from burning a bit of rubbish the way I wanted, and I began to think that things were getting beyond a joke. I really am perfectly capable, thank you, of assessing whether or not it is sensible to burn something, giving it a whirl, and removing it again if necessary. But no, I had to be told. So I am beginning to get a bit fed up with being treated like a child on all sides, by one or two in particular, though I think it is probably better to stay tight-lipped for the moment.

Some people are obviously much better at doing everything and can't really handle not doing everything themselves, so the best thing is to let them get on with it. On the whole, that is what I have decided to do.

I raised one or two things at the campfire last night, from comments made to me by other people. This led to an interesting discussion about our team and its tactics. A rather more laissez-faire attitude seems to have been adopted, without my having been aware or involved in deciding it, which doesn't bother me, although I would like to have known what was happening. I still feel instinctively that I would have been happier in the other team, even though ours works more efficiently. Ken described it the other night as being like the Wind in the Willows - the other team are like Moley and Ratty and we are the Weasels. It's a good analogy, but I am not naturally a Weasel.

Tonight we have ended up camping on a ridge which we had not quite conquered before it began pelting with rain. It is quite exposed and I think there is a high potential for us being cold and probably wet tonight. The rain is just about letting up now but it has been bucketing, we are all soaked and I've got the shivers right now.

At least I'm on a flatter site, but much closer to the ground than before. There are leeches on this site whereas there haven't in the past, so I'm going to have to be more careful about the whole business of camp shoes, bare feet and all that sort of thing. But presumably we won't be around long as we are striking camp and setting off again first thing tomorrow.

I think morale will be a bit low, at least until people are warm and dry again.

ALEX

Rain! It did rain today!

Not that it mattered; we were so hot when we got here. I was terrified. My blooming backpack must weigh fifty pounds. I mean, you can't practise with that at home, because at home you can take it off and rest, and start again. But here, it's a nightmare!

I suppose all the easy bits are over now, and I found the easy bits hard enough!

We were up at six. I watched all the girls filling themselves up with noodles and porridge, and I wished to God I could, but I couldn't.

Do I keep this to myself, or do I tell somebody?

No. I keep it to myself and just get on with it. They can't leave me behind, we're in the middle of nowhere.

I can feel myself wobbling all over, feeling sick. I suppose it's that walk into the unknown. I find the heat quite overpowering. I knew I would, because I've never been in heat like this before. I hope that slowly everything will fall into place and I get used to things.

We walked towards the river, and suddenly we turned directly left, and walked down an extremely steep bank. 'Oh, God,' I thought, 'this is only the first twenty minutes, but it doesn't matter, Ken says we'll be there by half past two. It's now half past eight in the morning I'm sure I can carry on. I'm number three in the queue.' I think to myself, 'Stay at the top, if you stay at the front girl, you'll be okay, because everybody will be behind you, pushing you on.'

We had to walk across several rivers, tributaries of the main rivers. Of course, we got wet boots. Going up those hills, and cross trekking down the sides. And just when you think we might get a flat bit, no, up we go again, and down. Two o'clock comes and I think, 'Well, why aren't we here?'

Two thirty, three o'clock, half past three, and we're still trying to find where we're meant to be camping. I'm absolutely exhausted. And of course, in order to be safe, in case the river floods, we have to be on a ridge. I have to heave myself up the top. And then, because I'd moaned and groaned so much and puffed and panted all day, I felt I must do something to compensate.

I said I would go and get the water!

I don't know what made me say it, and I didn't know how the heck I was going to do it, because it meant going down from that ridge, collecting the water and climbing back up again with it. The strong girls – Izzy, Dicky – are the ones who always put their hands up to go and get the water. But that's not fair; I've got to join in, I've got to be part of this team.

I've noticed that even when I am so physically exhausted it only takes me ten minutes to recuperate. And once I know, mentally that I'm in the right place and this is where we are going to stop for the night, get that wretched backpack off, give me another ten minutes and I'm fine and ready to get cracking again.

As soon as we got the water back up the hill, the heavens just opened and we had iron stair-rod water pouring down on us. We managed to get most of the tarps up, so, at least where we were sleeping, we could try and keep that patch dry. I remember putting my mug up outside, and it filled up within eight seconds.

PATSY

Ken comes round and talks to each of us every evening, to check that we haven't been struggling too much. He is carrying almost twice as much weight as us, as well as being responsible for the back-up and television unit.

We were pleased to get going, away from the mud of 230alpha.

Alex had to be cooled down at every stop.

I was asked to give a speech about litter, and preservation of the forest. There is a spectre hanging over us - Dr Wong - who is in charge of the health of all the forests in Brunei. He has given us permission to go in, but we have to look after his jungle in return.

Every time anyone cuts down a little tree or steps on a bug, someone says, 'Dr Wong's watching!'

I am happy to look after the jungle. I would hate to see it spoiled, but I'm a bit concerned that I might be doing all the clearing up myself. The native *Iban* hunters don't appear to have the same middle-class concerns; they have left plastic bottles lying around their abandoned hunting camps.

This evening, it has been pelting down again, while I have been reviewing the medical problems.

There are already a lot of aches and pains in the group, and trouble with contact lenses. Nothing serious yet, though.

CATHERINE

I was awake before dawn. I was on cooking duty, and had to be up by the fire and cooking before anybody else. Claire was up with me and it took us three quarters of an hour to light the fire because everything was very damp from the night before.

I was very excited about setting off, but nervous about the packing and unpacking of the bag. We were cross-graining today.

Some of the terrain was very steep and muddy, and I am becoming very conscious of how easy it would be to break a limb, or at the very least to sprain something badly. The real problem is the pack. It's unbelievably heavy, and we have to be very careful to keep our balance. The loads on our backs could easily topple us, especially if we're carrying water bladders. They slip and slide all over the place. Izzy and Fiona have showed us the technique of bending right over on to our sticks whenever we stop, which seems to be very often, because we're at the back at the moment. They've also promised to help Sally and me to pack our bags, and show us how to do it properly. I know that this is the one thing that is going to drive me insane. I'm an extremely disorganised person, the sort of person who takes something out of a drawer at home and leaves it open, I don't shut it. So you can imagine what packing and unpacking of the bag is like for me.

We are so busy with day-to-day chores that there is very little time to appreciate our surroundings. Nevertheless, they are beginning gently to insinuate themselves into my consciousness. The shapes in the jungle are fantastical. And I'd love to take some of the weird and wonderful things I see home, so that Lucy could draw them, and make some sort of sculpture from them.

FIONA

It's just started pissing down with rain. We've got the top bits up, but they're pretty useless, and they leak. I thought everything was okay, I'd got it all sorted and we had a nice little area where we could all shelter. We were all sitting under Jules' *basha* and we had a brew going – very civilised, but when I went to check on mine, it had a pool of water in it and that was just the final straw!

The day had been fine, but thinking that now you were

going to spend the night in a pool of water, just wasn't appealing. Unfortunately, everyone else was the same. So, we went round as a group, and mopped each others beds up, to make sure that everybody had a dry place to sleep. And we just carried on talking.

It's amazing how you can still laugh even when you're wet. I mean, the rain's just ridiculous; it's just like a sheet. Sergeant-Major Bhuwani came and joined us for a chat and a roll-up.

He gave us a bit of helpful advice, which was good.

But I'm not looking forward to tonight at all I have to say. It's going to be fairly miserable.

GWENDA

Here I am in my hammock at eight o'clock pm. A very wet hammock, wet and soggy, and I'm wet and soggy.

We had our first proper trek today. One point two kilometres. And it took us one hour to go a hundred metres. Can you believe that? One hour to go a hundred metres! And yet when I was fourteen, I could run a hundred metres in twelve and a half seconds.

We also had to wade into the river, up to our bottoms, so I got my boots wet for the first time. I'm looking at my feet now, they're very shrivelled and pickled.

We got absolutely soaked again, and of course we found our *bashas* were all wet but we rallied round and got a little *hexi block* stove going under Jules' hammock, and had some chicken dupiaza for supper with a good old chit-chat, and laugh. We're all wondering what on earth we're doing here. It's not as if we were made to come, and it's something we've all paid to do.

We must be, barking, *barking* mad!

Anyway, it took ages to get undressed and dry myself and powder my feet. Now I'm sitting here feeling a bit better than I was. I wouldn't exactly say I'm enjoying the experience, but I am enjoying the comradeship of all the girls.

WENDY

Thought for the Day:
When you feel terrific, notify your face.

You wouldn't believe I'm doing this audio diary tucked up in my sleeping bag, in a very wet hammock after a heavy rainstorm. I'm talking into my navel, right down in my bag, because it's quite noisy outside and also because I don't really like talking out in the open.

Today was the first day of our trek. It's been a bit of a struggle for some people but I think we're all struggling in our own ways. I never thought it was going to be easy, I don't really want it to be easy, because I want to push myself and see how far I can go.

I think Sally struggled today, as did Alex. Sally's pack was very high and she's of very slight build, so she's got to repack her rucksack. She seems to have a sort of inner strength and always keeps going. And Catherine just keeps going regardless.

Our group of six is really nice; we seem to get on well though we've all got very different personalities. Catherine and Sally have been friends anyway, for twenty odd years and went to the same university. They just make me laugh. Catherine is always losing things.

Patsy seems to keep herself to herself, which is fine. She's always there if you need her and she's really good at her duties. I feel much more comfortable with the six than I do with all twelve. There are some very strong personalities in the other group. I know I wouldn't feel so comfortable there.

chapter ten

Is It Uphill All The Way?

DAY 8 - Tuesday 11ᵀᴴ July

The expedition sets off on its second full day's trekking.

Ken Hames is determined that the Ghurkas, who were engaged strictly to provide a safety back-up, must not get involved with helping the Jungle Janes. If the exercise is to prove anything, it's vital that the women should do their own navigation and administration.

He's aware that Sally is already struggling, albeit without too much protest and he's very worried about Alex.

She's determined to complete the trek, desperate not to let down the rest of the team, but she was in a state of great distress after the first day's proper walking.

He's frankly doubtful that she'll make it. Besides that, she's holding up the whole team, which is bad for morale and creating potential resentment.

By the end of the day, some of the women are wondering if it's worth going on.

SUSANNA

Today really was a very long day. We set off at eight thirty am, terribly slowly to start with because the going was tough at the front. A lot of chopping had to be done which means that those at the back of the line end up standing around, and I was towards the back at that point. The packs are undeniably heavy, particularly since most of us were carrying half bladders of water as well, which adds a further ten pounds or so, so that was quite tough.

My shoulders are holding out even though I did get a touch of sunburn when we erected the washing line at 230A. Things generally seem to be going well, though.

We are now doing this trip by ourselves: navigating ourselves, and putting up our own *bashas*, although, of course, if there's a problem the Ghurkas will come and sort it.

I went down for a swim once we got here. There was a bit of a muddle around lunch time about the navigation and we didn't get quite as far as we thought we had so things got slightly stressed up front and Ken got narky with us and we got narky with him. I think he is very tense about the whole thing. Anyway, after a horrendous descent we finally got down to an idyllic river with a pool and brook running into it over little waterfalls - very pretty.

Catherine, Claire and I went down after we'd got our *bashas* and everything sorted out up here. That was very nice and very interesting talking with them. Claire is a very clear-thinking person and has spotted a lot in terms of undercurrents and psychology that is always interesting to hear. And Catherine too is quite wise. I think we are beginning to realise that she was right when she said that she was very disorganised. It has become quite a joke and she seems to quite enjoy being the butt of it, so that's fine.

We also had quite a chat with Ken who reported that some of the girls have apparently been talking about aborting the trip a bit early as they don't see the point of going on for two weeks like this. I did take the opportunity to ask him whether the terrain was likely to change at all - whether it was going to get more open or whether the vegetation will alter at all, but he said no, it will all be broadly the same. I think it is difficult psychologically that we have no specific target, that we don't have a hill to climb, a lake to visit, or some other specific aim. We just seem to be heading off each day without a clear idea of what the real game plan is. But he says that it is quite difficult to indicate without showing each of us individually. Well, personally, I would like to see it individually. We are about to go down to the river so I will take my map and ask him to show us. But I think aborting at this stage... I don't know - some people are definitely struggling - but then Sally, bless her, is carrying two thirds of her own body weight which is just ridiculous on paper, and one does wonder why - why are we doing this? It is alright for me. Alex is doing better now that she's hanging at the back with Bhuwani, so she comes independently and is able to go more consistently. But it's still terribly stop-start-stop-start with all of us and that does make it much more tiring. Psychologically, too, Alex finds it much easier that she doesn't have to push herself to keep up with us - which is good.

Personally I think I would find it much harder not to be part of the team, but she is doing what suits her and the main thing is that she sticks with it and doesn't have to go out of the jungle early, nor do we have to adapt to her speed.

ALEX

I wake up and think, 'I don't know if I can cope with this.' Again, terrified.

We've got to march on, two thousand metres – just two kilometres.

It's hot and everyone has stuffed that blinking porridge down them. All those ghastly noodles, I can't face duck noodles or prawn noodles at seven in the morning.

Patsy says to me, 'You've got to eat.' Everybody's saying, 'You've got to eat.' But I can't swallow anything. I try and have a cup of coffee, and then I'm asked, 'How many pees did you do in the night?' I lie, to shut them up. We've done a course, you see. I'm not being responsible, though. I've got to make sure that the kidneys work properly. I've got to make sure that I do eat in order to have the energy to climb these hills. I can't get anywhere here, until I start getting my head around this.

But something happened today, which has changed my whole view of the trek. It was done without me knowing, before I realised what had been going on. Ken had been watching me deteriorating mentally, and Bhuwani, who is the Ghurkha Sergeant-Major, went to see him and said, 'Why not take Alex out of the queue and put her at the back with me? I'll pace it with her, and she'll be fine.'

Of course, when I was hauled out of the queue, first thing in the morning, I didn't really understand what was going on, but I said, 'No, no! I've got to stay at the front, because then I know I can get there.'

And this little face said to me, 'No, Alex. You come at the back with me.' These piercing brown eyes stared into mine, and I suddenly thought, 'Yes, I think I'd better do as I'm told.' So the team moved off, and I stayed behind.

I watched them walk into the distance without me. And I was here with this man, who I'd seen about the camp, but didn't know. I'd watched how hard he was working, how much he was carrying. And how his soldiers respected him. Suddenly it was my turn to be part of his team, and slowly as the day wore on, I realised what was going on. He would sit me down, every twenty minutes. And I'd rest the pack on a log, so it wasn't straining my muscles all the time. He said, 'When the ladies are standing in a queue, waiting for the first ones to move off, they are all standing there with their backpacks on. They are not resting. These backpacks are too heavy. When the trek stops, backpacks off.'

I thought, 'Yes, that's right.'

Slowly I realised that if I stopped for ten minutes at a time, my legs had time to recover, my mind had time to recover. And I found myself walking straight into the next bit, where the girls had already stopped. And after a day of this, the girls all said, 'Gosh you look so much better! You're not so red in the face and heaving and humping.'

And I thought, 'Well, shall I keep this a secret, or shall I tell them? No, I'll keep it a secret for a few more days to see if it works.'

Well, it does work. It's the most extraordinary thing. Suddenly I appreciate that this is the man who lives in the jungle, with his students. This is the man who has seen army sergeants and soldiers being airlifted out, through lack of pacing, through lack of understanding. Alex, you have the mental capacity to do this. That's why you have to look after the physical side. So, Bhuwani and I have become good friends, and when I have my ten minutes breaks, we talk about his life and my life, and I tell him about all the things that I have done with poetry and Shakespeare. He's very interested, and I think that perhaps I am teaching him just a little bit, and he is teaching me everything to cope in this far-off land.

As I began to realise that my walking at the back was helping me no end, I wondered what the other girls were thinking. There are eleven of them, walking forward, and one who is ten minutes behind.

Is she part of this trek, or is she being held up, being helped by the experts?

What do they think? I've no idea. Maybe they're too tired to even worry about me.

But I'm worried. Does it look as if I have a privilege above them, by being helped. So, I did try and say in front of them all one evening, I hope that you realise, all of you, that I can't do this without this pacing with Bhuwani, but maybe if I get stronger and stronger, I *will* be able to walk in the queue again.

And I looked into their faces and hoped that they were on

Ariel view of the jungle

Example of the size of the leaves

Sunlight fighting to get through the trees

Examples of flora and forna

Making camp.

Laundry Day.

my side, and still think we're a team, that the twelve of us must finish this together. It isn't a question of, "Who's the strongest?" and, "I want to do it on my own and I don't give a damn about you girls."

There's none of that there, although there are definitely the strong ones and the weaker ones. And there are more strong ones than weaker ones. Now, I do feel that I'm part of the team, I can see in other people's faces, the anguish and difficulties that they're facing. And that's not to say that I'm not, because I am. But I have more courage now and understanding of the jungle. And a greater love and respect for it. It isn't just a place of heat and insects, and nasty crevices that you have to climb over. It's a place of great peace and beauty, and I would never have learned that if Bhuwani hadn't taught it to me, because I would have been too busy with my head on my feet, watching every move that I made, sweating, sweating, sweating, getting more and more tired.

He's given me something that I have got to thank him for, by giving me the strength and understanding of the forest and I just want the other girls to learn what I've learned. I don't feel guilty anymore. How on earth I'm going to get everybody at home to understand this, I'll never know.

PATSY

I am carrying forty-five pounds and I think this is too much for some of the smaller women.

We arrived at a beautiful river and filled our water bladders up before walking up to our campsite – not far but very steep.

There was one fall and a minor ankle twist on this bank – a result of tiredness.

We were cheered up when Ken told us tomorrow will be a rest day, although I think that the cameraman would like us to push on.

I can sense the separation between the two groups. Some of group B, unable to get things together, look a bit ground down by the whole process. The other group just want to get on and was declaring independence. I am sad and cross about this. In some ways, I think I have more in common with the efficient group, but I don't feel inclined to go with the crowd. It'll probably end in tears, but I don't want to make a scene. My way of dealing with this tension is just to withdraw into my own self-sufficiency. It's not my problem.

I am relieved by the decision to put Alex at the back where she can walk more slowly with Bhuwani to advise her. Alex is certainly in better shape tonight.

IZZY

I found the going a bit easier today. We kept pretty much to ridgelines, and dropped down to a river, in the early afternoon, in through a steep path, just after lunch. It was very well navigated. I think we're starting to take a lot more responsibility for checking our bearings, pacing, and timings.

I don't think we're doing too badly when this is just our second day of real walking in the jungle. It's a lot to take in, it's a lot to get used to. It's completely different, living in a rucksack, putting up a *basha*, and getting organised.

But like everybody else I've got doubts about my ability to keep going. I have worries and fears about letting the group down, or not being able to pull my weight. But I do have a definite advantage. I'm quite fit. I don't have anyone to think about at home. Whereas I'm sure other people, when things are a bit unpleasant, get terribly homesick. If they've got children and husbands they must wonder what they're doing in a *basha* in the jungle.

We lit a fire in our lower camp this evening, because we

wanted hot water to wash. But I think some people felt quite strongly that it was anti-social to have a separate fire down here. But I hope not. It was all resolved and we had dinner altogether at the top, which was fine. I just really don't want there to be any kind of atmosphere of difference between the groups. I think we all mix pretty well, and I just hate, any kind of atmosphere, and any kind of argy bargy, and to be honest, its pretty unnecessary. It's not about big things, it's about little things, but unfortunately in situations like this, perhaps it's the little things that grind and gripe that matter to people.

I've got a nice *basha* set up and some decent flat ground to step onto for a change. And I have to say, it's perfectly pitched, thanks to the help I've had.

I asked Bhuwani to check the weight of my pack, before I took the water out, so I've got an idea of how much I'm walking with. With a full bladder on top, he reckoned it weighed about sixty five pounds. I haven't quite worked it out, but I weigh about fifty kilos at the moment, so, I think that's pretty heavy, and I can't say I want to walk with a full bladder for very long.

CATHERINE

Today was a hard slog. I don't think there's any other way to describe it, though sheer, grinding slog comes to mind.

I think I'm beginning to get paranoid about this rucksack. My pre-occupation with it is all consuming; I can't imagine why I thought this trek would be easy. There are times when we're cross-graining when my muscles just refuse to function. I have to use my hand, to help lift a leg over a log or up some sort of steep incline. I've also become very aware of how easy it would be to hurt myself doing something stupid. I have to be very careful not to grab the first thing, which can either come away in your hand or be covered in nasty spikes. Concentration is the key, concentration and patience. Sally and I have been at the back for two days, which can be very wearing, because we do a lot of standing around. We'd like to try going nearer the front, sort of beating our way through the jungle.

Walking isn't so difficult in the morning because we're fresher, but towards the end of the day it becomes much harder. And then of course, we have to set up our *bashas*. So it's a real effort for us all to keep going, and smiling at the same time.

Rain makes a huge difference. If we can set up camp without it raining, we're very cheerful. If the rain comes, just as we're setting up, it casts a great shadow over everything. Tonight that happened. When I managed to get my *basha* up, I just sat under it. Crouching down, wondering what on earth to do next, my mind just refused to function.

Then, I decided to enjoy it – just sit and watch the rain, and the light changing.

We're usually so busy at home, we don't stop and stare. But here you have to. You can't rush things. I think I'm beginning to relax into it.

I've discovered another thing, the lure of water. Even though I was exhausted when I got up to the camp, I couldn't wait to get back down to the river, to cool down.

DICKY

Aagh, this morning was dreadful, we were soaking wet, having been wet all night, and we had to climb out of our reasonably dry hammocks and get into very wet clothes, wet boots, wet socks, load up our very wet hammocks, and wet tarpaulins and stuff it all into our already wet *bergens*.

Everybody was quite tetchy because we hadn't managed to have very good suppers last night, as none of the lighters would work. We couldn't get the fires going very well, so we all stomped off in silence.

The most important thing that happened today was that dear Nabi gave me two squares of chocolate. It felt like Christmas. They're such nice chaps, these Ghurkhas. Like fairy godmothers. Nabi is such a nice guy, he knows I'm always hungry, and every time he sees me, he gives me a big smile, and says, 'Are you still hungry?' And I say, 'Of course I'm still hungry!'

Anyway, I gave him a cigar in exchange for the two pieces of chocolate.

FIONA

I've had my third leech. It got quite big, but apart from that, they don't bother me. I mean, they used them in Victorian times for bleeding for medicinal purposes, so they can't be that harmful.

But when you have a leech, everyone comes at you, and a fair whack of lighters, and spray to zap it off for you, slightly over-zealously.

The stream where we are now is really beautiful. We had to walk across a log, we've walked over quite a few log crossings today, getting our feet wet. And our final ascent was really steep. It's not quite vertical, but it looks it from down here.

GWENDA

Quite a hard day for me, though I wasn't fully concentrating on the actual walking. I was missing Katie and Harry so much this morning and feeling totally sorry for myself. I was completely hopeless with counting steps and navigation and everything else. I'm still crap at navigation. Every time anyone asked me if I was okay, I just wanted to go off into a corner and cry. Eventually I did have a little weep, and gave myself a good talking to. By lunchtime I wasn't too bad, though I kept thinking, 'Gosh, is this all worth it?

Why am I here? I'm missing all the things the children are doing this month. The morning went well; I think we did much better than yesterday. When we got down to the river, we knew we had about a hundred metres to go. So we filled up the bladders. We were already carrying forty pounds, and this water must weigh about ten pounds, putting that on top of your haversack. Susanna could hardly lift it to get it on my back. But I had such a huge burst of energy, I went shooting up this hill, which was probably the most difficult part, it doesn't make sense, really.

SALLY

Today was very, very, very hard, and I woke up this morning feeling battered. I was in a car crash when I was about seventeen. The car hit a bank and rolled over a couple of times, and I remember feeling shaken up like chocolates in a box. And the next day I felt bruised and battered; I had the same sort of feeling this morning. Most of the time I'm concentrating on what I'm doing though, because you have to think every time you put your foot down and every time you put your hand down. Sometimes, unless the uphill is very difficult with huge steps to be taken, if I can just plod, then that's all right. And I tend to think ordinary, everyday things. Or sometimes I think of poetry that I like, and that makes me feel a bit mournful, so I go back to pacing.

I think we did about one and half kilometres today, which sounds absolutely nothing at all, but it took us from about half eight, to two o'clock. With a few breaks. One thing happened to me on the walk, for which I still have the scars to show. There was a big, big piece of deadfall on the way down a slope. A few people had gone over in front of me and I put my foot on this one piece of dead wood, and just when I transferred my weight onto it, it gave way, and my foot went through a few inches, and got wedged. It wasn't the foot that hurt; I must have banged my shin on something else when I lost my balance and now I've got a huge lump on my shin. Tonight there was the most wonderful moth in my hammock. I desperately tried to photograph it. It was about five inches long, thin and absolutely beautiful. It had shaped wings and looked like a ballerina in a classical ballet.

Something about the jungle that's surprised me is that there isn't more colour. I expected very vivid flowers and fruits, dripping off the trees, but in fact, we've hardly seen any flowers at all, a couple of purple flowers were near the landing site, and a tiny glimpse of an orange, sort of honeysuckle type blossom. And that's been it. Otherwise there's just greenery, but it is very beautiful.

WENDY

Thought for the Day:
Remember that a person who steals an egg will steal a chicken.

We've been in the jungle a week now, which seems quite amazing. It's very strange how quickly we've adapted to this way of life. The big ants that seemed so big at first are now little ants compared to those we're seeing now.

Julie was told this morning that as leader she would be in charge of navigation, too. She looked at me and I looked at her and we thought, 'Okay, we'll do it together.'

It worked out really well, we were a good team – Jules was very good at spotting the tracks and I was good at keeping her on track by studying the map quite carefully. I got a bit frustrated at lunchtime when we were coming down along the ridge and we decided to stop for lunch but no one had been counting so we didn't know how far along the ridge we were and we couldn't really prepare for the next stretch. I thought Ken had agreed my position so I took a bearing from that. Of course, it was wrong but it was only out by a little bit.

Some of the girls carried full bladders up to the site this evening. I could have carried them okay, it's just my feet are so painful at the end of the day from being waterlogged. It's strange there are so many noises in the jungle. Sometimes you listen in the dark and you think you can hear church bells. And then another time, in last night's camp I could hear something that sounded like people – like choral singers.

The hornbills make a really piercing sound at a quarter to six. There's a powerful shrieking noise throughout the night, but you get used to it. The noises themselves don't frighten me – I don't feel afraid of the jungle at all. I feel quite safe in my hammock.

I'm apprehensive about the next few days – we've got a week's worth of walking. I know that's what we're here for but sometimes it can get a bit monotonous.

Sally hates any creepy-crawlies or anything and today we were sitting having this revolting soup and inspecting for leeches. There was one on my boot. I told Sally and instead of sort of jumping to help me, she just run away from it. I thought, 'Oh – brilliant!' So Dicky stubbed it out with a cigarette. She got it just as it was going under my bootlaces.

I'm really glad we've got a rest day tomorrow. We've got another four or five kilometres to do before Saturday. On Thursday we do a long stretch which is a climb of about five hundred feet and then a long ridge walk and a descent down to the river.

KEN'S LOG

This morning, after a pretty damp and grotty night sleeping in a wet blanket, I was glad to get going.

We took the decision pretty early on to put Alex at the back - because it was judged that that was where she would feel able to keep up better, rather than feeling the pressure of being within the group. I did talk to a couple of girls about Alex and whether they thought she was becoming a liability to the group.

She's very well aware herself that she's struggling.

At the end of the day, they said they were a group and they wanted to finish as a group, and that's a noble aim. What I've got to ensure is that we don't injure her, that she doesn't get heat exhaustion or anything like that and also that we don't break her - because it is possible to break people's spirit in this environment if you're not careful, and that's not the idea at all. People are supposed to be here having an enjoyable experience - not a glorified route march.

The day unfolded quite interestingly because we climbed on top of the ridge. I had a bit of an argument with Gwenda - over nothing really. She was feeling a bit down today - she told me she was missing the children, which was to be expected.

We started descending some fairly steep ground and the girls were navigating up front, leading and cutting the bush away, but tempers began to fray a little when navigational errors occurred.

I had to give them a bit of a gee-up three quarters of the way through the day to say that it's not just up to the two people at the front, it's for everyone to contribute to the navigation. I thought Wendy and Julie did exceptionally well - really trying hard to read the map - trying to get it in the right direction.

Poor Claire fell and twisted her ankle and I thought at one point she had broken it. I thought 'here we go - Helicopter! Winch ho!' - all that sort of thing, but luckily it's just a slight sprain. I think she's a real star Claire - I'm very impressed with her. She's very solid, very reliable, strong, focused and I think her style is complementary to the group. The others respect her for her single-mindedness. Sometimes she seems not to be a team-player but she has her own style of working in a group. Clearly she's been very successful in her job at British Airways. It's been a real pleasure for me to see her work in this environment.

'The Dangerous Sisters' - Catherine and Sally, keep me amused every morning with their shenanigans. Taking down their *bashas*, they seem to have this most incredible array of paraphernalia which they tinker with for hours.

They're obviously happy with each other's company but I think they're a source of frustration sometimes to the rest of the party because when it's time to gather wood or water and time to be up the hill, they always seem to be deep inside their rucksacks.

Susanna seems to have settled down and now we're on the move she seems much happier. She was a little frustrated as she hasn't been able to take as many pictures of flowers and birds that she perhaps expected to. So I advised her to go and sit by the river for a while. I'm glad she has picked up the pace now.

Patsy's also very relaxed. She works like a Trojan, gathering wood and gathering water and I know she's been a real rock to her group. I don't know whether she gets much support - she could do with a little more when she's doing those sort of

134

chores but she's highly organised and in contact with her professional life.

Wendy seems to go up and down like a yoyo. She's one of those people who likes to be in the front, likes to be in the lead. I think she gets rather frustrated when she's pushed to the back not in the limelight.

'The Spice Girls', Fiona & Izzy are as happy as Larry, enjoying every minute of this. In fact I think they probably want to stay here forever.

Dicky's also a very solid character and moving along. I think she gets frustrated listening to all the banter that goes on. She's a decisive person and likes to get things done, but she's very stoical and listens to the constant negotiations with great patience. I think a number of subgroups have formed. You can see it in the evening when everybody splits off into their little parties.

I think each of the main groups is a little frustrated with the other. Group B, with Catherine, Sally and Dicky in it, are still much slower with their administration. There are a few divisions, and it's one of those things that you've got to resolve so that they're able to work in harmony. I set the groups up back in England on the basis of what I knew of existing friendships and a mix of abilities. There are a hundred ways you could do it. Maybe now there's a case for re-jigging the groups and I should consider that. I might throw that into one of the talks that we have and see what the reaction is.

KH 11-07-00

chapter eleven

Bliss

DAY 9 - Wednesday 12TH July

The Jungle Janes have a day off. Although they've walked only two days from 230alpha, Ken feels there's no point in forcing the pace, particularly as some of the women are still struggling. They spend most of the day hanging out around a jungle pool, where they swim, wash and play around. They're pleased with their campsite, and glad to be there for two nights.

But the morning gets off to a bad start, when differences between the two groups come to a head.

SUSANNA

It is 10.20 am on Wednesday twelfth, a lovely sunny day. It didn't rain last night and we are in quite a good site as far as I am concerned because I've got on the flat again.

When we got into camp yesterday evening after a long day's walking, there was a mad scramble for the slope and everybody was sorting themselves out while Patsy and I dealt with the water, so we didn't exactly have first pick of the sites. What struck me as extraordinary was that no one had taken the obvious ones, which were dead flat and right by the communal fire area. So Patsy and I are up here and that's nice. I slept reasonably well last night, although it is jolly difficult to get the *basha* one hundred percent right first go. Mine developed right-ist tendencies, and I've got a cricked neck this morning. But the hammocks are extraordinarily comfortable when you do get them right.

There were quite a few tensions last night and this morning and tempers are beginning to fray. It's difficult, because the teams have developed very different operating styles and both are getting slightly frustrated with the other because the other often finds it difficult to see their point of view. I feel a bit pig-in-the-middle, because I can see the advantages of both methods, and my instinct is towards the method that the other team has adopted.

I think I have also caused a few ructions by staying up here at my *basha* site, but I wanted the flatness. I'm not up here to get away from the others, I just function better on a flat site - as simple as that – but I'm not sure it's being seen that way. We are going down to the river now. We'll have lunch down there and re-charge the old batteries in every sense of the word.

It is now six fifteen pm on July twelfth. We've had a lovely peaceful day down by the river, in practical terms. However, tensions are growing between the two teams over simple things and Wendy is getting very upset over quite a lot of things. I think some of it is personal frustration with her own inability to reconcile the fact that, although she has been leading her group and leadership is her thing, her group is not as efficient or as well-bonded as ours. Even though ours is ostensibly very disorganised, it seems to work more efficiently and this is causing some unhappiness, which is a shame. Everybody is still too tired to handle it as well as they should, but when feelings run high it is not really surprising that there are going to be sparks. I get the impression that we are brewing a bit of a storm. However there will be a change in leader tomorrow, and if the right person is chosen and handles it the right way - though goodness knows what that is - then perhaps we can get back on track. A lot of people are ceasing to enjoy the expedition because they feel permanently under pressure to reach unnecessary deadlines. They're asking why we are having to do everything against the clock and why should it have mattered so much that some people weren't ready to go down to the river at ten thirty am when it is a day off - that people should be able to go at their own pace. However I hope we can get through without a rumpus today, but then perhaps it might be better to have a rumpus today and have it over by tomorrow. Who knows?

It was gorgeous by the river. The camera was a bit omnipresent which was irritating but there was a wonderful jacuzzi bit and swimming bit, although the rocks were hellishly slippery which made access quite hard. There was a lot of swimming and sunbathing, and it was really very hot. Unfortunately, though, we have no sunblock. We thought that the army stuff was a mixture of insect repellent and sunblock but it turns out that it has no sun protection factor at all. No wonder we burnt on the landing site the other day.

We are all feeling a bit better on the personal front if not on the psychological front. Personally I feel quite calm. I am outside most of the 'rumpi' and am trying to be philosophical about it all. I had a nice half hour in my *basha* looking out at all this greenery and listening to the insects which make such a racket all the time. But otherwise, it was very peaceful. There was silence from most areas of the camp although there is one contingent that seem to be either singing or shouting to each other most of the time.

I hope there won't be too much trouble between now and tomorrow. We'll have to see. We've got an early start, then three days on the trot of hard graft.

ALEX

Oh, we've got a day off, I don't believe it!

Such a relief to wake up in the morning and think, cor, I

don't have to pack everything up in my backpack. Ooh, peace!

We've found another bit of the river, far more beautiful than the bit we crossed over yesterday, just around the corner. There's a waterfall, and it was idyllic. It was like the set for a Pirelli calendar shoot, the only trouble was, we didn't quite look like the models in the shots, but we don't care.

It was covered in very slippery stones, and of course madam here goes crash, bang, wallop. I have the bruise to prove it. But it was blissful sitting in the shade, being able to stop and reflect and be cool in the water. I was thinking to myself, how many rivers in England do I know that I can go and wallow in? Something I never even dream about doing in England, but, oh boy, it's beautiful here. There was a wee bit of a tiff today because we hadn't seen water for a few days and we were desperate to get the washing done.

Because we've been split into these two groups, it was decided by the first group that we'd meet by the fire which is always our meeting point, at ten thirty am. Ten thirty am came and there we were, desperate to get to the water, and the other group wasn't ready to go.

We were making a concerted effort to go together so we didn't have this split between us, so we waited and waited, and waited another ten minutes and kept being told, 'We'll be there in ten minutes.'

Obviously the other group weren't taking it as seriously as we were, and of course this blew up into something really distressing. It shouldn't have happened. If everybody took everything seriously and did what they've decided to do, then these little hiccups wouldn't happen. But it resulted in group B, who were late, getting lost, trying to find the place, so they missed out on three quarters of an hour of blissful swim.

We're beginning to eat separately, too. Some people get worried about this but it doesn't bother me in the slightest. You can't all eat in one big circle anyway; there are twelve of us.

When we got back to the camp, Gwenda got out her mini-disc and to my utter joy, she had all this wonderful seventies music that we'd all grown up to. I was in seventh heaven. Of course with those funny machines, you forget that nobody can hear, except you, and I started singing out loud. I was making a right pig's ear of it all, but I didn't care. Just to hear that music! Ooh. It was an hour of sheer bliss. Everything is beginning to loosen up for me now.

CATHERINE

This morning we woke up very early, which was blissful, because we didn't have an early start. It was really pleasant just to lie, swinging gently, and listening to everything. When I did decide to get up, though, it was a problem. I felt like crying because I just didn't want to put on wet socks and shoes again. I was very stupid, I'd kept my boots dry for so long, that I used my trainers to go swimming, even though the boots are bound to get wet, we cross too many rivers and wadis for them not to. There was also a column of ants going into my trainers. I squirted them with Micel foot powder and that seemed to do the trick.

After I'd got out of the hammock, I had breakfast, which was a fairly horrible start to the day. Due to lack of communication and because I was over tired, I was still very sensitive to things. But I had a long talk with Sally and sorted myself out.

This evening, I can still hear the discussions going on about food, and what people are going to take tomorrow. I can't say that I'm looking forward to tomorrow very much. I want to go on; I want to see what's around the corner, but I know that it's going to take a real effort of will.

PATSY

It's a beautiful day. I find my feelings of last night being aired by others. We all agree that we are much better off behaving as a single group and we felt more relaxed after this.

I held a foot clinic this morning, to check how people were getting on, and I found no problems there. One of the women who had a hole in the seat of her trousers has found that the leeches are making a bee line for it, thus ending up uncomfortably close to her private parts. The women who are phobic about leeches shrieked with horror when they heard this.

I've been getting over-confident in my hammock. Last night I attempted a complicated manoeuvre that tipped me out with a thud. Only my pride had been hurt, though.

Each pool and glade is more beautiful than the last. The one we visited today was long and straight, a natural thirty metre swimming pool, framed at each end by stony, gurgly bits, ferns and vines. We spent four happy hours there.

FIONA

The camp is fantastic – the best camp so far. It's very easy, it's nice, it's fun. All the stuff is strapped up, the beds all up, probably the best beds we've had, and it didn't rain, so it was easy to get things going. There's been a little bit of discord, as I think the groups are splitting a little. I really don't think it's a problem at all. We're a lot of strong personalities, and we're all getting to know each other.

I think Patsy had a point when she said we should all eat together. It's an important time of day, that communal time, but I really don't think it does any harm if we do go off and set up our own little camp fires later.

Claire comes and visits a lot, I go and visit. I think that's nice, people need their quiet time as well as their social time.

Everyone has done their washing today, so we can have

clean, dry, nice smelling clothes again. Nice smelling means not smelling of horse! Someone said their clothes smelt of cat's piss! It's horrible, just rank, but after a while, you do get used to it, but it's not very pleasant at all.

It's interesting. Inhibitions are breaking down, very much so. I've got Catherine and Sally pulling faces at me. But, when we first met, everyone was hiding; now everyone's wandering around in knickers, and some people are going naked.

Alex admitted that she's finding it tough. But she's so much part of the group, that I couldn't be here without her; she's a joy to have around.

Dicky is playing her harmonica; everyone is really relaxed and talking about any grievances they have, and dealing with things. And we'll be ready tomorrow. The only thing I wish for is no rain.

The peace didn't last. We've had World War III with the ants this evening. We were attacked by sugar ants, termites, fire ants, red ants, coupled with a tarantula and a few big spiders. In fact, more wildlife than we've seen in the entire time we've been here. We fought back with flame throwers, we had powder, we had DDT. We six girls probably wiped out ten generations of ants. It'll go down in ant history as the massacre at Ridge 38.3. But it was absolutely hysterical. Alex started it off with a thigh-slapping dance, followed by a squeal. Gwenda's rucksack shot down the side of the hill. Mine was infested with ants. It was a very amusing evening.

We're all a little bit hot and flustered now. We've run out of tea, so we can't make a cup. Jules and I are worried about this tarantula, Boris, who has made his home under our *basha*. I'm just looking down Boris's hole now, to see if I can see him. I can't, which is a relief. We've built a lovely shelter, free-standing, it looks like a Greek taverna, with Izzy's sarong hanging out down the back.

The outcome of this whole evening was an incredible amount of laughter. Slightly hysterical some of it, but it was good, raucous laughter. We've all agreed it beats a Saturday night out in town.

Alex is back, I can see her diminishing bottom as she's about to cocoon herself, while Julie and I are going to examine every inch of our homes, in case anything has managed to insert itself. Although with the amount of Napalm we blasted around this area in the last hour, I'd be surprised if anything could.

IZZY

This evening we've been invaded by ants. There were termites underneath Fiona's *basha* and spiders on her rucksack. And we had an infestation of red ants that I think they call fire ants. Anyway, they bite, and it bloody hurts.

That started off underneath Alex and Gwenda, but I think we all got a nip off one. We also found a spider that Ken rather reassuringly thought was probably a tarantula. It was nesting in the base of the tree where both Fiona and Julie have their *basha*. They're not going to sleep very much tonight.

JULIE

We've just had a bit of drama here in the camp. Loads and loads of different species of very, very bitey ants turned up under everyone's *basha*. And the most enormous spider I have ever seen in my life was about two feet from my elbow. Bhuwani came and squirted it with ant stuff from an aerosol, which he then turned into a flame thrower, so, three *bashas* have been scorched.

We're all trying to calm down a bit, before we turn in for the night, because quite a few of us are petrified of spiders, me in particular. I'm hoping I'll get over that fear eventually, but we do keep shining our torches down the tarantula's hole, just to make absolutely sure. Fiona had a leech as well, last night, in her private parts, which not a lot of people can claim. It was quite a shock to her. We just want to know where the leech dropped off, or is it going to go back for seconds?

But we've been assured they don't travel upwards, so that's quite a relief. Though as Izzy so rightly pointed out, there's always a first time. Fiona could at any moment give birth to lots of little leechlings. Aaghh!

I'm definitely going to turn in now, so that's goodnight from me, and it's goodnight from all the beasties from the forest. Even though it's been tremendously difficult this past twenty-four hours, we've all survived. I just hope it just gets better and better.

WENDY

Thought for the Day:
Don't let a little dispute injure a great friendship.

There's been quite a lot of upsets within the camp. Lots of, "I did this" and, "You've done that", and sort of quiet attacking of our group, which is getting very petty. I've tried to sort it out this evening but I think what we really did was just brush it under the carpet and it will rear it's ugly head when things get stressful again.

I think the two groups are very, very different. Our group gets on with things quietly and we support each other, whereas the other group are very vocal, very noisy. I just sense that there's a bigger split between the two groups than people really dare to admit because obviously we were never meant to be a group of twelve. And really we're just two groups of six – we make gestures by going down to each other's camp and so on, but it doesn't feel really one hundred percent. Maybe it's just me; I'm not having a particularly good day although it was a meant to be a rest day. I don't think I'm very comfortable in the group of twelve really – not yet. I still have mixed feelings. But I feel very privileged to be here and I think I'm very lucky and having the experience of a lifetime. I get on in the jungle quite well but I don't feel as well with the rest of the group as I thought I would or should. I think it all started with the discussion and it's still upsetting me.

KEN'S LOG

The two teams didn't get on particularly well today.

They ought to try and understand that living in this sort of backwoodsman way is always going to raise problems of logistics for lighting fires and cooking. What's interesting from a sort of group dynamic point of view is that it's not the mountains you have to climb, or the rock faces you have to traverse, it's not the wildlife you have to deal with - it's each other - that's the most difficult thing. And quite often the things that get people agitated in the jungle are where they've got their house. Have they got the right two trees? Are they the only person digging the latrine? Are they the only person fetching water or gathering wood?

And it's that last mosquito bite that can send someone over the edge.

I'm glad we're moving on tomorrow. We've got one of the longer marches, but it follows a nice ridgeline. The next few days are going to be quite testing because we're going to an area where there isn't so much water, and we're going to have to carry the stuff. That's more pressure on the women. But I think this day off has done them some psychological good - given them time to relax and get their kit sorted out.

We've got a new leader tomorrow and that's Fiona. She spoke very wisely this evening when she got up to give the group their first briefing.

It's clear she wants to make sure that everybody gets in there and pulls together. She's a good team member in that way, but she's very scared about navigating. She knows she's not good at it. But we'll see if we can boost her confidence tomorrow.

KH 12-07-00

chapter twelve

Follow My Leader

DAY 10 - Thursday 13TH July

This is the third full day of serious trekking.

Ken is conscious that some of the women have grave doubts about carrying on. They can't see the point of always pushing on to meet arbitrary deadlines.

The arachnophobes in the group, who thought the tarantula had been zapped last night, weren't too happy to find it this morning, dead, but dangling by one leg, twelve inches from the end of Fiona's hammock where it must have been crawling when it finally expired.

SUSANNA

It's been an interesting day. We got up horrendously early, at five am, which meant getting dressed in the dark which I don't like at the best of times, but it is particularly bad when you have to grapple with wet socks and wet boots. But we set off up a ridge that was quite gentle and we were able to achieve our target by lunchtime.

Patsy and Izzy did a fantastic job on the navigation, although there was a bit of an upset with Wendy who is still very uptight about life in general. I think that one of the problems is that she has a lot of theoretical knowledge of how teams and leadership should work, and we just don't comply with them. I think she is also finding it less easy than she thought and she is obviously a lady who is used to being in control. But I think we have weathered the storm and we have had a nice calm afternoon. She has been able to be quiet and read her book and I hope she will enjoy the trip a bit more in the future.

Our site is in a very nice position, quite close to the river, so we can hear it. In fact it smothers quite a lot of the insect noise, which makes a change, and it is really very attractive. We are within easy striking distance of it so we can just potter down and bathe when we want.

I have enjoyed today. I was 'Tail-End Charlie' and had time to enjoy just being in the jungle and I am beginning to feel more at home in it now. I have also seen some nice insect life. Talking of which, there was a nasty incident last night for Fiona who discovered a tarantula within a few feet of her *basha*, and although it was supposedly put to an end, in the morning it was still alive and within one foot of her *basha*.

I have felt very calm today and quite detached from all the activity. The teams are still functioning rather separately and there are still snide remarks flying from both sides, which is a great shame. I am taking a firmly neutral stance. As it happens, for the second night running my *basha* is about as far as from my own team as it could be but again it was totally unintentional. However, I think they are perfectly all right about it. I need flatness and space, and I spend time with them, as and when, which seems fair to me.

ALEX

I'm waking up now, and although I still can't eat anything in the mornings, I don't feel the terrible nausea that I did to begin with.

I'm beginning to come to terms with where I am, the days are going slightly faster, and I'm feeling physically stronger. I think

I can get through this now.

It's the most extraordinary thing when you have to dig so deep into your mental capacities to scrape out that last little bit of effort and thank the Lord there's still a little there to scrape out.

DICKY

There was a real scramble this morning when we got up at half past five. We were supposed to leave camp at seven, so we jumped up in the dark, rolled up our *bashas*, tied everything in knots and chucked it all in our bags.

We were up and ready to leave at ten past seven.

Patsy was navigating today and after about an hour, I was promoted to the chief slasher, which means I went in front with my *parang*, and hacked away at everything to clear a path. That was exciting and passed the time very quickly. It was a really good day, and we walked for about four hours, from seven to eleven – steady ridge walking, not too much cross graining, or too much climbing.

I'm getting to know everybody a bit better every day. We stopped and boiled up our *hexi-blocks* today for lunch, which was fun. It's all becoming a little like Steptoe's back yard. We've all got bits that we want, or don't want, and a lot of bartering is going on. I did a very good swap last night – a small carton of lemon and lime tea, for two bags of coffee. The interesting thing is that one isn't quite as permanently hungry as one was. I still have this overwhelming desire for a slab of chocolate, but apart from that, I have my iced lemon and lime tea for breakfast, and a slimy crab soup for lunch, and a silver bag for supper. So I'm not that hungry, but if anybody offered me chocolate, I wouldn't say "No".

We've camped above the most beautiful river and we did some swimming this evening. I climbed a log across the river and sat on it thinking how lovely it was to be here. The hornbills come in at twenty past six each evening, on the dot, sounding like police sirens. They start at twenty past six in the morning, too, and just make the most extraordinary noise. We saw a pair of them today for the very first time – great big black birds, with a four foot wingspan.

On the whole I think the two groups have got on better today, we've integrated far better. Fiona's been a very good leader. She rushes around being frightfully jolly to everybody, calling everybody 'darling' and 'honey pie'.

I'm sitting here under my *basha*. It's warm; I've got my T-shirt on and a pair of lycra knickers, and I can't think of anywhere I'd rather be at this point in time.

I can hear Alex in the background; she really is worth her weight in gold – which is a quite considerable weight, I might add – because she really does liven up the campfire in the evening. She's very chatty and sings, and keeps everybody going.

The scenery is quite extraordinary, if you can look up from under the weight of your backpack. The trees just seem to stretch up and up and up and up. It takes a real effort to stand straight and almost bend over backwards to see them reaching right up into the sky. You feel just like a little insect walking along.

It's the most beautiful place - primary jungle they call it. There's not too much tangled undergrowth, though a lot of fallen deadwood, and prickly things that grow across the path. There's a quite extraordinary feeling of peace, too. One doesn't have a huge amount of time to think, because one's always thinking about what one's going to do tomorrow, where one's candle is, where one's plastic knickers are, or where one's last piece of food is. But it would be a very thought-provoking place if one was maybe here for a week, in one place. Possibly with just one or two other people. One could very easily sit and write a book here, or compose a song or just be at peace with the world and with God.

I wonder how everything is at school. It's getting on towards the end of term, the pace will be hotting up, everybody getting frantic and Richard writing his speech, ready for Prize Day. All the cups are being polished, the books are being given out, leavers are coming back from leaver's camp. I'm so sad to be missing all that. I feel a little guilty too, about missing time with the children, but this is such precious time here, it's overwhelming really.

PATSY

After a five-thirty start in the semi-dark, we travelled two kilometres in five and a half hours. We had lunch when we arrived.

I navigated with Izzy. We found we had to check our position every hundred metres, and even then it was easy to make mistakes.

I'm glad we were walking along a ridgeline, which meant there were occasional views across beautiful precipitous valleys.

The lighter women are already losing weight. They're not taking in enough calories. I'm encouraging them to eat sweet things at each stop; dried fruit is good for this, but it is heavy to carry.

GWENDA

It was quite a heated day, because people from the two groups started to feel that we were two groups when we should have been one. A couple of the girls are feeling a bit miserable at the moment – annoying, really. This is to be expected. Everybody is going to have good and bad days, but we must be patient and understanding I think.

Last night we had quite an exciting evening. We started a new dance called the ant dance, leaping all over the place, because ants were biting us.

I felt much better today, full of energy; it was a much more enjoyable walk, even with the backpack on. A lot easier terrain, because we were walking along the ridgeline. I suppose too, that my backpack weighs less than it did a few days ago, because of the food having gone, but I still had to carry water.

We got to camp about half past one, so we had plenty of time to do our *bashas*. And there was no rain! And I feel really perky, and I think I might be enjoying this a bit.

One lassie's not feeling good, but I think that should be sorted out today. I hope she is alright. She doesn't want to talk to me; she said she's okay.

IZZY

We managed to leave on time at about half past seven this morning, which surprised us. We had a long day's trek ahead of us, but we set quite a good rate. I helped to navigate with Patsy; we only made one small mistake, but it took us about twenty metres down a steep ridge, which wasn't on our route. We had to backtrack a bit, and do a little rock climbing to get down to the ridge we should have been on. People weren't too pissed off, but we had a bit of an odd incident today. I think it was to do with pre-menstrual tension and a bit of tiredness. Somebody got upset and thought they were being left out. But it was all a bit of miscommunication and I'm sure by tomorrow it will all be sorted out. It's inevitable, really, if you put twelve women together that there's a bit of pre-menstrual tension, and your emotions get mixed up, and little things can make a very big difference.

Navigation can be quite an onerous task when you've got twelve people following your directions. If you go out of your way, you can feel hugely guilty, dragging them up or down slopes or into difficult places where they have to retrace their steps. But I quite enjoyed it today, and it does at least take your mind off the weight of the pack. We had to walk part of the day with half bladders. What we've been trying to do is to swap them between members of the group, but a couple of people are either carrying other things, or they have an ankle injury. Alex has got the frying pan, and also, she does find the walking a bit difficult, so we try and share out the bladders among people who are feeling better or stronger that day.

I'm getting more used to carrying the weight. I think that in one respect I'm getting stronger, but in another, I'm actually losing weight. This is a worry, as I only weighed fifty kilos to start with. But it's only a matter of having to tighten the belt on my trousers to stop them falling down. And the belt on my backpack is getting closer and closer to its final notch. Patsy has decided that I should try and eat more rations, which is great. Everybody gives me their extra boil in the bags, or any extra scraps of food, so I'm not complaining.

WENDY

Thought for the Day:

Remember that no time is ever wasted that makes two people better friends.

We've camped up here after doing just over two kilometres today. They said it was going to be relatively easy, but I found it quite tough.

I don't feel one hundred percent. I felt a bit out of sorts all day, so I just sort of struggled on, didn't say very much and just got on with the job.

KEN'S LOG

We had a lovely day up on the ridge with some great views over to Sarawak and Gunung Mulu, the big mountain over there, 8,000 feet high. And it was good to see everyone talking about navigation and getting their pacing, their compass bearings and timing sorted out.

Some of my concerns about some of the women were alleviated today, though I am worried about Sally because she's quite an emotional soul, and very close to the edge. I think she copes admirably when we're on the march, but when we stop.... perhaps it's just a release of adrenaline. She seems much perkier today though. And my concerns about Alex seem to get less and less. She was storming along today. Okay, she's had help, but she's needed it.

Some of the women are still disappointed with the scenery, I think they expected more sort of paradise-type landscape, with beautiful flowers and humming birds hanging off every tree. Of course, we make so much noise that all the wildlife probably runs away and it's difficult to spot it - although we spotted two lovely hornbills flying by when we were near a river junction.

I think the person I'm most concerned about now is Wendy. Wendy's a real scout and tries very hard for everybody. Sometimes I think she sets her standards too high. And she gets disappointed and she feels rejection in some way. Perhaps she feels that people don't take enough interest in her as an individual. I'm going to have to talk to her in the next couple of days to find out just what's eating away at her.

We're reaching the stage now when we're going

to turn away from the pattern of landing sites that punctuate the southern part of the jungle and go into unknown territory where there are no landing sites. This does add another danger element to our expedition in that if we did have a problem, we would have to chop a winch site in the jungle, which is very hard work. It takes a long time, so it's more dangerous. We've also got a water problem looming because we're climbing onto much higher ground and to get to water will be more difficult. We're going to have to pack up tomorrow and carry full bladders onto the top, and that will be hard.

Our leader today was Fiona. She stomped off in front wielding her machete wildly, chopping everything in sight. I gave her a bit of advice from time to time and tried to get her to look more closely at the route she was taking. I told her to try to go round trees and not through them, but she was very enthusiastic as leader and a pleasure to have at the front.

She got everybody moving after the breaks and we covered a lot of ground, much quicker than we have done before. She'll have a hard time tomorrow though because we're climbing quite a steep hill with a lot of difficult navigation to do.

Gwenda and I had a good chat today. She's a very good judge of character and is able to sum people up quite well. She's concerned about Wendy, too, and rather sad to see her low when she's usually so enthusiastic and effervescent.

KH 13-07-00

chapter thirteen

Empty Bladders

DAY 11 - Friday 14th July
The Jungle Janes have a tough day.

They're climbing, and they're carrying a lot of water.

Early on, two bladders burst, making water shortage an even greater potential danger. Finding water on the ridge will pose a serious problem.

Personal relations improve though, as Wendy apologises for yesterday's moodiness.

And despite the hard going, the women recover enough in the evening to indulge in charades and singing.

SUSANNA

This was the first day that we had to carry full water bladders, and that was hard. We got into a bit of a muddle at the start of the day because we had a lot of the bladders draped over the top of people's rucksacks as they hadn't got room for them inside.

Dicky was leading the way, chopping and she and her bladder had a contretemps with a spikey 'Wait-a-While' plant that slashed the bladder in three places - cuts of about an inch. The water just poured out and that was the end of that. There was not a lot we could do about it.

Ken was not very pleased.

The food is still alright but I'm beginning to get a bit bored of beef jerky and I gave a huge stack away to one of the Gurkhas tonight and will probably give away more tomorrow. That has relieved the pack a bit. It doesn't weigh anything because the bags have air in them, but it's a bit bulky, which is annoying.

We walked uphill most of the morning. I was navigating with Izzy and Wendy. Wendy put us on to a slight red herring on our interpretation of our location - we weren't wrong but she confused us a bit on where we were at one point. She had a different theory, which was justified - these maps are jolly difficult because they are not accurate. You just have to read indications and make various possibilities fit and then eliminate the possibilities as you move on to the next point.

Alex kept up reasonably well, although she finished off with Bhuwani towards the end with the final slog up hill. We have come to quite a good arrangement: she takes the frying pan in return for not taking any water, so at least those of us who are carrying water don't have to carry the pan as well, which would be adding insult to injury. I have to say Izzy is astonishingly strong for someone as petite as she is. She carried water virtually all the way.

We had a jolly evening with charades because the camp here is flat in most places which has made it very good for a lot of people - much more comfortable, and we are all quite close together, so there is less sense of 'us and them'. The Gurkhas came and joined us towards the end of the evening and they were very jolly. We are beginning to tease each other, which is nice. They're beginning to grasp our sense of humour and we theirs. We're winding Bhuwani up about his wife and what she would think of Alex. But in fact it looks as though Alex is chatting them all up. She's got them all round the fire, topless.

There is a lot of preoccupation with scatology. I have been having no problem on that front whatsoever. Once a day, no trouble! However, one thing that has finally struck home is the smell of my feet, or rather my socks. They have now got beyond the point of no return. They are quite unbelievable. Not cheesy any more, but putrid. Anyone would think my feet are rotting but they're not – they're fine. Okay, they get wrinkled like prunes at the end of a walking day, but I don't have blisters or any torn skin. But, oh, I'm going to have to have clean socks tomorrow because I just can't stand it!

Everyone is very obsessed with losing weight, but I don't seem to have lost a thing which is very depressing, as I am the one who could do with losing some. Nobody has said to me 'You are looking thin', or 'Oh your bottom is disappearing', or 'Ooh, you look nice', as to others, so I can only assume that no weight is coming off and that I look pretty grim, which, seeing as I haven't looked in a mirror for the last two weeks, is probably the case.

Despite the racket coming from the campfire it is quieter up here and the insects and the bird-life have been much less obvious. If the chatterboxes shut up in time I may not need my earplugs tonight which would be nice, as they are not terribly comfortable. At the moment I wouldn't want to be anywhere else, but then, this is the best time of the day, lying in your *basha* when you've done it all. If we can just persuade party animal Alex to call it a night, then peace will reign.

FIONA

I was leading today. Wendy, Izzy and Susanna did the navigation. We made a few mistakes, but they were mistakes that anyone could have made, Ken said. It was a good day with some tough walking, but everyone just got on with it – grinned and bore it.

I'm feeling okay now but I had a bit of a grump this morning.

Izzy just winked at me. It's been one of those days where you feel that you've proven a point; you've proven that you can stay out here, face these tarantulas, spiders, ants, scorpions; you can drink purified water, you can wear clothes that smell like cat's piss, and you've done it. Why do any more?

But then you turn round straight away, and you know you're here for this amount of days and nothing, and nobody will stop that happening. Even though Jules had a mad cow day today.

We've just got on with it and laughed. Izzy hurt her shoulder and got on with it, Claire hurt her foot, and got on with it. Everyone gets on with things. And it was my day to moan this morning. I hacked things down, and swore a bit, and now I'm fine again.

I had fun slashing yesterday. Ken called me an axe murderer. Ha ha. The way I was chopping, I don't think I'd be able to do much more than maim someone.

Today, with Dicky chopping, Izzy and Susanna navigating, me pacing, Wendy probably a little way back today, helping us with navigation, we kept up quite a good pace.

I'm supposed to be leader, and it's been a pretty tough day. As far as I'm concerned, I've done my job. I give it up tomorrow. Quite happily. I just hope that the rest of the trip carries on like this. We're a group but I don't know how we're going to feel tomorrow, because I don't know what tomorrow holds. If it carries on like this, then it's going to be brilliant. Whoever takes on after me is lucky, because they're a damn good group of girls, and they're going to stay like that.

Right, I'm going to ask everyone how they're feeling.

Okay guys, one by one - How are you feeling?

Happy.

Mellow.

Cheerful.

A lot calmer.

Fantastic.

Great.

Spiffing.

Hungry, always.

Orgasmic, wahey,

Stupendous.

It can't get any better than that, can it?

One minute, hold on, I've got one more to go. How are you feeling?

What am I, how am I feeling? Ooh er, oh um, er, terrific.

I went to see the Ghurkhas this evening. They were busy cooking their food. I haven't used my camera, and I thought it would be nice to get some pictures. I had a chat with them, and I think they're proud of us and what we're doing here.

What came across more than anything else is that they desperately want us to succeed.

IZZY

We had a nice campsite last night. It was an old army campsite, but not used for some time. So it was lovely and clear, by a river, a really good opportunity just to wash some clothes, and enjoy being without our packs for an afternoon. And this morning, we had a late getaway, because of lots of factors, and we were only anticipating walking between, one and one and a half kilometres, so we didn't set off until around twelve, by which time it's pretty hot. During the day I think it gets up to thirty something. And with high humidity as well, you certainly feel the difference, starting at that particular time.

Today's been pretty much all uphill, especially the first ridge which seemed to take forever, though it probably took about an hour and a half to two hours to get to the top. Because of the heat of the day, I think it exhausted people, and as we're camped today high up on a saddle between two knolls, we won't have any access to water. We had to bring full bladders up with us, which has been quite tough. And one of them has a slow leak, so we only half filled that one. Another one got punctured by some plant, so that's got a big tear in it and is past repair. We were at one stage a little concerned about losing so much water, but now that we've actually got to our campsite, I was one of the reccy party that went down to find a stream that we could perhaps use to fill up the bladders. That was quite good fun. I really enjoy clambering about up here. Without a cumbersome pack on your back, you can move a lot faster and its quite good fun.

I carried a full water bladder all day today. That's partly because some people have got sore ankles, or just blisters, and all their packs are heavy enough really. I don't mind, it adds a bit extra to the challenge, but I must admit my legs feel it at the end of the day.

Tonight our campsite is actually on almost flat ground, which is a bit of a first, so, if I fall out of my *basha*, I'm not going to roll halfway down the hill. It's been very hot tonight, there's no wind and it's about twenty-eight degrees. But I'm slowly acclimatising to the heat. I'm very happy. We had a very nice evening, playing charades and singing songs. The group's getting on well at the moment. The issues that we had about cooking in two different groups, and the stuff perhaps dividing us in two, seem to have dissipated.

I hope that we all make it through to the end, and don't lose anybody along the way. Claire twisted an ankle the other day, but it seems to be holding up okay. And Julie's got a slight swollen ankle from an injury that she doesn't even remember doing. She's been walking on it for a day or two anyway, but we've given her a 'tubigrip'.

I can't think how many days we've got left, and to be honest I'm not sure that it's a good thing to dwell on.

We had a little visitor during the night. I woke to hear quite a lot of scrabbling around, and it was a civet cat, eating what was left of the boil in the bags. I can't say it's got much taste, especially as it was going through the Lancashire hotpot. Anyway, it was completely unperturbed by having a light shone on it, so eventually I managed to get out of my *basha* to root around for my camera and took a picture of it. I hope it comes out.

PATSY

There was a lot of singing tonight. Ken likes to sing, and he has a nice voice. I think if I ever did anything like this again, which I won't in a hurry, I would bring song sheets. We all know one or two words or lines of a song but we'd love to know more.

It's coolish under the canopy, even if it's baking up above. But once we're loaded and walking, it's absolute hell, though sixty pounds up hill is manageable.

The site we've reached today is lovely, but a long way from a good water supply. We have found a little, which we have to filter.

The Gurkhas tell me they think the cameraman wants to push us on a bit harder. I guess I know why, but my absolute priority is that the trip should be completed without injury.

KEN'S LOG

What a day it's been. We started off this morning from the LS at 363. We had pretty heavy *bergens* and full bladders of water. This was the first day the ladies have been fully laden. When we'd crossed the LS, almost immediately one of the bladders burst. I wasn't annoyed, but I was slightly nonplussed that they had managed to pack one of them right on top of a *bergen*, so it was sticking out. I'd pointed out to them that if you do and the water bladder gets caught, it will simply rip and burst, and that's exactly what's happened.

We were down a couple of gallons straight away. And then about another 50 metres up the track, another one burst, so we're down 4 gallons by that stage. The difficulty was that we really needed the water because we were going to go and sleep up on the ridge.

As it transpired, we were able to find water up here, which was fortunate to say the least considering the weather conditions. It was a pretty hard push up the hill and navigationally it was quite difficult. But I'm pleased to say they have persevered with their navigation and they actually got it right, eventually, by a process of consultation and perseverance.

Wendy came to see me this morning to apologise for being in a bit of a state yesterday.

I said to her, 'Wendy, if you do have this sort of up and down personality then it might be good to talk about it sometimes because people might be able to help or suggest ways where you might not sink into this depressive state.'

It's very obvious when she goes into it and I think she has had it on more than one occasion on the trip so far. I didn't expect her to be that way inclined. Anyway, that's it. She's snapped out of it today and seems a lot happier. I think she's probably accepted her position within the group - not always as leader, but quite often as someone who just contributes, and that, of course, is the strength of a team.

I had a terrible night's sleep myself last night. I was worried about something subconsciously and couldn't figure out quite what it was. It's probably natural anxiety about getting everyone through this safely, and not getting anybody injured, because the responsibility at the end of the day rests on my shoulders. I sat up in my *basha*, smoked about ten fags and tried to work it all out. This morning I felt much better and I ate a good breakfast and got cracking again. Tonight we're *basha*-ed up on this beautiful ridge which is not far from twelve hundred feet. I think the ladies are in good spirits tonight, singing and laughing. It's funny how their mood swings between depression in the morning and elation in the evening when they've stopped.

They've got some hard yards in front of them. They've got to drop down to the river. It's quite a long way, some tricky navigation at the end down to the river for more water, I hope, though we can never be certain that there's any in it.

We're in unknown territory now. I've been here before, although my memory's faded but we're as far off the beaten track as you can probably get, miles from anywhere. There are no landing sites around here so it's pretty inaccessible.

Over the next two days people will certainly begin to feel tired and perhaps a little tarnished. And I have no doubt people's tempers will fray a bit more because it becomes harder to motivate yourself and to get along and gather water. And water will be an issue for the next few days.

Over the last few days, Patsy's really impressed me. She works like a Trojan; she's always doing the cooking, gathering water and is a real mother hen around the place. You need that sort of person. You need someone who's going around crossing the T's and dotting the I's.

Claire's also impressed me; very strong, she carried an enormous weight today - probably more than she weighs herself. She does it uncomplainingly.

Dicky and Julie are the life and soul of the party. Dicky walks round most of the time topless which can be a bit disconcerting. You spot this half-naked woman through the trees drifting along.

Izzy and Fiona are having the time of their lives and I think they're really enjoying the experience. Fiona's been leader for the last couple of days and has done a fantastic job - bags of enthusiasm, bags of get up and go, and it's been a pleasure to see her at the front. The good thing about Fiona is that she gets people going, gets them motivated and doesn't waste time.

KH 14-07-00

chapter fourteen

Tail-End Charley

DAY 12 - Saturday 15th July

The expedition breaks camp and has left by 8.00am. They are heading for a twelve hundred foot hill, which they reach before dropping down towards a river.

Unluckily, they get badly lost, and have to resort to a lot of cross-graining and slashing.

They're into densely undergrown secondary jungle, and their campsite, when they reach it, is dark, damp and nasty, with only a dribble of a dirty stream to provide water.

ALEX

Two days now without any fresh water. It's a bit of a fiddle for those who have to carry it, because we have to rely totally on the water that we have in our packs.

We were told that we would be walking until about two thirty and it was an extremely gruelling walk. Boy, we had to go down a very steep, rocky bit. I was so frightened. I would never have been able to do this in England!

Again, two thirty comes and goes. "Sorry, we've come to a part in the jungle, which isn't where we thought it was. We've got to find another way."

Earlier, Bhuwani and I were sitting down having a rest. We always sit on a log so I can rest the backpack; it just takes all the strain off me. And the log collapsed on my left calf muscle. I thought for a minute, "Ooh, my leg's completely trapped under here." I've never seen anyone jump off a log so quick as Bhuwani. He was terrified that I'd twisted my ankle. As it happened, I hadn't, but I'd been left with a nasty big bruise on my leg, which doesn't really matter, it just adds to the other twenty five bruises I've already got. I did think, though, that I could play up to this a bit. But I didn't.

We're in the back of beyond here, it's dark, it's swampy, it's smelly. But I did see a monkey – the first time I've seen a monkey in a tree. Even that didn't cheer me up. I'd had it, I was absolutely exhausted.

I had Catherine behind me, and Susanna in front. Both were carrying water, and wimpy old me in the middle.

When I got to this camp, Patsy took one look at me. "Sit down Alex. Backpack off; shirt off." She started fanning me. I was so hot, I burst into tears again. I'm quite good at that. I've never burst into tears so many times in all my life.

CATHERINE

As usual once we'd got our *bashas* up, everybody recovered their spirits. There was a lot of laughter and jollity, after an extremely tough day.

But when we got to this campsite, we were really shattered. Added to that was our extreme disappointment at the site. It appeared to be next to secondary jungle, and the river we were all longing to see and leap into, turned out to be a dank little tributary, not flowing and overgrown and the area surrounding it, very damp and murky.

To put the *bashas* up was very difficult and involved a lot of chopping.

The plan had been to spend a day here by the water, having

fun, and resting up. But I think, to a woman, we all decided within two seconds of being here, that we wanted to move on the next day – no matter how difficult.

What is interesting, (and I think perhaps as it gets more difficult, this will be more apparent) is that the two groups which have to stay two groups for administrative purposes, are actually becoming one in every other respect. I think that probably happens, when things get tough or difficult.

Ah, I can hear the tweet of a bird, which is very unusual. Perhaps this isn't so bad after all. I think this is more like what we all imagined jungle to be, very overgrown, trees close together, lots of low lying bushes, and I've seen a lot more insect life here, than I have anywhere else; which I don't like much.

Everybody is pretty exhausted, so we were all into bed without a murmur.

Today I felt very strongly, if I saw Robert appear over the hill, I should be very, very glad to see him. He would be surprised to hear me say that. But I would.

CLAIRE

Today we are walking endlessly up and down hills. Can you imagine placing one foot in front of the other, with your head down, and a very heavy load on your back?

I'm here to see the scenery, I'm here to see the rainforest, but I feel that all I can see are my feet, one in front of the other, and the back of the person in front of me. I can hear them either clicking, which we need to do for pacing and to keep a count of how many metres we do, or I can hear them huffing, and puffing – very heavily, just as heavily as me.

I'm teetering as I walk, with my ankle. But even without a difficult ankle, I still feel I'd be teetering. It's almost like being a little baby, when you're learning to walk. I'm using all my strength, utilising my stick, hanging onto vines, trying to find the right foothold. It's so difficult at times, but onward we go.

That's not how I'm feeling inside, though; I'm glad to be here, so glad to be surrounded by all of this!

DICKY

We left at quarter past eight, after a fairly decent breakfast of hot chocolate, and we walked two and a half kilometres.

We finally arrived at about four o'clock at the most shitty, ghastly place you've ever seen. We had to lop down lots of trees with our *parangs*, and I think today was the first day that everybody, *everybody* was at the end of their tethers. The last little thing we had to do was to cross a river, balancing across a log, which we all did quite successfully. We filled and lugged six bladders another fifty metres, which doesn't sound a lot, but which is a huge distance when you're absolutely dead on your feet, and psychologically, once you've finished, you feel you just want to stop.

It has been the worst day yet, but still, every now and then, there's a lot of laughter and people giggling, and we're all gradually getting to know each other a lot better. I spent quite a lot of time up at the front as lead scout. There wasn't a huge amount of clearing to do, and it's quite fun to be up at the front, because you can more or less set your own pace.

I've been thinking a lot today about school. It's Prize Day, at half past five there this evening; Richard would have been launching into his speech. All the parents would have been there. Hopefully Douglas would have been there, too, listening to the speeches, ready to pick up Lucy. This evening he will have taken Lucy and Jane over to granny's house, and it will be the end of term. I know that feeling so well, when nearly all the children have gone, except for the Spanish, and it's just total relief and exhaustion; no more prayers in the school chapel until next September when the new year starts.

In a funny sort of way, I was relieved, because life at school isn't going on without me anymore, which I felt badly about over the last two weeks.

We had planned on having a rest tomorrow, but this is such a ghastly place I think we're going to move on. "Outwards and onwards!" And, as Douglas would say, "If you can't take a joke, you shouldn't have joined."

I'm not going to give in, and give him the satisfaction of saying, "This is a girlie's outing."

Because if and when this comes out on the television, one of the benefits is that he'll see this is nothing like a girlie's outing. There's real tough stuff. I bet there are a few men I know who wouldn't want to be here.

PATSY

Last night we played charades, with everyone in incredibly high spirits in front of the fire on a lovely flat site. Then we had an eight o'clock start this morning.

I've found that the group is gelling, perhaps because skill levels had risen, putting everyone more on a par. Navigation has been hell today, and eight hours after we started, we've arrived at a very bad *basha* site, boggy, dense and littered with vines and tiny trees which needed a lot of cutting.

I'm the most tired I've been so far. There's generally a lot of exhaustion and a few tears from the others.

One of the girls is carrying close on two thirds of her own body weight, which is risky.

I'm rattling from anti-malarials, vitamin C and now antibiotics for a skin infection caused by poor hygiene, and in the rest of the group we have a *carpheobatoma*, a twisted ankle, two eye infections, grumbling constipation, a crunchy shoulder and a recovering minor ankle injury.

I think Ken's exhausted, as well.

FIONA

It's quarter past seven in the evening, and we're all knackered. It was a really tough day today.

We've got a couple of injuries – ankles, bruises, and exhaustion, but generally everybody has been pretty incredible. It's amazing what inner strength you can find when you have to. There are things that people have done that they just wouldn't do in normal daily life.

Catherine actually turned around today and announced to us that she thought the ants were quite friendly. When she first came, she'd have run a mile, now, when they run all over her – no problem, she just deals with it.

Sally is scared of heights, and when you watch her strolling on past a huge drop, you've got so much respect; she just gets on with it without even hesitating. It must be pretty hard for her to do that.

Today was my last day as leader. I asked if anybody else wanted the job, but no-one did, so I nominated Dicky, who was very happily seconded.

Last night, I had a really weird dream, with a big cat, a puma type cat. And I woke up to find Izzy had her torch on, shining across to the campfire. And when I looked across there were two shiny eyes. And focusing more, I saw my first bit of real wildlife, since living in the jungle - a wild cat. It was about two foot high, three foot long, with a very long, stripy tail and short legs. It was rummaging through our rubbish, having a good old nose around the boil in the bags. It was there for ages and though Izzy had her torch shining on it, it didn't seem at all perturbed. It must have been very hungry if it was on Lancashire hotpot. Then it went off with a bag in its mouth.

Jules has seen one of these civet cats, but unfortunately when she went tch tch tch, it failed to come to her, and just ran away.

Izzy's got a leech. In fact, shall we all check for leeches in a second?

Alex just deals with leeches now. It's like, "I've got another one, and I can't be bothered to get it off. It will fall off when it's had it's fifteen minutes." And off she trots.

GWENDA

This morning I started out as the slasher, (now known as the lead scout, which sounds much grander).

I did it for about two hours, and by the end of that two hours, my arms were killing me. I could hardly lift the *parang*; then Ken told me I had gone off track and I said that the girls told me that we were near the edge of a cliff and wanted me to move away from it.

He said, "Well, get back on the path."

"What do you *think* I'm trying to do,' I said.

I was in a no-win situation.

This time last week, I would never have thought that we would manage to walk five days in the jungle with so few injuries.

Julie has hurt her ankle, Alex has had a log fall on her leg, but everybody has done really well.

This evening, everybody is still laughing and joking. I can't believe the morale of the girls. Even when they're exhausted, they find time for each other. And everybody is so good at cheering everybody else up. I know that when we're all in our bunks, we're all thinking about our families and our homes, and it can get a little bit lonely at times, but I just think, 'Well everyone's in their bunk, maybe feeling a little bit like me.' And I take comfort from the fact that I'm not alone.

We do laugh, and laugh, and laugh at times, and tell the most outrageous jokes, and take the mickey out of each other. I must say that this trip has made me become very close to a lot of fantastic, strong women. I had a few reservations about some of them, but I think they've all done incredibly well.

IZZY

It's been quite a challenge today.

We reached a high point at about twelve o'clock and we were looking for a ridge to take us down to the river, and the place that we were aiming to camp. But we've had real problems trying to find it, and in the end we had to go cross country, rather than sticking to the ridges.

Everyone found it hard work, and by the time we got to the campsite here tonight, I was absolutely 'cream-crackered'.

Now Alex is being her usual bubbly self, so she's obviously recovered, and spirits have soared. She's got Dicky and Claire and all that lot as an audience tonight.

Fiona's done a great job. I think there have been some tensions in the group over the last few days, and she's helped everybody pull together. We've had some tough days, and her style of leadership sets a pace, and her tone is good. And I think it's helped everybody adjust, and everybody is feeling quite comfortable now. She's now giving me a hug "yeah, because you're saying nice things about me." Wait until you're not here.

SALLY

Day twelve was very, very tough.

The down hill parts I always find very difficult, because I don't like heights. And I always suddenly become aware that there's nothing on, say, the left side of me, and it sends me into a panic. I don't know which foot to put where and my legs become frozen.

The other thing we did yesterday which was quite alarming

for me, was crossing a tiny steam, which was black, boggy and rather dank, at the bottom of the valley, just before we came up to our camp. We had to walk along a log, which was like a bridge over the stream, and although it was only just clear of the water, I felt as though I was walking a tightrope. These logs are covered in moss and after a few people have gone over, they tend to get muddy and slippery. If it were on flat ground, I could probably do it, but as soon as you think it's a few feet above the ground, with water underneath, it sends tremors down your legs and it all becomes quite an ordeal.

SUSANNA

On our hardest day, we had a gruelling two and a half kilometres. The second half of which was very difficult from the navigational point of view. And I was in the hot seat, doing the navigation with Wendy and Izzy.

We had to climb a lot, and there was a red herring that got in the way. It wasn't our fault; these maps are very frustrating. (I'm having an absentee love affair with the Ordnance Survey, with their little public houses and churches with spires, and little copses. Oh for a map like that now!)

You never have any time to rest yourself when you're navigating, and I got a kink in my platypus' water pipe, which meant that for the first hour, I couldn't drink anything. It was a very gruelling climb to begin with and, because I was on navigation, I didn't have time to take my pack off, and get it sorted. I got very behind on my drinking, which concerned Patsy. But I've caught up now.

Having now done two solid days of navigation, I'm ready for a day or two off, and I shall do a bit of Tail-End Charley-ing.

KEN'S LOG

We managed to get away from our last campsite by 8 in the morning, which was a nice site high up on the ridge.

The aim today was to climb a 1200 foot hill, then drop down to a river. The whole route is about 2 1/2 kilometres.

We got off to quite a good start although the ladies are having some difficulty seeing a track, which is natural. I did try to offer advice and was just ignored a couple of times. Eventually, though, we hit the 1200 foot feature and even at that stage some of them were looking a bit harrowed - in particular Sally. Alexandra of course was bringing up the rear - 'Tail-End Charley'.

They had navigated quite well up till then and I think they just lost a bit of concentration as we were coming off the top of the feature. They turned left too early. I remember shouting 'Are you on the right bearing?' to be greeted with silence.

Things were getting a bit fraught, though, eventually, we ended up at the river having gone down some very steep ground.

I explained to the ladies then that they'd done jolly well. Even if they were a hundred metres out, they still knew the general area they were in and they'd hit the river - so that was the main thing. I've been in these jungles many times and trained soldiers would have struggled with that route and they would certainly have struggled with the navigation, too.

The ladies were absolutely whacked after today and it showed tonight, when they came to cook their dinner. They found it difficult to muster the energy to do even that, but I think they should be pretty pleased with themselves.

Most of them remained pretty patient today. There was the odd flare-up here and there, but that's inevitable.

When we got into camp this evening, Sally was absolutely tired out. I think emotionally she finds it quite difficult at this stage of the day but it's probably just the elation of getting to the end of a hard day, and the body winding down. We managed to get some fairly decent water out of the river using filters and we'll have to carry that up with us tomorrow. And our problems aren't over yet because we've still got to negotiate quite a difficult stage where water isn't a certainty, until we make our next river point which is two and a half or three kilometres north of here.

I think today just proved that it's not always the same. It's a landscape of traps; you think that everything is ticking along fine and then suddenly you find yourself in a very difficult situation. It takes a cool-headed person to choose which is the best path to take. Some of the ladies were saying... "When I go on my next trip, I think I'll go to Africa," but every country has its hardships.

They've certainly entered the first division here. Really only special forces and people who are very highly trained come into this area and I think those who looked on it as a bit of a joke or who saw it as a lot of girls running into the forest for a bit of a laugh will have to look to their laurels. We've now been in here longer than soldiers who come here for jungle warfare training, and I think that's a massive credit.

I hope they can sustain this; they've got quite a way to go yet and it's at the stage - coming up to the two week point - where things could start to break down, both physically and mentally, and it becomes easy to let things slip - personal administration and looking after each other. What I'll have to do is to make sure that we maintain our standards as we go along. I must be sure that the water's purified, that people do powder their feet and change into their dry clothes, otherwise it's easy to fall down. And if one falls down, we all have to stop.

KH 15-07-00

chapter fifteen

Bleeding Trees

DAY 13 - Sunday 16th July

This is another tough day for the Jungle Janes. They start in the morning, still slashing through dense vegetation, until they encounter some massive deadfall. Alex came close to doing herself some serious damage.

Later, they walk along an open ridge, which is easier.

In the evening, the women are worried that they haven't bathed, or washed their clothes for more than three days.

SUSANNA

I think most of our shirts have reached a point of no return. I don't think the strongest of biological powder could get the stains out of mine now. They are completely ingrained. Some of them look more dramatic than they are. I've got two magnificent red stains on one of my sleeves, which look like blood stains from leeches, or wounds encountered on route, but in fact it's only red sap from a tree. There are one or two trees that bleed when you stick your *parang* in them, which is tragic.

One of my hands is dyed yellow, and despite having washed all the laundry, it is still as yellow as it was beforehand. In fact, it's my hands that perhaps have suffered most. I've tended to wear long sleeves, because the flies love me and the mosquitoes love me, and I don't want to have to spray myself the whole time. I also don't like getting scratched, so I'd rather have my shirt torn than me. But my hands, because I sweat so much, are permanently wet, and they've peeled, so I have great tracts of peeled skin. It doesn't feel at all sore, but it doesn't look very attractive. I've also got blisters and calluses from using a *parang*.

The peaty earth in some areas of the forest seems to get into every crevice of one's fingertips, and my hands are just a mess. Fingernails are permanently filthy, and however much you clean them, it's back within two minutes. My hands are also fairly scratched from 'Wait-a-whiles' and things. In fact, my hands have suffered far more than my feet, which is not something I expected. I hope I won't be required to shake hands with anybody that matters, otherwise they might wonder what I've been doing.

The campsite is better today. We've had time to relax this afternoon, so we're feeling better, too, but tired. And we're desperately hoping that the promised land that we're heading for tomorrow will materialise and be as good as we've been told. We haven't actually had rain for four or five days now. That hasn't helped the rivers and they're very low now.

One disadvantage of the water not actually flowing is that we can't just *steri-tab* the water, we have to filter it. The little hand pumps that we have are extremely effective, but very slow. It takes a good half hour with both pumps being handled to fill one bladder. And that takes three people – one to balance the two water carriers so that the little tubes go into the water at both ends, and two people actually to pump.

It's been a pain having no running water, as well as what it does to morale. But the teams still seem to be working well together. There is still the odd candid remark, under the breath, on both sides, but I think we're working much more effectively. A sort of *modus vivendi* is being established, and people are more settled in themselves and how they're operating. I certainly feel that I'm more in control than I was when we were back at 230alpha. It's partly because I'm sleeping properly now. I think that's down to the earplugs. Which is rather sad; I hate the idea of shutting out the lullaby of the jungle, but I don't seem to be able to take it, and sleep is more important. I shove these, very grotty now, bits of foam into my ear, and I'm away. It's a huge relief to me, because that was what I found so difficult for the first four or five days here.

I was 'Tail-End Charley' today. I've taken myself off navigation and it's been much less stressful and very peaceful. I've begun to realise that my brain has relaxed into the tempo of the jungle.

I think my life at home is very busy mentally. I live in two places. I lead a freelance, peripatetic existence which is hard. I'm on my own, so all decisions have to be debated with myself. And a lot of the time, the stresses of the day aren't necessarily relieved by talking them through with a partner.

Out here, I don't have to worry about any of that. My day is ordered for me, and the only things I have to worry about are so basic, and so straightforward, they don't really require planning and background thought. You're either in the right place at the right time and ready, or not.

While some people might find it slightly worrying that they're mind is emptied, I think it's a very good thing for me and the jungle is providing the ultimate relaxation.

Ken described the jungle as being womb-like; it surrounds you, you can't escape it. The outside world is irrelevant, anything could be happening, World War III could have broken out and we wouldn't have a clue.

I'm giving very little thought to what is happening back home. There's a lot of chat from others about their families and partners, but a lot of the time I think about nothing. On the walk today, I overheard somebody ask someone else, "What are you thinking about?" And I wondered what I would say if they asked me. The answer would have to be: "Nothing." I concentrate on putting one foot in front of the other.

I look around the jungle, constantly on the lookout for wildlife, in the hope that I might see a bit more than we have so far. It's all very hidden away. They hear us coming, which is not surprising; a gaggle of talkative women is not something this jungle is used to. We're probably the first here, other than *Iban* women, and I don't know whether they're great chatterboxes, though human nature suggests that they are.

Each camp we come to now may have been occupied by soldiers, either Ghurkhas or special forces, but they are very unlikely to have had the feminine touch. Not that we're exactly putting vases of flowers everywhere. Chance would be a fine thing, but we just haven't seen any flowers, though Bhuwani produced the petals of an orchid the other day, which we all stuck our noses into. It smelled just divine, particularly in comparison with the way that most of us are at the moment.

I think I've scored highest in the scent stakes when we do come to washing, because my shower gel seems to have a slightly stronger injections of chemicals than the others, so it has a fresher, smell than some of the soap. Anything to cover up the smell of me.

I tried to wash my socks today, but I don't think that the slightly stagnant water helped, so I've put them away in a plastic bag, well sealed, until I feel strong enough to tackle them.

PATSY

We've done two kilometres today, not gruelling, but across terrain that's very difficult to navigate. People are tired and stumbling and there have been some tears.

We haven't washed in three days, and there's been no rain for two. Any water we find will have to be filtered and purified.

We're beginning to think of the homeward straight, which is when people relax and stop taking care. I'll have to be sure to remain vigilant.

This evening, I'm lying in my hammock when Sally comes up and knocks on my tarpaulin. She says she's found a lump.

I examine her and find she has a hernia. This was something I should have anticipated, though, in fact hernias aren't very common in women.

It isn't a dangerous one, but Sally's very anxious about it, and it's giving her quite a lot of pain. I feel she can go on with the trek; we only have a few more days walking, and I decide we can manage the pain with painkillers. But, I have to weigh up the possibility of it becoming complicated. On the homeward straight, we will be a long way from any landing sites, and to evacuate Sally, we would have to cut down jungle. I let her choose if she wants to go out, or go on. She wants to go on, which I'm pleased about.

We have taken any surplus weight we can from Sally's ruck-sack, and Buwhani is taking her out of the group, as he has with Alex, which she doesn't like, but he's given her little choice, and I think he's wise to do this.

CATHERINE

Each day seems to get harder and harder. This morning I had to carry a bladder again. The bladders make you lopsided, because they scoot all over the place, and whenever I had to climb up a log and walk across it, I was very nervous of slipping. I would hate something as stupid as that to happen, to put me out of the race as it were.

I tried navigating for the first time today, with Izzy and Patsy. I found it very interesting; it's important to pace and use the compass, because the map doesn't always match the land. And it's reading the land that I find difficult. When you cross grain it can become very hard; if you get it wrong and make people go even a hundred metres in the wrong direction, it can be very disheartening.

We found a good campsite today. Once again the water isn't brilliant, but it's enough and it's not as bad as last night's, which was horrible.

Tomorrow, we should have an easier trek to a lovely river, I hope.

A thought: each day gets harder and harder, but we're doing the same thing – going up and down, carrying these enormous great water bladders. And the thought does cross my mind, "Why, are we doing it?"

It's relentless. Nothing changes. In the sense that the jungle remains the same, the terrain remains the same. It's just up and down, up and down. I don't know the answer to that question yet, but there must be an answer.

CLAIRE

Today I'm at the front. I've decided to do the chopping – lead scout.

I take out my *parang*, which I must admit I'm apprehensive about using. But slowly and surely, I'm getting more confident with it. Now I'm at the front, I've got to chop it right through so that the ladies can follow. As I lift the first ever chop, I can't believe it, oh, I'm in my stride, ooh, at last, I can get at this undergrowth, because it's been getting at us.

I swish, and I swash – swash-buckling, like the TV shows – but my goodness, I've got to use so much strength!

But I cut through, knocking vines out the way, trees and leaves, but nothing dead. The dead plants I'm able to just snap off, use my feet, kick them aside. Swish, swash, using that *parang*, I have to be careful.

But, oh my goodness, how much of this can we keep taking?

I can't believe it, we get a chance to stop, but I'm still really perspiring, drinking so much water, eating so much, but then, on we go with our packs again. No time to rest, no time to think about it. I go on a 'reccy' with the others, so I can see exactly where we're going, so I have an idea where to chop through.

Oh, now I'm getting really angry with this!

First it was a nice easy path, now it's harder, as the blade cuts through the vines, as it cuts through the jungle, you should see the height of some of this. It's just sapping my energy, I haven't had a chance to think about my ankle. I am just pushing forward. We've been going hours. Gosh, how much strength have we got as women? They say that we're the fairer sex, the weaker sex. I don't believe it! We are definitely the stronger sex. Think of it, men don't give birth. Look at us here, as well. We can do almost anything. The strength of a woman is not just her physical strength, it's her mental strength too.

Think of the force behind twelve women, all of us here; we're formidable! We really are.

DICKY

It turned out a good day. We did two kilometres quite quickly and finished about lunchtime.

This morning we had two huge logs to circumnavigate. It was a bit like the Grand National course. On one occasion we had to get right up on top of a log, and then walk along it, covered in moss and quite slippery, for about forty metres, three or four feet off the ground, which is quite high when you've got a very heavy backpack on. You're trying very hard to balance. If I'd seen that in cold blood, there's no way I would have got onto it, and walked across it with a forty pound *bergen*. But you see everybody ahead of you just resignedly climbing onto it, heaving themselves up, and you just do the same.

On another occasion, we came to a huge log right across the path too high to get over, so we had to get down on our hands and knees, which again is jolly difficult with a huge pack on your back. You feel absolutely like a donkey or a beast of burden as you get right down and crawl under the ruddy thing.

As I say, a bit like the Grand National. Some wag started singing the theme of the Horse of the Year Show.

We walked into camp at about half past one, and it's jolly nice to be here. We've had a nice afternoon; some of us have played cards. The winners were supposed to collect goodies and sweets and things from the three losers, but I daresay we won't be paid off.

We wrote our diaries; we went down to the river for water, which was absolutely disgusting. Somebody saw a small crocodile, but I'm not sure that I believe them. And we filtered a lot of the water, because it was so disgusting. We've had the usual supper, and most people turned in about eight o'clock. Poor old Izzy fell twice, so she's not had such a good day, and Claire disappeared off to her *basha* really early and slept all through supper.

We're all gradually getting more and more exhausted but I think everybody is determined to bash on.

SALLY

Today, I was quite proud of myself. We had to walk along a very long piece of deadfall. It must have been an ancient tree. I was doing pacing today, and when I paced my way along it, it was well over thirty metres, something that you simply wouldn't come across on a walk in the UK. You might come across a telegraph pole type log, but this was of gigantic proportions. It must have had a girth of about a metre, so it was quite hard to scramble up onto it, with

185

your pack on – a sort of hands and knees job, with possibly a shove up behind from the person beneath you – before very tentatively inching your way along it.

Yesterday I felt very, very weary at the end of the day, almost sick with tiredness. Today, because we only walked for about four and a half hours, we've had quite a nice rest and a leisurely time this afternoon. I even played a game of gin rummy, which was a bit of fun. I feel much better tonight, in much better spirits.

FIONA

It's a pretty cool campsite; there are some big trees, though we can't go in the middle because there's a bit of deadfall. But we're camping further down and we're back as a big group again. Everyone is very chatty, talkative. Dicky is now the leader.

Oh fuck it, I can't remember what day it is!

I lost my watch today, but it was found again, which was a huge relief, because I'd have been very upset ,even though I'm a strong believer that if you do lose things, you're meant to.

We had a great night, listening to Capital FM with the boys. We talked and told loads and loads of jokes and got told off for making too much noise!

GWENDA

It should have been a rest day, but because last night our campsite was so grotty, and there was no decent water, we decided to move on today. So we said the Lord's Prayer today, which brought a tear to my eye, and made me think of home a lot.

I hope God will keep us safe on this expedition and make sure we all get out safe and well.

Although we had a fairly easy walk today, while I was carrying the water, I felt so weak. I had no strength at all and it was a real effort to put one step in front of another. I nearly fell over at one time.

I smelt my socks today, and they made me retch. They were absolutely gopping. They smelt like pure ammonia. I can't believe that my body has made them smell so much. I haven't been able to wash for a couple of days now. I've used baby wipes and I put some water in a cup and used that to wash. It makes me feel a little bit better, but I don't know whether the smell improves.

We've had some time to ourselves today, so I've been able to sort out my pack, and read for ages, and listen to my Walkman. I taped all my favourite songs before I came away, from my CDs and tapes and my 45s. The children made a little tape for me too, with singing and reading, and Harry playing the violin. They're so funny and good kids.

We're halfway through the expedition and we're all still here. Apparently it's pretty amazing that no one has gone out. We've had a sore leg, a swollen ankle, lots of bites and things, but nothing major. And Ken is chuffed to bits.

If we can keep laughing, especially at ourselves, then we can't go too far wrong. But let's hope it carries on like that. We haven't got far to go now.

JULIE

Oh, I do find these tapes difficult…

And I haven't really done a tape for a couple of days now, mainly because yesterday when we arrived at that camp – that hovel, more like – we'd been trekking for about eight hours, probably more, and cross-graining, which was an absolute nightmare. Walking down, and walking up, and stumbling all over the place. You just get down, and you think, ooh, great, perhaps we're going to find a ridge, and then, you look up, just to be faced with climbing again, and you know you just haven't got the energy to pull yourself up anymore.

I got stuck climbing over a dead log today, which was quite funny. I just couldn't move at all. Ha ha. Ooh, it was so funny! Those bits I can laugh at, and by and large, I can laugh most of the time, but trudging up those hills - Oh, God, it's an absolute nightmare!

It was awful yesterday. Absolutely awful!

One of the good spots yesterday was coming across this wonderful gully where we really felt like explorers going into the unknown.

Now everyone's busy sorting Alex' clothes. Ooh, she's getting dressed this evening!

No she isn't; she isn't putting on her best clothes tonight after all. I think she's going to save them for later on in the trek. Ha ha.

KEN'S LOG

Yesterday I felt some fear and trepidation. We were crossing a piece of jungle that had no landing sites on it and in the morning we left through an area which was full of secondary growth - really thick jungle and a low canopy. The only explanation was that it was a big bowl and a water catchment - a real sun-trap. Perhaps that had killed off the bigger trees and left the smaller ones. It was an impressive place, full of insects and hot and sticky and not very pleasant at all. It was really good to climb out of it into the fresh air and to be able to see out over the canopy. I was glad when we hit a good ridge and were able to set off.

As the day went on, I grew slightly easier because we hit a good track and we had about a couple of hundred metres to ascend at the end of the day. But we hit another problem where the navigation was really difficult. There were lots of hidden gullies and difficult ground – we had to cross-grain and got stuck in some thick country for a couple of hundred metres until we hit a ridge and came down into an old camp. It had an air of sanctuary about it, and for me it was a bit of a turning point because I recognised it from when I had been here before.

It was a hard day for me mentally because I was worried about someone getting injured and then having to chop a winch hole to get them out. There was a distinct lack of water as well and we really had run out of water by the end of the day. Lucky we found some.

KH 16-07-00

chapter sixteen

Shrangi-la

DAY 14 - Monday 17ᵀᴴ July

After four hard days' trekking, the Jungle Janes took an easier ridge route, dropping down to a river near a designated landing site, before heading up to a British Army jungle warfare training camp.

The women were delighted to see plenty of fresh water again, and the mood was generally buoyant. During the day, though, fresh cracks had begun to show in unexpected places.

DICKY

We left camp this morning at eight o'clock and had a relatively easy walk through what I consider to be a real jungle – not a lot of undergrowth to hack, fairly good paths, lots of dried leaves, lots of big frondy palms and masses of fallen dead wood. There were also some beautiful butterflies, flying ant things, like huge spiders with long spindly legs, and big wasps. We had about three hours walking. Wendy was navigating and did very well.

The only problem at the moment is that Ken and Patsy aren't getting on. Patsy is being a bit starchy about things. Ken criticised the navigating yesterday. He said they needed to hurry up and not be so pedantic. Patsy took it very personally, and she's gone all sniffy about it now. This morning somebody had an eye infection; when Ken light-heartedly suggested putting tea bags on, Patsy took offence; she said it wasn't an infection, it needed Chloridamide C or something, so they very nearly had a blow up.

I managed to get Patsy walking right at the back today, so we've avoided a confrontation, but at the moment Ken can't stand Patsy, and Patsy can't stand Ken. So that really needs sorting, and as I'm leader, I suppose I ought to do it, but really I don't know how to do it. I'm just going to let things slide and hope that it will sort itself out.

Otherwise, today was a good day – nothing too strenuous, a river crossing right at the end, but a nice river. A lot of people fiddled about and clambered over slippery rocks, but I'd had enough by that time, so I just waded through about knee high.

We walked about another thirty metres up from the river and came upon this most wonderful camp, with little *rattan* shelters and pits, and ready-made latrines, and masses of clear trees to swing our hammocks from. It really is the most lovely place.

It was such a relief to get here, almost like when you're a child, going to the seaside, and Dad's saying, "We're nearly there, we're nearly there," and all the kids are sitting in the back shouting, "Who's going to be the first one to see the sea, who's going to be the first one to see the sea?" And suddenly you come over the hill, and there it is, blue and sparkling.

It was just like that. After ages, and ages, suddenly there was the most wonderful sight.

There's a helicopter dropping us in some new supplies tomorrow, so it's a complete rest day, and we can just lie in our hammocks. I've said I'll do breakfast tomorrow at eight o'clock.

There's a real mood of relaxation and bonhomie and everyone is getting on fine. A little bit like the lull before the storm, because we know that Thursday and Friday are going to be really bad days. We've got to go up some hugely steep hills, and Bhuwani said we're going to suffer. We've got to carry six full bladders between us. And those full bladders add on between eighteen and twenty pounds to your already full backpack, because by then we'll be fully loaded with eight days supplies. Each silver bag weighs just under a pound. And so, with eight of those, there's eight pounds, plus your ordinary *bergen* weight, plus every half hour carrying a full bladder up some very steep hills. We're all going to suffer so we're having a lovely time now.

A lot of the girls don't like Paul being around with the camera all the time, but he's such a good fellow, and so unobtrusive. He's a normal guy, doing his job, I think exceedingly well. And he's got a very good sense of humour. But, honestly, some of the girls get so stupid about covering up their boobs, and things.

Susanna says, "Nobody's going to see me without my bra!" and the moment he disappears she takes everything off.

But he's seen it all before, he doesn't bat an eyelid, and he's not out to make a smutty film.

Ken's getting on fine, and being an inspirational leader. He just needs to keep his hair on as far as Patsy is concerned and not get wound up. But everybody has these bouts.

I don't think I've fallen out with anybody yet, though.

I had a good game of cards with Gwenda and Catherine, who's an absolute hoot, and Sally and Alex whose legs are covered with bruises. We chatted, and smoked with everybody around the fire. And it's been a really nice, relaxing afternoon.

ALEX

I don' t mind being at the back of the queue anymore because I feel so much better now.

I saw the Sarawak mountains today, and the borderline, as well as green dragonflies, and two more monkeys.

The girls walking in front of me have all got their heads down, and I think, 'Girls, you're all missing all this!'

I find myself able to reach them where they're having their rests far quicker than I could a few days ago. Mind you, it's an easier walk today. We're walking the tops of the ridges. There are pathways! Ooh, what utter bliss!

Cor, I'll be glad when I'm in my hammock that night. Where is this Shangri-la that Ken has promised us? We seem to be going on and on and on in the heat. We've been promised that we would be here at twelve o'clock, but where is this Shangri-la? Five days we've been now with no swimming, no running water near us. I need that river! I need to get in that water, just to recuperate!

Then at the top of the ridge, around the corner, you can hear the waterfall. Music to my ears. As I look down, I think, "Oh god, I've got to climb down there now!"

Never mind. We've done it many times before now, and at the bottom there's going to be our Shangri-la, for two days off. Sure enough, there it was. Of course, we had to climb over these rocks in the river to get to it, and poor old Jules slipped and went crash bang wallop, on her bottom. She hasn't really got much of a bottom now because we're all losing so much weight. She was more worried about getting her backpack wet than she was about her bottom. So we heaved her up again, and went to the other side, and waited to turn the corner to this wonderful oasis that is going to be ours for the next two days.

The minute you arrive, you get your backpacks off, you put your notch in your tree for your *basha*, check you're sleeping next to the person that you want to be sleeping next to. I thought, "Stuff this, just get me in that water! Come on girls, we've got to get in that water, please, please, please!" They don't seem to realise how desperate I am to get in and swim and cool down.

The joy of being in that water was amazing. I think I washed my body with soap four times. Utter heaven.

PATSY

After a comfortable two kilometre trek, we've arrived at, by our very different standards, a paradise, with fire-sites and existing logs to sit on, by a beautiful stretch of river.

We've all been down to luxuriate in the water. I saw a small turtle there.

CATHERINE

We arrived at the new camp after a fairly easy walk. I don't think we could have been gladder to hear the sound of running water, which meant that we could finally wash and change our clothes, and make some semblance of getting clean again. We lunched by the river, and weren't allowed to go into the camp for at least twenty minutes.

I'd got very tired on this walk, although it was easy. I think it was a cumulative effect of previous days and I was feeling quite bolshy when I walked into the camp, and just sat there. But Ken was very excited and wanted to see the expressions on our faces when we walked in.

I was surveying the scene, as we've often been told, to decide on my two particular trees and I felt slightly cheated that we didn't have to do any chopping. My first impression was that the place was brown and bare and dead, compared with the jungle around it and all the other camps that we'd been in. However, that feeling only lasted about five minutes, when I saw that we were going to have quite an easy time of it in setting up our *bashas*. And, of course, the thing that we were all longing to do was to get down to the river. When we did, I don't think that apart from plonking me in a modern shower, I could have been better pleased than just getting into that water.

Looking around now, one of the things that strikes me about

the various campsites that we've had, is that there is a huge possibility of being garrotted by guy ropes, which seem to be strung out all over the place. And there are times when I do feel I'll never walk straight again, either bowed down by the rucksack, or crouching to get under my *basha*, or somebody else's.

Another thing I've noticed about the jungle which is rather a worry is that I sometimes feel quite clumsy. I'm forever tripping over roots, or guy ropes, or branches, or slipping and sliding, and grabbing onto trees that don't stay in the ground. Gracefulness and agility are not things that come to mind as far as human beings in the jungle are concerned. We have to learn to take things very slowly, watch where we step, watch where we go, there's no need to rush anything.

One reason I found today difficult is that quite a lot of tension had built up in me. I was trying to work out why, and I think that I'm not used to the intimate company of so many women for such a long time, also, I now realise that, at home, I do have explosions of temper. If I'm irritated or annoyed about something, I vent my feelings. But in public I control myself, as so many of us are trained to do, and I've had to control myself now for two weeks, which is quite a long time.

I'm sure it's the same for a lot of the others people as well. Other ways of expressing oneself, or expressing annoyance become quite important.

Fiona has just discovered some animal on a stick by Sally's *basha*, and it looks remarkably like a cockroach. It's munching on brown biscuits. It's absolutely horrendous!

If I'd discovered it first, it wouldn't have been just a mild shriek.

Oh, my goodness. It's like a rat!

We want Poo (Susanna) to come and take a photograph. She's been trying to take photographs of insects but she's been singularly unsuccessful because as we tramp through the jungle, everything disappears. Apparently we have to stay very quiet for five or six hours, in one place before anything will come out.

So, this is a real muncher. It's not at all fazed by a bright light being shone in it's face. It's continuing to eat.

We've got Poo out of bed now, and Dicky.

Oh, it's gone!

We've had no rain for about four days. As we're in the dry season, I guess that's not unusual. We're going to make the most of tomorrow in the river for the last time for a couple of days, because we're going to go very high, and we'll have to carry our own water with us. Everybody seems very jolly and relaxed, and I think we definitely need these two days to recover.

CLAIRE

Well, what an easy day this is! I should have been at the front today! Can you believe it, I chose yesterday, of all the days!

It's almost like a motorway here, the track is so perfect. The *Ibans*, the natives of this wonderful rainforest have left the most amazing paths. You know it's them, because of all the natural homes and shelters they've left behind. And here we are following in their footsteps. Don't get me wrong, nothing is easy in the rainforest, but let's say it's easier than it has been. We know that we're going at a very good speed, because in the first half an hour we covered six hundred and fifty metres, which is excellent. Our top speed so far has been approximately five hundred metres per hour, so we're going well. That's because we know that we're heading for Shangri-la!

We just can't wait to get there, we're dying to get to some water because we're all absolutely filthy. We hope that we're going to get somewhere today that is really beautiful. We need another picturesque site.

The navigating is going extremely well. No wrong turns so far, though we had to think twice a couple of times, but we're doing well.

And finally we arrive, my goodness, it *is* Shangri-la!

It's lovely, no chopping, no felling, no *parangs*, all the trees are there, ready for us. It's an old army camp. Bhuwani says it's approximately three years since it was used by the SAS. Ken assures us that it's very safe here, and it's one of the best camps in the jungle.

We've got our *bashas* up, and at last we're going down to the water. You cannot imagine how wonderful this feels. We're like mermaids; we're back in our water. Water babies, that's what we are. It's wonderful to be able to wash, at last. This was top of my wish list, along with ice-cream, and aromatherapy.

That's the most important, just to feel clean, to feel the wonderful ice clear water on our bodies. It's beautiful, it really is, to take off your clothes and walk straight into the water and get clean. Lots of soap all over, lots of bubbles everywhere. I hope we're not polluting the rainforest river. I doubt it. How can we, there are so few of us and so much of the rainforest river.

It's the night of the fourteenth, and what a beautiful night!

There's the biggest full moon I've ever seen. Gosh, it's so beautiful, casting a wonderful fluorescent light down upon our camp. And the camp is so peaceful, so still.

I can see stars as well for the first time since I've been in the rainforest. We've been much lower down, so there's been a massive canopy over us and lots of foliage around, so we've been unable to see the stars, the moon or the sky, whereas here tonight, it's come out, just for us!

FIONA

Yesterday we got up and we knew we had a long walk, but we were told there were some pretty good tracks to follow. I was lead chopper slasher, and pretty much redundant, because it wasn't a hard track to follow.

There were a few injuries, which make it tough going, but we finally got to where we were going after a few sing songs, and a few stops for navigation checks.

We hoped and prayed there would be a rest day, only to turn the final corner and find the camp. And it is absolutely awesome. It feels like being in the Maldives or something. There are steps down to the river. They're basic, but they're steps. There is plenty of room for your *basha*; there are huts that you can eat in.

The thought of spending the night here was absolutely fantastic.

We spent the evening chatting to the Ghurkhas. I think a very important part to this trip has been spending time chatting to these guys. I've learned more about Nepal, the Ghurkhas and the Nepalese way of life in the last week than I would ever have learned from a book or a documentary. They are very strong, individual characters and they love to laugh as much as we do. Those of us who have made the effort to talk to them have really benefited from spending time with them.

Alex has spent a lot of time with Bhuwani because she's been walking with him. And some of the stories that he's told her have kept her going. I know it is as important to them, too, that we finish this as a whole team.

I'm looking forward to tomorrow, and our first full day off for a while.

IZZY

We've called the campsite Shangri-la, and we've got two and a half days to make the most of being near a river. We've actually been about four or five days without having water to swim or wash in so we're all a bit whiffy. I know I am, but as everybody's in the same boat, it doesn't matter hugely. But I think a lot of us are quite tired. Personally speaking I am, though I could put on my backpack and keep walking, and it wouldn't bother me. But I think it's quite nice to have a couple of days to recharge batteries and stock up on a bit of food. I'm having occasional double rations in the evening, a few chocolate drinks, stuff like that, so as not to lose too much weight. It's funny, because I've lost complete track of how I look. I'm sure we all look as if we've gone native. Most people have got sarongs; they're quite nice to put on, they make a nice change from the trekking trousers. And I seem to have adopted this headscarf from Fiona. It's rather manky-looking, but it does keep my head cool and my hair out of the way. I doubt I'll be setting any fashion trends though.

JULIE

I really don't know what day of the week it is, I think it might be Monday.

We've had quite an easy day, just trekked and carried on until lunchtime. Everyone seems to be in really good spirits. And then we were told we were going to have lunch by a river, and from there, not very far, would be our camp.

But we had to cross the river first. I was really careful in finding out which stones were slippery, and which weren't, in order not to get my boots wet, and not to fall in, but I stepped on this flat stone with absolutely no mess at all on it and no slime. And I promptly lost my footing and fell straight on my bottom. Needless to say I got my boots wet, but fortunately my pack stayed dry. And the only way to stop myself from screaming and crying, was by shouting Ow, ow, ow, ow, and trying to make light of it. Fortunately I didn't hurt myself badly; I haven't even got a bruise.

We had lunch – the usual soup and noodles. We were told to wait by the river, and after what seemed like absolutely ages, we were told to come on up this path, which looked like a staircase, and got to the top, and absolute bliss! Staircase to heaven! Shangri-la or what?

We immediately felt better, especially after we were told that the next day was going to be a rest day.

Later we all trundled back down to the river looking like bag ladies and had our first swim in about five days. I don't think I've ever smelt so badly in my entire life. I'd hate to be a tramp!

It was wonderful and really refreshing to have nice soap around your armpits and your parts.

After the swim, for the first time since the trek started, I lounged in my hammock in the afternoon and read my book.

In the evening, we went up and sat with the Ghurkhas, which we're not really supposed to do, but who cares. We had little dried whitebait things. I also had a very nice cup of coffee with a slug of whisky in it.

I don't think Ken's going to be too pleased.

SUSANNA

I'm delighted to report that Ken has brought us to paradise. We've nicknamed it Shangri-la. It's heavenly after the campsites of the last couple of days, though there are one or two built in hazards, from the jungle warfare side of things. You suddenly come across a load of spiked sticks on the way to the latrines, which are in fact areas for soldiers to defend themeselves from the enemy by sitting in the middle of all these spikes, and there are little sort of shell holes, where in the event of being under fire, the soldiers can dive in – little trenches really. And it's said that there are some underground tunnels around here, with the entrances well hidden, so I hope that nobody is going to fall down any of those. We're very happy people, particularly since there is an attractive river, with a good pool for swimming and a waterfall at the end if you swim around the corner. And it's a joy to find flowing water because the last few rivers we've come across have been nothing much more than muddy ditches. And although you can wash to a certain extent in a muddy ditch, it's not really as satisfactory as being able strip off, and have a swim and scrub down. So, morale is very high, and we want to stay here. However, we know there's a really hard couple of days to come after this, so our pleasure is tinged with anxiety.

There are some lovely butterflies around, which I have been trying to photograph, rather unsuccessfully. They just don't seem to settle, unlike the English butterflies that find a flower and sit on it to sun themselves for hours. These guys keep on the move, which from a photographic point of view is very frustrating. But it's just lovely to be here, and enjoy the peace, though of course, the insect life still keeps up the background noise – there's no escaping that dentist's drill!

We ended up lingering over supper longer than usual. We've now got time to start talking to each other as human beings who don't actually know each other terribly well. We've been talking about people's lives and experiences back home and our hopes and aspirations. This is a luxury because up till now, we've been so up against it to keep on top of the practicalities of living in the jungle that we haven't had time to develop relationships on a deeper level than, "Who's going to do the fire tomorrow morning?" or, "Who didn't bring up their share of the water?" It's good to be able to take it to the next stage.

I was trying to remember what my fears were, when I was back in London, thinking about this trip – what I was afraid of and whether those fears have come anywhere near being realised. My brain is so addled, that I had quite a lot of difficulty remembering what I was frightened of. I seem to remember that one of my main concerns was whether I would cope physically, because of my fractured right foot, and it hasn't squeaked at all. It's absolutely fine so far, and though it would probably be rash to say so, I hope it'll be okay until the end of the trip.

It would be very rash, so I won't.

So that fear, so far, has not come to fruition.

Now, the eight legged problem, arachnophobia. That again hasn't been a real problem. I think it makes a huge difference being outside. I always feel worse when I'm in a confined space with a spider. But the jungle is a very big space indeed and even when a really quite large spider is not very far away, the anxiety isn't there in quite the same way. Mind you, having had a spider in my *basha* the first night, and having heard of Fiona's near escape with the tarantula making it's way halfway down her hammock string, I would never risk sleeping without my mosquito net.

KEN'S LOG

After an uneventful walk over some nice terrain and a good track we arrived near Landing Site 236bravo. We've occupied an old army camp which is exciting for the ladies. It resembles a typical jungle, Viet-Cong type out-post, with towers and bunkers, and all the jungle's been cleared except for the big trees. It's close to a pretty marvellous river with pools and lovely swimming. We've been incredibly fortunate to find these things because it is supposed to be the dry season and a lot of these rivers might have been dry but there's been water in a lot of them.

There's quite a good mood in camp tonight - it's a very airy place and the breeze is wafting through the trees and the moon's overhead and I was talking to some of them this evening.

They were predicting what was ahead were a couple of hard climbs and then back to our base camp but all the time I was thinking, "This isn't the end; we've still got quite a long way to go."

As an individual I've got to keep my guard up and make sure there isn't a sort of end of term feeling, when people's concentration wavers and they start to make mistakes. It's a bit like climbing a mountain; the ascent is usually the period of the greatest concentration and it's only in the descent - after the euphoria - that the major mistakes are made.

We've still got quite a few kilometres to do before we get back to our base camp and then we must try to address the problem of getting downstream.

We've got a few niggling injuries. Sally's got a hernia which is quite serious, because it could get worse. She's going to have to take it very steady. Claire's ankle's swelled quite a bit, but I think she'll make it with a good bit of strapping. I don't think she'll let that put her off. She's a very determined person.

People were saying tonight that we've been incredibly lucky, there haven't been any major injuries, nothing's gone wrong. This is tempting fate. I almost wish the conversation hadn't taken place because it takes very little here to cause an injury or make you ill.

Although everybody's in good spirits, I think there is an air of tiredness - they look drawn, some of them look positively emaciated, they've lost so much bodyweight. Then again, others look the picture of health.

We have a re-supply coming in tomorrow and it's a long time since we saw anybody from the outside world. We are about as far off the beaten track as you can get. And I told them today that they definitely were the first women to ever be in this place, which is quite an achievement and something to be proud of - to have trod on bits of jungle where nobody's been since the beginning of time.

The jungle still holds its delights for me, because you never know quite what's round the corner. This evening, I wandered up the track to the landing site which is near here. I couldn't resist just going off the other side of it to see what lay beyond. That's one of the fascinations for me about it, you don't know what's fifty metres ahead. It could be a cliff, it could be a river, it could be a snake, it could be a fallen tree. It's full of surprises.

We're just over half way, and I am proud of the women. They've shown great determination and courage. Many of them have had to confront their greatest fears, whether that be wildlife, or the proximity of other people all the time. Some still escape to their hammock for the evening and I wonder what they think about when they're there. "Should I be up the hill, laughing and joking with everybody else or should I just lie here in my own little world?"

The jungle's a great place for facing yourself, because it levels you. It brings you back down to basics, you see yourself in a different light and you tend to pick up on your weaknesses. Usually, you try to rectify them or make some sort of pledge to improve in the future.

I think the women have been incredibly selfless - a quality that's often lacking in men. They think about each other all the time. They look after each other well.

I hope this trek is turning out to be all that they expected. It's hard, yes, but if it wasn't hard, it wouldn't be worth doing.

KH 17-07-00

chapter seventeen

Star Gazing

DAY 15 - Tuesday 18TH July

Day fifteen, spent resting at the camp they had christened Shangri-la, represents a watershed in the course the Trek. More than half the journey is behind the Jungle Janes, but they have two of the longest, toughest days in front of them. Ken's concerned that they don't relax and unwind so much that they can't get going again.

While they wash, swim and talk, ceaselessly, Ken takes himself up into the hills to reccy the route ahead of them. He comes back fairly exhausted, but he has called a meeting of all the Janes to talk about their reactions to the expedition so far.

ALEX

Gosh! Imagine waking up and thinking, I don't have to get out of my hammock at six in the morning. I can actually lie here for another half an hour.

It was bliss. There was peace all around us, we were in this camp with the sort of house that Tarzan might have built, little places in trees, ladders, tunnels and traps. It's wonderful, airy and light. The shadows are exquisite, and the moon is full tonight.

It's absolute heaven, being here, and for the first time in years, I haven't got to do anything except what I want to do. Which, in my case, is swim, and swim, and swim. And wash, and wash, and wash. And laugh, and laugh, and laugh. And we've done plenty of that today. And we don't have to do anything tomorrow, either. We've got another day off. I think that's because this dreaded Thursday, the twentieth of July is going to take it out of us. Ken thinks we need this mega-rest, in order to cope with it.

He reccied it himself, and ran up and down the hill that we're going to hike up and down. He did it in two and a half hours and came back alive, although he was covered in sweat, so maybe it won't be that bad.

One of these shelters that's sitting in the middle of this Shangri-la is like a little school room. And we were asked to meet Ken there at five fifteen. We were all rested, we'd had a lovely quiet day. We'd actually had time to lie down in our hammocks which are the only comfy places in this jungle, and read.

We all made our way to the schoolroom, with Dicky in charge.

Sometimes when Ken calls us for meetings, we all get ticked off, and it all gets a bit tense. So we were all rather nervous.

Oh God, what have we done now? Why, where are we going wrong?

Please, let it be a nice chat, because we've had such a lovely day. And Ken had his glasses on, and we hadn't seen him with his glasses before, and I could see there was a nice calm smile on his face. Sometimes he's a bit like an angry bear, when he comes scooting round us all, telling us things, and telling us we should have shaped up and done this, and done that. But today was different, his clothes were clean, and dry, his hair was washed, and he had his posh new glasses on.

He wanted to know how we all felt, how we'd changed, and how we all got on with each other.

He was asking us questions, which was rather nice, actually, because it was the first time that we'd ever had a talk with him, not him talking at us, or telling us what to do, or instructing us.

Of course, we didn't all agree with what everybody else was

saying. Some people thought they wanted to push themselves to the limit, to see how they'd react.

Cor blimey! That's the last thing I wanted to do! I don't want to push myself to the limit; if I push myself to the limit, I might explode and never come back.

I want to know what it feels like, but actually, on reflection I think I *do* know what it feels like. At the beginning of this trek, in that dark wood, I was pretty low then. But I don't want to get lower than that, I don't want to find out what it feels like to drag yourself up from the depths.

I felt we were seeing how our everyday life at home had been stripped away, and everyone has become twenty years younger, and free. All the hassles of life have disappeared. And it's lovely just enjoying being you when you haven't had a chance to be you for so many years.

It's strange though, that you have to go through this traumatic experience to feel like this.

It was a very happy meeting, though it's a shame that Patsy didn't say anything.

I worry about Patsy. At home, she and I are very close friends. We've been very good friends for a long time, and I respect her enormously. But she's out on a limb at the moment. And I can't get close to her, though I know her well enough to know that she needs to be left alone.

It made me very sad that she didn't join in the discussion. I don't know if she's been hurting; I don't know if she's being stubborn; I don't know how her mind is working, I just hope that she's finding her own way through this.

IZZY

We had a discussion this afternoon about what we thought

we'd achieved so far. Most people contributed. I asked those who didn't why they hadn't. They said it was because there were so many people ready to give an opinion that quite often everything had been said. We're starting to work as a real team; we think alike as well; there's not much dissent, and we're all getting on .

I hope we've surprised a few people. I hope we've surprised ourselves really. I didn't think when we first started out that we'd all still be here at this stage. I'm very pleased that we are and I hope that it lasts through to the end.

It will be quite something to have completed just over three weeks in the jungle and I wonder whether a group of men would have achieved the same, and got on so well together. I think men are more competitive, and women better at compromising.

I spent quite a few hours talking to Wendy and Claire. God knows what we were all talking about but it was really nice to have a little bit of time just to get to know each other. A lot of the time when we're trekking, we've got our heads down, because you're watching where you're going, and you don't have those deep meaningful conversations.

Sally is not feeling tops at the moment. She's had an injury, and I know that she's quite worried about it. But, I don't think it will stop her finishing.

We've been through her rucksack, and thrown out lots of bits of extras that she was keeping for emergencies, which gets rid of quite a bit of weight. I hope that when they share out the rations they'll try and keep her extra stuff to a minimum. She's so lovely, and she desperately wants to finish.

I know that we've got a tough day on Thursday; I've been looking at the map. We've got to cross a couple of rivers, then go up a pretty steep escarpment to about fifteen hundred feet, which doesn't sound much, but it's probably going to be a long hot day, and I think we'll start pretty early.

It's come as a bit of a surprise that we've only got about three more days trekking left before we're back at 230alpha. I could quite happily stay here for another couple of weeks really.

I'm having a lovely time, and I don't really miss home, because it's all going to be there when I get back, and this will be over all too quickly. It's such a unique thing to be able to do, and it's quite something when you think that we're the only women that have ever have been to this jungle.

CLAIRE

Fifteen days in the rainforest! Can you imagine?

As I watch day break over the camp, I wonder, was I the last to fall asleep, am I the first to wake?

I can see hammocks swinging very slowly, people turning in their sleep. Somebody else has just got up. Is that a light I can see? Or is it the flick of a lighter?

Slowly the camp is coming to life.

We haven't set any schedule; everyone's free to take their time. Yes, actually to take our time, wake, have breakfast, move around the camp, go down for a swim, do what we want – sit around and have a chatter; get to know someone else, find out how someone else is feeling, just enjoy each other's company.

What a lovely relaxing day and of course, lots and lots of time to go down to the river and have a swim, to the waterfall, just to enjoy the camp. What a wonderful day.

DICKY

We've just had a really nice quiet relaxing day, at this old SAS camp with the *rattan* huts, swimming and lazing around.

We did a Telegraph crossword. Susanna's pretty good at the crossword. Julie and I tried to roll a cigarette out of some old leaves, but her papers wouldn't stick. We borrowed some super-glue from Alex, but unfortunately she managed to spill it all down my neck, and stuck my hair to my back, so I couldn't move. And it all spilt down my shirt as well, which was quite irritating. The cigarette itself was absolutely disgusting.

We've had a long talk with Paul. People have been talking about emotions, what they miss, and what they don't miss. If there's one person I'm really looking forward to sharing all this with, it's my mum. My mum is really my best friend, and we laugh and giggle a lot. I see her every week because I go home for my day off on a Tuesday. She's a bit forgetful and doddery at times, but she's so just how a mum should be, and I can't wait to get back and tell her all about this.

I can't wait to sit across the kitchen table with a cup of coffee and tell her about some of the things that have happened. Like lying in my hammock the other night, absolutely stark naked, waiting for the Orang-utan to come, and that sort of thing. She'll giggle, she'll understand and she'll know exactly how my mind works. She'll splutter over her prunes and her apricots, and I'll tell her I've been eating dried prunes too, and she'll giggle.

Sometimes, when we're talking and there are other people around the kitchen table, she'll catch my eye, or I'll catch her eye, about something that somebody has said, and we'll just go off into the biggest fits of explosive laughter. Talking about laughter, I've never laughed so much as I have over these last two weeks. There've been such moments of real, gutting agony and shit, but I've been weak with laughter today. Poor old Wendy, she's like a bull in a china shop.

Sally and Wendy, and Catherine and I went down to the river to do some washing. And Catherine and Sally were sitting quite primly in their sarongs, and their tops, scrubbing away at their clothes. And suddenly Wendy came down the bank, absolutely stark naked, with this most enormous white bottom, sort of wobbling around. I looked at Sally, and Sally looked at me, and we both went into fits of giggles. I had to turn round, because I wouldn't hurt Wendy for the world, but of course, three steps into the river, she then tripped over a boulder and went absolutely flat. There were sploshes everywhere, and just a minute ago, there was this great crash as she'd tripped over and knocked the pan of water into the fire. Somebody said without even looking, 'Is that you, Wendy? Are you all right?'

'Yes,' she said. 'If anybody ever trips it's always me.'

So there are these special moments, where you catch somebody's eye. You don't laugh at anybody – well, I suppose you do laugh at them, but you're laughing at them in the nicest possible way.

I'm lying here, looking up through the canopy, and there are a few little stars twinkling.

I could just as easily be lying on my back, on top of the Brecon Beacons, or Bredon Hill, near my home. My brother and I used to camp out a lot on Bredon Hill. We never had tarpaulins or anything. We just had an old sleeping bag, and a ground sheet. We'd go off up the hill with some porridge, bacon, and a frying pan for a couple of days. I could just as easily be up there on a summer's evening – Bredon Hill on the borders of Worcestershire and Gloucestershire. One of the loveliest places on earth to be. Maybe, when I get home, I'll take the children camping. I think I'll do that, show them how to put up hammocks and build a decent campfire, because we haven't really done much of that before. They can use my *parang*, and chop down a few trees.

PATSY

We're having a rest day today.

At ten there's an aerobics and stretch class, but there's nothing else on the agenda.

It's extraordinary, but I've never had a day with nothing to do! At home I find I have five things to do every second of the day.

We have to fill time; we dig a new latrine, fill a few water bladders, read a bit, do a crossword and rest by the stream.

We've just had a big chat about where we've been, where we're going and what we think about it. We're all very relaxed with each other as a group.

FIONA

It's day fifteen, our first day of rest and relaxation, and I woke up at six o'clock. As did quite a few people from the heads I saw, but I didn't have to get up. And to be honest, I haven't even cleaned my teeth all day. I've been lounging around, I've read a couple of hundred pages of a book that I have to give to Catherine in a minute. I've been for a swim, collected some logs, filled in a latrine, done some water, and, to be completely honest, I'm bored. We've got another day off tomorrow, and I really wish we were cracking on again. We've had a rest, most of yesterday afternoon, today, our clothes are all dry, and mine are definitely coming in from the washing line tonight, in case it pisses down with rain. But I'm ready to move on. We know that we've got a big strong climb ahead of us, and we know we have to get our heads around the fact that it could be quite tough. But it's only a day, and then it's downhill.

It's nice, though, seeing everybody relax, people spending time pottering, and doing their own thing and, don't get me wrong, I know I'm a bit restless, I do think it's important that we've had today.

GWENDA

I'm lying here at ten o'clock at night, with this beautiful palm tree in front of me and the moon coming up behind it. I can hear all the insects and noises in the background.

We didn't have to get up until about eight. I slept without my muslin again, which makes it much cooler, and you end up not sweating, for a change. Then I spent at least an hour in my hammock, listening to my Walkman, playing some of my favourite songs. I felt at peace with myself, and home, and Ken, and everybody else.

Then I went swimming in the nude, which was very liberating.

This evening we had a group discussion led by Ken, about how we felt, whether we thought we'd changed or anything. Some people didn't join in the conversation at all, which surprised me.

I said that I thought the TV programme would be great for all the women who watch it. I hoped it would give a huge boost to their confidence, because they would see us, just ordinary women, doing something very difficult, and it might inspire them to go out and do the things they want to do.

I do feel that I have changed in a way. I feel very calm, which I wasn't when I first came out, because I'd been so busy. I'm more accepting of people and their idiosyncrasies. I hope I'm becoming more tolerant, which can be no bad thing. But most of all, I realise that I've got to spend much more time with Katie and Harry, not just time, but good quality time. And I realise that it doesn't really matter if I don't do jobs around the house straight away, they can wait.

Looking forward to the drop tomorrow with all our goodies. I've got some choccys and stuff coming in. And I'm wondering how I'm going to manage to climb that bloody big hill on Thursday. But until then, I'll just enjoy the peace and quiet.

SALLY

I didn't contribute to the discussion tonight about the expedition. I've thought about it since, though.

When I decided to go on this expedition, I did say that I thought I hadn't lived. I'd gone from school desk to office desk, and in forty-four years, I felt that I hadn't taken any real risks. So, I thought this was partly an escape from predictability, and partly to do something bold.

But after our talk today, I've realised that the essence of survival is risk assessment and caution, driven by the basic instinct to survive. So, in the end, risks aren't taken, and boldness doesn't come into the equation at all.

Perhaps boldness is more of a fault than being cautious.

Who said, *"Boldness is the child of ignorance, and an ill keeper of promise."*

I've had time to realise that's probably true. On this trip, the real dangers that have presented themselves are tiredness and carelessness, not snake bites, scorpions stings or deadfall, because all of those can be avoided if you're careful.

I've always thought of being careful as being boring. I'm not showing much spirit out here, and I've felt a childish sort of disappointment over that. I've always thought that I've hidden behind excuses, that I've not been adventurous enough or tried different things, maybe, because of the fear of failure. But, I feel now that perhaps I just had the wrong image of adventure and boldness. This jungle trip has been a test of endurance, of how a group performs, of how people cope with a challenge.

I feel slightly thwarted at the moment, although perhaps I'm growing up and realising some basic things about life that haven't been plain before.

When you read children's stories, they're all about dashing and exciting people. And it isn't real adventure. A successful adventure is based on careful planning and caution, in order to get to the end of the expedition and learn something from it.

I feel I have learned something from it, but it's not what I expected to learn. That's all.

SUSANNA

Today I was told that there was a large poisonous spider down at the river, in case I wanted to photograph it. So I duly trundled down there with my camera, and stood in the water, because it was lurking on a log, and the best vantage point was from the water. I paddled into the water, but it was very much underneath the log, and it was all dark, and rather difficult to take. It was about five inches across, with very thin legs – a sizeable grey thing, with the odd yellow bit, nothing spectacular.

Bhuwani asked if I wanted him to sort of encourage it further out onto the log, so I could get a better shot. He poked it, at which point, it swam towards me, which was alarming; I didn't realise that spiders could be amphibious. But, I must say, I got a much better photograph of it.

Bhuwani reckoned it was nasty and a bite would not be a good idea, so that's livened up our swims, now we know these spiders can take to the water.

I went up to the landing site, to see if I could find any more insect life. But other than a couple of grasshoppers and a stick insect, there is frustratingly little. I had thought there would be far more around us – birds and monkeys and boars trundling about. But they are totally absent. The birds are particularly frustrating, because one can hear them everywhere, and other than one bird of prey, at 230alpha landing site, I haven't seen a single bird. I've been carrying a little bird book, which has glorious photographs of every sort of kingfisher, and hoopoo, and the ever-audible hornbill, but actually to catch sight of them is proving almost impossible.

I think this afternoon I might sing, just so long as nobody is around and listening. But it's been a good three weeks since I've sung a note, and I might. The landing site's a spectacular arena, and having gone up there this morning to take some photographs with Patsy, I thought I might just sneak up this afternoon and whack out a bit, just to see how the old voice is. And what it's like to sing in the jungle, because I can't believe that anybody has socked anything out in this part of the jungle before. God knows what I'll sing, but it will probably sound ghastly. Not having sung for three weeks, in this heat and being exhausted, the chords will be covered in rust. But it might just be fun, so I'll pop up and have a discreet warble and see what happens.

Maybe at least it will bring out a bit of wildlife to see what's happening; I doubt whether they'll have ever heard anything like it before!

KEN'S LOG

Day fifteen was a significant day in many ways because it represented a move into the latter half of the expedition. It's a rest day by the river and as usual the sun shone all day. The ladies had a chance to do their washing and drying and generally rest. They didn't do much resting, though they seemed to do a lot of talking, but I suppose that's resting in itself.

I've been very busy again. I went out this morning on a reccy of what will be the major obstacle for them on this expedition, that's the fifteen hundred footer - a very steep escarpment, about a kilometre from here, which they will climb on the twentieth.

I wanted to make sure that the route I've selected is feasible for them, that they'll be able to navigate their way over it. It's quite tricky - and consequently I have cut a bit of a track back through the thicker jungle. When I was climbing up the ridge, I had a young fit Gurkha with me who was pulling me along quite quickly and we were going at a pretty rapid rate.

Having got back, I felt pretty exhausted and I was hoping vainly that someone was going to stick a brew under my nose but that didn't happen so I decided to go down to the river and have a good swim, wash my clothes again and start planning for the rest of the day.

We had a good chat this afternoon - all the ladies and myself. At this halfway stage I wanted them to have the opportunity to talk to me on a one to one basis and get anything off their chests. Generally speaking, they were pretty forthcoming and made some interesting comments and observations but I still think some of them are a bit staid and hold back on some of their inner feelings. This is disappointing because what we're trying to do here is to show how people's psychological profile can change dramatically in an environment like this and how the mind adapts to coping with the pressures of jungle life. I think they're still a bit suspicious of me and maybe reluctant to bare their souls. But that said, they're a pretty capable bunch and I think that's probably women all over in adverse situations - they do become very adaptable and very resourceful and they just won't contemplate failure. They have a very positive attitude and collectively they are able to overcome most of the obstacles I put in front of them.

Wendy continues to stumble over things and every time I see her she's tripped over something or fallen in the river - she's quite accident prone so we'll have to watch her over the next week or so. Alexandra's in tremendous heart and warbles away all day and Sally seems to have perked up a bit. I'm still concerned about Patsy; she seems very quiet and a bit withdrawn, and of course I'm the sort of person who thinks it's my fault and I should be doing something to snap her out of it. We'll see what happens in the next few days.

I'm looking forward to moving from here. We have to give them these rest periods but the whole place becomes a bit of a Hi-De-Hi holiday camp and I find it a bit disconcerting. At least it gives us the opportunity to dry out and we have got a resupply coming in tomorrow which will bring in some goodies with it. That'll be another morale booster and then we'll be set to continue on. Some of the ladies think the end of this trip is in sight, but I had to tell them today that they've got to keep their guard up, because if they don't the jungle will turn round and bite them in the back. All the lessons they've learned about safety and hygiene - not cutting themselves and respecting the wildlife - all those things have got to be maintained and reinforced.

KH 18-07-00

chapter eighteen

Pig Fight

DAY 16 - Wednesday 19th July

The Jungle Janes spend a second full day at Shangri-la. Ken Hames wants them to have a serious rest before the final two days' hard trekking. He's also arranged a chopper to come in with final supplies which should last them back to camp at 230alpha and the three days it will take to get down river.

Sally's hernia is a problem. If she were a soldier, she would be taken out; but she's determined to finish with the rest of the team. It's unanimously agreed that some concession should be made in the share of weight she's carrying.

When the helicopter does arrive, though, there is an unseemly scramble for the treats and chocs.

ALEX

It's day sixteen and we're still in this lovely peaceful place.

Soon, we should hear the helicopter flying over, to drop in all the treats we have ordered. Pineapples, oranges and a birthday cake for Bhuwani. I never thought I'd ever be hungry here, but I am now, because I feel so much better and stronger.

It will be very exciting today because we have to eat as much as we possibly can, so we don't have to carry too much food tomorrow. It's all good fun, this living in the jungle business. I'd recommend it to anyone.

PATSY

It's been re-supply day and we're having a huge feast.

As Bhuwani has said that he likes the look of our ceramic water filters, we've given him one for his birthday, as well as a mini-disc which we've all recorded with our birthday wishes.

I've been down to lie in the pool by the waterfall for quite a long time. It's very soporific there but you still have to be alert for crocodiles and deadfall. There are some lovely dragonflies there too with purple, green and bright blue.

Although no-one usually drinks alcohol in the jungle because it's too dehydrating, a few bottles of beer came in on the helicopter for the Gurkhas, and they've been singing and dancing. I love the songs with an intermittent high pitched 'ting-ting', like chimes, interspersed with their male voices.

We've all been talking, and someone asked me about myself, so I've been thinking of myself with my maiden name, as if I were single. It feels very strange that my single self has been displaced by my identity as a wife and mother, and a new English persona. I don't mind about that but thinking about what to do with myself for a whole day is utterly unfamiliar.

CATHERINE

There was huge excitement this morning over the re-supply coming in. We had all ordered bags of things we wanted dropping off to us. We were looking forward to this very much indeed. We were all allowed up onto the landing strip, which was wonderful, because it's very open compared with where we normally are and the sunlight gets through. I love helicopters, and the sight and sound of one coming in, particularly for us, was great fun. Everything was unloaded, and we brought it down to the camp. The real business of the day began when we opened up our various bags. The other group failed to get coffee and tea, so we said that we would give them whatever they needed, as long as they'd give us whatever we needed.

Later, I got stung by a wasp, which was extremely painful. Patsy told me to take some anti-histamine, which I did. Those who hadn't been stung thought it was hilarious, and I ended up showing my bottom to everybody, because there's a rather nasty ever growing red mark on it. The pain lasted about twelve hours. I suppose I deserved it because I haven't been leeched yet. I've managed to keep those nasty little things away. As we were having a very early start next day, we were all in bed fairly sharpish, after a fantastic meal of chicken, rice and onions, fresh pineapple, and anything that anybody could think of thrown in. Absolutely delicious. And thanks to the cooks, Julie, Wendy, Claire and Alex.

We all trooped off to bed, very full and very satisfied, which was lucky, because the following day didn't quite go as planned.

CLAIRE

To my left, the fire is burning brightly. We always have a wonderful log fire. We stop, we make a fire and guess what, today we're cooking up a storm, because the re-supply came, we actually have fresh chicken for the first time since we left Sittang camp. We're going to have a feast this evening, for Bhuwani's birthday, which is in fact tomorrow.

We've already had a wonderful brunch, bacon sandwiches, peanut butter sandwiches, jam sandwiches, pineapple and orange. The simple things in life just cheer us so much and they give us a lot of energy for the next steps ahead.

I can just see the cooks over there, cutting, slicing, adding all the marinades, the seasoning – stock cubes which we bought to use as drinks.

Alex is laughing about something that she's just chopped up. What *is* she laughing at?

I just heard a clap of thunder. I wonder if a storm is about to break. It's been promising rain since we got to Shangri-la. But it just keeps passing us by.

Here I am in my hammock, listening to it all, watching it all. I'm not being lazy. I was helping with the chopping, but I've had to come back. And behind me I can hear Alex again, laughing. Such happy joyful sounds. Lovely smells, it's so tranquil, it's so nice here. It makes you wonder what happens when we leave and go back. But for now, just take it in, just look at it.

The re-supply was like feeding the five thousand. People were hoarding their bags. Nobody, but nobody would open their bags, lay them out and say, this is what we have, let's share it out. There are six in this team, I've got six of this, let me share. Nobody did that. Everybody huddled, and held their bags tightly and just put their hands out for more. It wasn't like a car boot sale, it was more like a bring and buy, no, no it wasn't even that, it was a "take whatever you can get". It's amazing how greedy people are when they haven't eaten proper food for a long time.

DICKY

We'd all been looking forward to the supply drop because we thought it was coming the day before. But of course it didn't come that day, and the anticipation was just like Lent when you're waiting for Easter Sunday, and you can start eating chocolate again.

It was a very moving moment, to see this enormous machine land so precisely on such a small piece of ground. But then in a funny sort of way, it feels rather like an intrusion, because we've got so used to each other's company, its like we're in our own little world and when you see these other faces in the helicopter, they're like visitors from outer space.

I'm very ashamed to say that I was so pleased to see the food, that as soon as somebody opened a packet of biscuits I stuffed about three into my mouth without even thinking. They were so delicious. They were digestive biscuits and funnily enough I'd been yearning for a digestive biscuit for ages. And then of course, luckily I got the bag of chocolate drinks to share out, and I counted them up very quickly and there were 64. It seems silly to be so precise about these things, but 64 divided by whatever, has to be very precise. Again I'm slightly ashamed to say there was one left over, which I sneaked. This morning, I was full of remorse, so I gave it to Sally. But food does become an overwhelming issue here for somebody like me who is always thinking of their stomach. And I did warn everybody at the beginning that if push came to a shove, I just couldn't be trusted.

Then we had the most delicious bacon sandwiches buttered, very sparingly, I might add, by Catherine, followed by fresh pineapple and oranges cut up by Patsy, who seems to have the most iron will. She doesn't eat until after everyone else. She doesn't just dive in, or eat snacks and bits off the end. She's just so grown up really.

Our delicious chicken dinner was slightly spoiled because we ate it from our blue plastic mugs, but fortunately I have got a silver spoon to eat with, because one has to maintain one's standards wherever one goes. So I ate my chicken out of my blue plastic mug, with my silver spoon and I went to bed with a full stomach for the first time in over fourteen days. I've been beginning to feel like Jesus on the cross, with all his ribs showing. Fortunately I'm not on the Cross on my own, although it does feel like it. A bit like the agony before the ecstasy, only the other way round, we all had to go to bed a bit early, because we knew we were going to get up really early and set off on this huge ascent of fifteen hundred feet, with full water bladders.

GWENDA

When the helicopter arrived, it was like a pig fight; a bun fight, I should say, with everybody trying to sort out their rations. It's amazing how people change when there's food there, and it all has to be given out. Everybody demanding to know where their amount was. And why wasn't this there, and why wasn't that there. But I think it's quite understandable, considering the circumstances.

IZZY

I think we're all quite looking forward to setting off, quite soon as well. We've got a long walk ahead tomorrow and it's going to be tough, but nothing we haven't done before.

Bacon sandwiches have been brilliant. It's so nice to have something different. The boil in the bags are great, but it is nice to have variety.

Dicky has managed to work her way through all the chocolate bars that are available, but she's very amusing and she keeps us all on our toes.

I'm just going to enjoy the river, and chill out until we leave tomorrow.

SALLY

We went up to the landing site. I was excited to see the helicopter, but I was actually quite relieved that it left without me. I didn't want to leave the trek early. When the food came, all the bags were rummaged through to see which were whose, and which bag belonged to which group. There was quite a lot of ribbing, because we thought we were going to have a lot of chocolate, and a lot of rummaging in all the bags to try and track some down, but we couldn't find any.

SUSANNA

It's going to be very sad to leave here, because we've had a very nice time.

We've all enjoyed ourselves hugely, doing absolutely nothing except pottering up and down to the river.

I particularly like swimming there, because it makes me very nostalgic for the days when I was a child and my father and I did a lot of river swimming. In those days you could swim in the Cherwell in North Oxford. When he got home from the office he used to sling his swimming trunks over his shoulder and take my hand, over the fields to the river. Totally on our own, swimming in the natural water, which is so much nicer than a swimming pool. I wished very much that he was with me today, as I swam in the pool.

It's been very hot, and I think actually for the first time that most of us are really quite longing for some rain. Well-timed rain mind you, we don't really want it while we're out and about. But in the night would be nice, because it's got very close and the sweat pours off us, even though we're doing virtually nothing.

The only thing that's got on my wick today have been flies. Despite being cleaner than I have been for days, and clean clothes and all the rest of it, I seem to be one hot favourite with them. Maybe I should just be more liberal with the old repellent. But it feels so awful, when you've just got out of the river, and you feel clean, and your skin is actually feeling fresh for once, to cover it in a sort of greasy mess. So, I haven't been using it much, and the flies have just been making a meal of me. They're so dopey, you can squash them, but it takes forever, because they come in their droves. I also got stung this evening by something. Catherine got stung almost simultaneously, but on her bottom, so I think she's probably more sore than me.

I was stung just below the elbow by some little blighter. I don't think it was a wasp, because the wasps make their presence known by buzzing. And there was no buzzing, I was just fiddling around below my *basha*, and suddenly, ouch! and it's really quite sore tonight. I've taken an antihistamine tablet on Patsy's advice, and I hope it won't keep me awake.

I had a long chat with Claire about her life at home, her ambitions, and all her business plans –a very switched-on lady.

We also discussed what we felt about the trip, and we're both very much in agreement that while everybody else has found it challenging and stimulating, we've also found it physically very challenging. But mentally, it's been very restful for us, because we're both single women running different strands to our lives alongside each other. Our lives at home are mentally very challenging – Claire's particularly, because she has a son, and she's doing a part-time psychology degree. She's a senior member of BA cabin staff, she's also about to start a new business, which is a totally separate activity.

My life is also complicated. I live in two different places, which in itself is quite a challenge, because I have to make sure I'm in the right place, with the right kit at the right time. And I lead a freelance existence, which is challenging in itself, with career decisions to be made. I have no help with the domestic chores, and I have a few legal hassles with my properties. I also started a singers' co-operative, and I still have some input. So I find the mental challenge here is minimal, when all you have to worry about is if you've remembered to put your *steri-tabs* in your rucksack before you go down to the river.

The jungle has been a huge release from our home tensions,

because the phone doesn't ring, you can't ring the solicitor, you can't take a major decision about life when you're out here. And life is so far away. So, we've both found it very relaxing. It's been great to be stimulated physically, because my instinct is to be a lazybones. One of the things I wanted from this trip, when I think clearly about it, was to push myself physically, because I am such a couch potato. That has certainly happened, although having puffed myself up from the river with nothing today, no pack, and just clutching a sarong in one hand, I got to the top absolutely panting. I thought I was somewhat fitter after carting sixty pounds around for the last week.

I have rather reluctantly been appointed team leader from today and the next two days. Reluctantly because, while I feel quite capable of leading, I think that the fact that I have found this all so relaxing and I've been able to have a month off from the pressures of my life, has been such a plus. Galvanising myself, if only for three days, into getting other people on the move is something I don't much want to do. Actually having to engage the brain, and set the alarm clock for ten minutes earlier than everybody else, in order to make sure that I've got them up, and to summon up the jollity which will be required to encourage them tomorrow, is going to be quite hard. I just hope I can get myself going enough to drag them through it, with some pleasure on their part, and not kicking and screaming.

FIONA

It's been a really good day. Everyone is really relaxed and they've had time to read, sew, repair things, make, or do whatever they have to do. And I'd say that considering we've got quite a tough day tomorrow, everyone is in good spirits.

It's Bhuwani's birthday tomorrow, but because tomorrow is

going to be a long day, we thought we'd celebrate tonight. And it also meant that we didn't have to carry the Sara Lee chocolate and carrot cake. We gave Bhuwani his water filter, which he really loved. In Nepal they just go out and get drunk; I don't think they really celebrate birthdays, but I would say that everyone is in fine form. I'm certainly raring to go. It's great sitting around, but there comes a point where you don't want to go at all, because it's easier to stay, so I really want to get going now.

I can't believe that I'm yawning! It's not even eight o'clock. But out here, ten o'clock is a very, very late night, eleven o'clock is like four o'clock in the morning. But you're up at five or six, most mornings, and it's great. Tomorrow, we've a good walk ahead of us. We've clean clothes, clean everything. It will be good, we can do it. We're a team.

WENDY

Thought for the Day:

Don't dismiss a good idea simply because you don't like the source.

Tomorrow I'm navigating. We've got a very difficult climb of about twelve hundred foot up the mountain, and it's very steep. I think a couple of the girls are really apprehensive about it.

We're a good team now, we work very well together, so I've no doubt we're going to make it, but it's still quite scary. It's going to be very hard, especially with full bladders because we're staying on the top of the hill, to descend to base the following day. I'm not looking forward to it because it's going to be the stiffest challenge, but that's what we're here for and I feel this is where the real teamwork will come into play. I think it's really important, and I think we'll get there, so I'm having an early night.

chapter nineteen

Come On Ladies

DAY 17 Thursday 20TH July

The women agree that day seventeen, the second last day of their circular march, has been the toughest of the lot.

Ken knows it will be tough, and he's given them plenty of warning. But he leaves them to make their own mistakes, and a single, major navigational error doubles the effort needed to get to their camp tonight, and almost finishes the journey for Alex.

ALEX

The end of Shang-ri-la!

Up at five-thirty am. At home, we would be milking the cows.

It was really dark and hard to pack up and get cracking. But we did, and stood in our line, me at the back with Sally this time. Everybody had to walk through the river, but *we* managed to keep our boots dry because we found a log further down stream to go across, so everyone had wet feet, except me and Sally, and Bhuwani of course.

But it was a nerve-wracking start because we knew we had to climb this steep hill. We'd all been told about it and the thought of it was all very terrifying.

As it happens the gradient wasn't quite so bad as we'd anticipated, and it wasn't so hairy until the very end, when navigation went somewhat awry. It wasn't anyone's fault. My God,

I'd be hopeless if it was my turn! But we found ourselves in front of this cliff face of rock, and when you've half climbed a hill, you don't want to turn round and go back down to start again. As usual, I capitulated in floods of tears, wailing, "I've had enough!"

When we'd been going for seven or eight hours, hot and exhausted, if anyone had said again, "two hundred metres to go," I'd have shot them.

But, like this whole trek, we got there in the end. How on earth we scrambled up these rocks, all of us, I'll never know. But we did, and then we found our way to the campsite. I don't think I've been utterly drained until now.

I can't remember much about the campsite because we were too busy getting into our hammocks and going to sleep.

SUSANNA

This is Susanna, at six pm on day seventeen, which has to be called our longest day.

Although I'd been dreading having to lead the group, they did me proud. And on the whole, we got through very well indeed. The rot set in this afternoon, though, when we had a bit of a diversion on the navigation front. When we thought we were nearly home and dry, we suddenly found ourselves having to cross- grain up a hundred metre gully, which felt like a very steep ravine with no real track. But everybody did very well. The stronger helped the weaker, as in all good teams, although I began to get anxious when there were one or two rather alarmed faces at the prospect of having to get up this slope. At one point it looked as if the group was splitting into two, and I was sort of stuck the wrong side of a ridge, and I began to think "Ohh, what's happening in this group? I'm meant to be holding it together."

But, they did come together – no thanks to me, though.

It was a feat for us to be proud of. We genuinely were challenged today. Dicky and Catherine said a couple of nights ago, they didn't think they'd been pushed to the limit yet. I think they'd say that they still hadn't been pushed to their limits, but they were a darn sight closer today. A lot of other people *were* pushed to their limits, but came through on top.

So I think we can really be proud of what we've done today. Particularly since I had to break the bad news, once we were here, that the water situation, although not desperate, was sufficiently serious that we weren't able to have boil in the bags for supper. I thought this might be the last straw and I'd be facing a lynch mob, but they took it on the chin.

On a personal level, I've enjoyed today. Those of us who are stronger end up carrying the water much longer than we should, and I do find that tough. I also have my photographic equipment, plus some extra bedding from one or two girls at various points, as well as the water. And it takes it's toll. There is no question about it, you can do the first couple of hours, but when it gets to the third, or the fourth, and it's still fairly steep, the body begins to shout. But, we did it!

I've been quite pleased with my own personal performance, physically, today. Considering I have been pushed beyond what I would normally think myself capable of. It's also been more of a mental challenge for me today, because I've been having to lead. And rather than just following along in a nice calm state, I've had to be a bit more pro-active.

But I've also been very spoilt by the way the girls have handled the day. I think it helped knowing all along that this was going to be our toughest day; nobody was taken by surprise by it, although I think the last, unplanned ravine was the last straw for a couple.

PATSY

Most of the women are fitter now, and able to carry sixty pounds.

But among all of them the number of minor injuries is increasing slowly.

My own legs are fine, but top heavy rucksacks have made my neck and back ache. I think they're poorly designed and I'm sure there's a better way to carry water.

We were anticipating a leisurely walk in the afternoon, but it turned into a nightmare after a navigational error. We've had to cross a steep ravine, with a hundred foot climb to get out. We've all done it, but it was hell.

Water is very tight. I've added up what we're carrying and it's not enough.

I've had to tell the rest of the group how to conserve our existing water.

We have had some fine views this evening from the camp site on a high ridge, across vast valleys on either side to bluey-green hills and we've seen our first tropical sunset.

Given our critical water position, it's very unfortunate that we weren't ready for the down pour and the chance it offered of replenishing our water stock.

I've been stung near my mouth. I brushed the insect off and it fell into my bed. I've searched and found a four inch centipede, which I've now evicted.

GWENDA

We all got up with much trepidation this morning, knowing we had a very steep climb ahead of us. We had to cross a river quite early on, so we had wet feet all day.

Once we'd crossed the river, we had to fill up water bladders.

I didn't have to carry one for the first hour, and I still found it very tough going. When I did get a bladder, it was even harder. Every step I took was a real thump, thump, thump, having to concentrate where to put my feet.

We had a difficult climb, then a nice lunch. After that, I felt really perky and we were on the flat for quite a while. All of a sudden, though, we went slightly wrong, and we had the climb of all climbs. You could describe it as the shittiest climb that we've done – a very steep, vertical hands and knees job.

People were finding it very difficult. Some had to have their packs off and carried up for them. I found that my knees for the first time were quite sore, and my back is still sore now, so I'm going to have to rub some tiger balm on it.

We eventually got to our campsite and we'd had to carry water all day because we were nowhere near a river. We've had to be very careful on the water, which makes you think of wanting to drink all day. We couldn't have our boil in the bag, either, which I really missed. So we just had soup again, and noodles, which left us quite a lot of time in the evening just to potter around. I had a good game of cards with the girls, and everybody has been very kind and generous, sharing out all their goodies.

I feel very privileged to be amongst this bunch of girls, because I think they've done incredibly well. It really is difficult and even though a lot of us don't have the physical strength, the mental strength is definitely there and we're going to make it a big success.

CATHERINE

We knew we would have a long arduous day ahead of us, carrying full bladders. I was one of the navigators, and I regarded this as a challenge – something that we're still only getting to grips with. It can be quite difficult and one of the besetting problems is that other people are relying on you to get it right and not to keep them waiting. And so, when we all concertina up, and stand and wait for people to find the right way to go, everybody takes it in quite good part, and understands why it takes so long.

We finally made it down to the river we had to cross. We got wet, but we're used to that by now.

We stopped at the top of the ridge for lunch, which congealed the minute I took my eyes off it. So my group had gloop to eat.

Once we set off again, navigation went slightly astray, for several reasons.

We were all tired, and you can't afford to be tired when you're navigating. We had assumed that it would be easy, straightforward going. But something we've learned, particularly today, is that you cannot for a moment lose concentration. You must pace, and the pacing must be accurate and constant. Your compass must be constant. You must stop at least every hundred metres to take bearings and to re-assess the situation.

In the middle of the afternoon, we took the wrong spur. On the map it's a tiny little blip, but that tiny blip, when it's translated into metres in the jungle, can become a very tortuous journey.

Instead of retracing our steps, which is what we should have done, we cross-grained – again, always difficult in the jungle, but we just happened to pick the most difficult spot too.

So bad that, once we got to the ridge that we wanted, we had a horrid climb to get to the top of it. But we managed.

We had a few grumbles and groans, but everybody at the end of the day looked upon it as a challenge to remember. Personally, I don't want anything too easy, or there's no sense of achievement.

We got to the top and had a rest, and then made our way up and down, and I'm very nervous this time, because again we were told this was very straightforward which made us very cautious.

We found a lovely campsite at the top. So that made it all worthwhile.

We'd carried full bladders up to the top here, and we're supposed to drink constantly, because we get dehydrated very quickly. But we've been told by Patsy to go easy on the water. So tonight we cooked tinned soup, because if we had used our boil in the bags, which contain a lot of fat, we would become even more dehydrated.

The trouble is, I don't normally feel thirsty here, which is quite dangerous, so you have to be reminded all the time to drink. So the instant Patsy said we should go easy on the water, all I wanted to do was drink.

DICKY

Well, I was very nervous about today so I woke up really early, like at half past four, and did a huge pee. I always pee when I'm nervous.

I haven't yet been fully tested physically, and I had a feeling that today might be the day. Despite all the excesses of yesterday, though, I was still feeling generally not full of beans.

We left camp at seven o'clock with Susanna in charge, and it was a very nice change to be called 'ladies', instead of 'guys'.

Susanna is very prim and proper and does everything very nicely, and makes me feel slightly heroic so she does pull the best out of you. Instead of saying, "Come on guys, let's go for it!", when you feel like answering, "Eff off,", Susanna says, "Come on ladies," and you feel you must respond.

For some reason I offered to carry a full bladder when we got down to the river, but Patsy insisted that she carry it for the first half hour, which fortunately was all uphill to begin with and then I rued my decision, because the next bit was flat, then, when it got to my turn it was very steeply uphill again. However, Susanna was still calling us ladies, so I continued to be inspired.

After lunch we thought we only had about another hour to go, but sadly the navigators got that a bit wrong. I can't say that too loudly, because one of them gets in a peeve. And then we missed a spur, I should say, by a matter of a hundred metres. Which doesn't sound very much, and when you run around the top pitch at school a hundred metres is gone in twevle seconds, but a hundred metres here in the jungle is a hugely long way out. And we then ended up climbing up a virtually vertical cliff face. One or two people had to take their backpacks off because they just couldn't manage it. But I was still feeling heroic because Susanna was being so inspirational, saying, "Well done girls!!", in a very gym mistressy voice.

I carried on and struggled up to the top with my backpack and said a few bad words along the way.

And what was supposed to be a very short stint after lunch, turned out to be a very long stint – another two or three hours, by which time I was getting totally fagged out, pissed off, but still hadn't reached my physical end, which I wanted to do.

But the thing that absolutely, very nearly reduced me to tears, was that when we got to the top of one very steep hill, somebody dropped a bar of chocolate in my lap, which was an amazing gesture. And just for a few seconds, I really felt like crying.

We had another fairly steep climb to get finally up to this camp, which is a very nice site and all quite flat. But, oh God, another disaster!

Susanna, who is being so sensible, declared that something to do with digesting fat was going to expend more water, so we couldn't eat our silver bags, which I've grumbled about every single night. And now the one night that we're not allowed to eat them, I'm just yearning for Lancashire hotpot, or sausage casserole, or even bacon and beans.

So they boiled up a whole load of gloopy looking pot noodles in a saucepan which I couldn't possibly eat. Sally and I had hot chocolate and biscuits for supper.

I'm not even looking forward to getting up in the morning, because there won't be much to eat then. Somebody, and I cannot think who – they must be out of their brain – said, "Why don't we set off without breakfast and have breakfast later."

How one can possibly be expected to get up and walk off without breakfast, when one hasn't even had supper, I don't know. But, there we go, tomorrow is another day, and upwards and onwards, a few more ribs showing. But never mind, I haven't cracked yet.

FIONA

We left the idyllic camp this morning at five thirty. It was one of those times when you set your alarm clock in your head. So, Bang, I was awake, at 5.30. I got dressed and was more than ready to get going again.

I took the role of pacer with Gwenda and Patsy, and we take an average of the three of us.

It went fine until we went a bit astray, and we were faced with a hundred metres of almost vertical going, the nearest to rock climbing that we've done since we've been here. For me this was the highlight of the trip. It was well within my means, but it was clambering and climbing, and helping and pulling, and everything I'd hoped to be doing more of. Don't get me wrong, I found it challenging and tiring, but instead of one foot in front of the other kind of walking, where you have to concentrate so hard, because it's maybe only a case of an ankle going, and you're out, this was up, this was climbing, and I like it! It's just made me realise that I want to climb even more when I get home.

Everyone else was fantastic, I think at points people thought, "No way!", but it's a situation where you're halfway up, and you've got to carry on up, because there's no way of going down.

Then when we thought we'd found Utopia, we were faced with another final ascent, and everyone sort of looked at it, it was probably twenty or so feet high, but we all just viewed it as a minor obstacle, and it was scaled within minutes.

We have one more day to go, a day that should get us back to 230alpha by mid-afternoon. Then we'll have completed our route. Reality crawls back really quickly.

I don't know how I feel about going back. I'm sure there's going to be some changes in my life. I'm not sure where they'll lead me, but there's going to be some changes. There's so much out there that I haven't even looked at yet, and I don't think I can settle without at least trying them.

Everyone is more than capable now of looking after themselves around the campsite. People are happy to drift off with their book, play cards, sit around the camp fire, or just be on their own. There's no pressure to be with people, there's no one group, or two groups. Everyone is mixing. We're all quite cosy tonight. The last few nights we've been quite spread out, but now we're literally within door knocking distance of each other. It's almost as if we could put our hands out and make a circle. I think Paul's slightly concerned about tonight, because we have a little bit of a reputation for being the rowdy group, and unfortunately for him he's surrounded by us. Though I think the only thing he really has to contend with tonight is Julie's snoring!

It's amazing after a day like this, laughter is the most important thing we've got. When someone falls over, everyone is concerned, but you can laugh too. And that's so important; that's what has got everyone through.

There's been quite an amusing conversation floating around

today about weight. Everyone has lost weight, although I think we're all dubious of some claims. But Izzy has lost a fair amount. We keep trying to feed her up, so she is the recipient of all left over food, and all boil in the bags and stuff.

Everyone has changed shape completely and the worry now is that when we get back home, everyone will put it all back on again. I think you'll see an influx of twelve women heading down to the gym, or hiking round Herefordshire with a backpack on, and washing in streams and peeing in their gardens, and not being able to sleep in their beds, and putting up the hammocks in the garden; recycling water by drinking the washing up water, which is what we're having to do tonight; wearing the same knickers for days on end, and the same socks; washing our hair and finding ourselves doing everything in streams. It's been a mad, incredible journey.

IZZY

It's been a bit of a tough day today – a little different from previous days. We knew it was going to be quite a long day, because we had some real steep ground to get up. And we were going to be aiming to camp at the top of this high ground. We also knew at the beginning of the day that there would be no water.

It was quite hard work, walking up steep ground with full bladders. So, what we tried to do was to stop every fifteen minutes for a brief rest, because it's really hard going, if you've got an extra twelve, fifteen litres that you're carrying, on top of your ordinary pack. So we changed water bladders over between people, every half an hour or so. Some people managed to carry them all the way, like Fiona Shapcott. She's strong as an ox; she can sometimes put the rest of us to shame.

After lunch, I was one of the navigators, with Wendy and

Catherine, and we just completely missed the spur we were looking for. So we were faced with either having to double back, which is what we should have done, or cross grain-up to the ridge we knew we were supposed to be on. We decided to cross-grain, which ended up being a bad call, and we reached more or less what looked like the foot of a cliff. It was only about twenty or thirty foot, but just sheer, so we couldn't get up it. A few people were quite pissed off.

The best thing to do was just to get our packs off and wander around to find a way up, which we did, and for those people who were really worried, which was quite a few, just to leave their packs where they were, or take them along the ledge as far as they could, leave them, and scramble up. Fiona as usual was first up there. I helped find a way, I went back, collected my pack and climbed on up.

We were very relieved to get to the top, but I think it was quite a useful lesson learned. Just a momentary lapse of concentration can have quite catastrophic effects. It certainly put quite a strain on us as a group. I did feel quite responsible but everyone was very nice about it, nobody complained.

Everybody was so shattered, some people didn't even notice the rain in the night. I had a nice little dip in my canopy that collected the water quite well, so at two in the morning I got up and rescued my clothes from the rain, and sat for three quarters of an hour and collected about three litres. I managed to fill about three-quarters of Claire's platypus, and another litre bottle. But then the rain eventually petered out, so I just went back to sleep. It's our second to last day of trekking, and I feel I'm just getting into the swing of it. I would be quite happy in a way to carry on. In a bizarre way, I even quite enjoyed today, apart from feeling a bit guilty for dragging people up a really difficult route. I thought it was quite interesting to test ourselves a little bit.

There are a few people nursing injuries of one sort or another and I thought that they were particularly brave. Claire's got a swollen ankle, from an injury a few days ago. So has Jules. Alex finds the heat and a lot of the walking quite tough at the best of times. Putting her through such a gruelling afternoon has been very tough on her. And Sally who is also nursing an injury, and who is in pain at the same time, has just been brilliant. Wendy has bad knees on occasions.

I wonder if a group of men would just get on with what we're doing, and get on so well together. I've got a lot of respect for all of the ladies here, and I think we're forming a good and solid team.

JULIE

What a bloody morning! I don't think I've ever woken up so bad tempered in my life. I just couldn't get anything right. I really should have changed my hormone patch yesterday. But I don't know, I just lose track of the days, so I woke up, and warned everybody that I was in a horrible mood. And then, halfway through Ken's little pep talk of what was going to happen today, I sort of walked off and burst into tears.

I haven't felt so low in ages. I'm sure it's the hormones.

The first hour was absolutely awful, really just trundling along, not climbing or anything, but in a bad mood. I had to try hard just to shake myself out of it.

When we got to the river, I didn't get my feet wet, which everyone else did.

We had to fill up the bladders, and that's when we started the climb. God, what a bloody climb it was! Never ending. It wasn't particularly difficult terrain, fairly straightforward, but just constantly climbing uphill. Sweat was just pouring off everyone. I've never been so wet in my entire life; I don't think I've drunk so much either.

And then, it just got steeper, and steeper, almost like a sheer cliff face. Awful! Just dreadful! I lost my temper at one point, and said not very nice words, I must admit.

But I looked at it, and I thought, "Can I do this?" and I decided that having done it before, I knew I could do it now.

Then I thought, this is it. We came to this little knoll, that was where the camp was. But no, it was down a bit, up another little pimple, down again, and then up another even steeper pimple!

Thank God we're here!

It's quite a nice camp actually. And everyone, which always amazes me, everyone actually manages to laugh at the end of each day, which I think is an absolute godsend, and no one goes to bed down in the dumps. Me, in particular, I never go to bed down in the dumps, I always have a laugh. I think that's really what has kept me going, these last, seventeen or eighteen days.

SALLY

Thursday the twentieth of July. Well this day had been built up as going to be very, very tough, with a steep climb. We'd all imagined we would be on hands and knees, crawling up the north face of the Eiger. But in fact, it wasn't as bad as we'd expected. Maybe it was a good thing to let our imaginations run riot and fear the worst, but when it came to it, it wasn't quite as bad as that.

WENDY

Thought for the Day:

Every so often let your spirit of adventure triumph over your good sense

We've had a steep climb and a very heavy day. We set off at about seven for what we call the big ascent, really about twelve hundred feet to climb. Things went all right until lunchtime, but by the time we got to the top, everyone was absolutely shattered.

We set off after lunch, having to go down a few hundred metres to the next knoll and somehow things went disastrously wrong.

I take responsibility, because I was the navigator in charge. I didn't do as much checking as I should; I let other people go in front too far away and I didn't follow them closely enough.

I was really annoyed that we cross-grained unnecessarily and I was annoyed with myself for putting the girls through quite an ordeal and extra distance unnecessarily. I hadn't done my job very well because after lunch I'd started to switch off and I don't think it was helped by the fact that my platypus burst. I'd filled up with water from Claire's bladder at lunch time, and by the time we came to set off, it was all empty again, so I only had about three sips of water all afternoon.

KEN

Today was a testing day for the ladies, and I wanted it to be so. It was an opportunity for them to have control of the navigation, tracking, water and their own destiny.

The aim of the day was to climb a thousand foot ridge which would put us onto the top of the ridge for the night and then we'd be almost pointing back in the direction of our start point.

We left at 7 and I was quite pleased that the ladies got themselves ready to go. I did a final navigational brief for them but we soon ran into difficulties as they went along the riverbank. They're still unable to see where the track goes, and they don't look hard enough. They just meander around and by now I would have hoped that they would have been able to pick a track out, but we went down a number of blind alleys before we eventually found the crossing point. There was quite a lot of faffing around there because people didn't want to get their boots wet but they had no choice really but to get in the river and cross it. They then filled bladders which seemed to take an age but eventually at about 09.10, having left at 07.00 we embarked up the steep ridge. They adopted a pattern of stopping every 15 minutes, which was quite good, it enabled people to get their breath back and rest. Navigation was pretty straightforward - keep going up and you'll get there - but it got a little more difficult when we got near the top and at that point they seemed a reluctant to send out reccies. There was bit of standing around and chatting for a while. Eventually someone took the initiative and dived off into the bush and found the right track up to the very top. It was a hard climb but I think some of them were very surprised how easily they coped with it. Others I think found it bloody hard. But some were carrying full bladders.

We got on top by about midday, had lunch and then the fun started.

I'd decided to leave them alone and let them get on with it and I was going to go forward and reccy a campsite about a kilometre away from the top so I set off and found the camp and then I returned back down to the ridge and dropped about a couple of hundred feet down and I could hear voices way down to my right. And I thought - that's strange and then the longer I listened the more I realised that the ladies had taken themselves off on a different spur. And were in fact three hundred and fifty feet below where they should have been.

The main reason for that navigational balls-up was really that they didn't pace properly and didn't follow the track. They made the ground fit the map and merrily trundled off down another ridge. They thought the easy option then was to come across country and climb.

Well having made that decision, they were then faced with - and I could see it below me - a very steep cliff and they then had to ferry their packs off to a point where they could walk with them again and by the time they got back on the ridge they all looked a bit sorry for themselves. What I had hoped they would have done then is to group together and try and let everybody know and explain why they'd gone wrong with the navigation. But it was more "Plonk down. You've done very well!"

But they hadn't done very well - they'd made a massive error and they were short of water anyway and by the time they'd reached the campsite tonight they were very short of water and they then decided not to cook their boil in the bags but just have soup. All in all it was a hard day, made harder by their navigational error but I hope they'll learn from that.

There still seems to be a sort of de-mob happy air, and maybe that's because they were returning from whence where they started. But they've still got another seven days to go and a lot can happen in seven days in the jungle and I'm going to have to remind them again not to drop their guard.

KH 20-07-00

chapter twenty

To The Limit

DAY 18 - Friday 21st July

On this last, longest leg of the trek, most, though not all of the Jungle Janes are more tired than they realise. The previous day has taken a lot out of them, despite the rest at Shangri-la.

Some have probably reached the end of their resources; only the knowledge that this is the end is keeping them going.

Tempers, so conspicuously controlled for the most part, are beginning visibly to fray.

This isn't surprising, after three weeks of close proximity in hostile surroundings. Twelve women thrown together in far more comfortable circumstances would have been expected to show internal divisions well within this space of time.

Or perhaps it is the very adversity which stifles the urge to air disagreement, or promote personal views.

Nevertheless, on this last day of walking, some simmering differences are coming close to the boil.

Disagreements between Patsy, as expedition doctor, and Ken as leader persist.

Patsy is anxious to ensure that nothing happens to jeopardise their short water supply. Her responsibilities as a doctor outweigh her regard for the personal ambitions of the group, and she insists that Ken himself should take command of the navigation.

He declines, on the grounds that the whole purpose of the trek is that the Jungle Janes should chart their own course, and deal with their own crises.

ALEX

This morning, we got ticked off because it rained in the night, and we didn't jump out of our hammocks and collect every drop. We got ourselves sorted, and I said a poem to get the girls going. And off we marched, me focusing on Sally's boots, if I can see Sally's boots, I can get anywhere. One hundred and seventy-five metres to the left, wrong decision. Patsy was getting a bit uptight, because we were short on water, and we weren't going to see water until we got to the end of this arduous trek.

Each of us had two and abit litres of water, to do about three and a half kilometres. In this heat that isn't enough, so we're all aware of the problem.

We trundled back up to the camp again, and got a mini-bollocking from our boss.

We needed to be about twenty degrees to the right. It's extraordinary how the slightest mistake in map reading can cause no end of trouble. And today, we could be walking into a wall of death with no water on us.

Landing Site 230alpha. Hmm. That's a big word in my brain. I'd never heard it before I came here, now I'll never forget it.

Like most days, we walked, and we walked, and we walked and certain trees became familiar to me. I remembered scrambling over logs that had been particularly difficult on the short trek before we left this alpha camp site. And slowly they came into view. If you remember when we talked about seeing the snake, we walked straight past the point where we found it.

I could recall, "I've been here before. That means I'm not that far from home." Cor!

It was a long day, though. Sally was walking with me. She didn't feel well, but she has a damn sight more stamina than I have. And provided I kept looking at her black heels and her black boots, plodding away in front of me, I kept going. But I needed a lot more water than I was drinking. And I was getting very hot, very quickly. I could feel myself overheating. And before long, my legs gave way beneath me, again. Bhuwani was really angry with me. He said, "You only have one hundred metres to go. Get up, get up you silly girl, get up and put a smile on your face." His job was almost over, he'd almost got twelve girls back safely to 230alpha. And there was this silly, dopey one at the end, who'd collapsed in a heap. It's a funny thing, when you think you're so close, and then suddenly you can't quite make it.

But I did. And those wonderful girls were waiting the other side of the landing site so that we could all walk in together. God, that was a triumphant moment, walking down that hill, together. Having done our circle round the jungle. I think that if we add up all the metres that we've done, it only comes to about eleven or twelve miles, which is nothing, but believe me, it's a heck of a long way in the jungle. And do you know what, we all came in together. That is something.

PATSY

We've had a long walk today, which has stretched from the predicted four hours to six. We started with around two and a half litres of water each – not enough, and not the best planning in my opinion.

I have formally asked Ken to take the lead himself, to avoid any navigational errors which could cause serious water problems, but he declined.

As a result, precious time *was* wasted on an error.

And now, as the day stretches out, the party has split into three.

Now, we have all returned safely to base 230alpha.

CATHERINE

We had very little to eat this morning, very stupidly I think, in hindsight. I had three biscuits and it wasn't nearly enough as I discovered by the end of the day. We had very little water, so I didn't have a hot drink either.

I was navigating with Izzy and Patsy, and we made a huge error to begin with. Even after everything had been drummed into us, we didn't reccy, so we went about a hundred and fifty metres along the wrong ridge before we discovered our mistake, and needless to say, people were very good, but deep down were probably very disappointed that they had to walk back up the hill. The extremely valuable lesson that we learned from this is that although there was a temptation to cut across grain, like we did yesterday, we didn't. Instead, we returned to the point from where we started, and then re-took our bearings, and then did the small reccy, which we should have done in the first place.

We had to stop and start, every hundred metres or so, which is very important here, and this is kind of depressing for the people behind, who just have to wait, and are not quite sure what's going on. But again, there is good humour and people try to understand why certain things are happening. I think when we finally reached our destination, everybody was enormously pleased, and we were all very, very tired.

It was a huge, huge relief, when we got back. I don't think I've been so glad to see anywhere as much as that landing site. I sort of collapsed onto a bench, and then helped Gwenda to build a fire.

I have to say the last two days when we were working hard and struggling was the first time that I have felt a sense of achievement, that I really felt that I was accomplishing something. That doesn't mean I want to do it again, because I'm not sure I do.

I'm amazed how quickly we all recover from all this, because it doesn't take us long. Once we've got our *bashas* up and a cup of tea in us, and we've had a chat, everybody is back up again, and I wouldn't say raring to go, but, if somebody said, "Go," we all would.

FIONA

Some people collected water during the night, when it rained. I personally looked out of my *basha*, checked that everything around me was under cover, and promptly went back to sleep again. Izzy and a few others collected water, but not very much.

We all had about two litres of water, I personally went for a little bit of tang in mine, to give it added flavour and set off for the last day's walking, back to 230alpha.

Jules was carrying extra stuff, and her shoulder was really hurting, so we ambled along a little bit at the back, just having a bit of fun. We stopped at one point, so I made the rash suggestion that we have lunch, which was a bit of a no go, because we had no water and no food.

We were walking along, and suddenly there were hand gestures, indicating to get down, down. Jules, Claire and myself and various others at the back were up and down like yo-yos, not having a clue about what to do, but giggling, and then sat down. Susanna went storming off with her camera, and we were told by various other people that there was a monkey in the vicinity. Which I have to say when you're sitting there like a complete idiot not knowing what was going on, it was nice to be finally told. Again people started to get a bit worried about how far we had to go and the water situation. But we carried on and got to a point where we decided to let a lead group go first, and we'd have a second group. We waited for Alex and Sally, and finally came home together.

One of the benefits of being in the back group was that the

fire was going, and the others had been to get water. We strung our bashas in what now looks like a Thai washing village. There are lots of little passages, with sarongs everywhere.

We had a nice evening round the fire that used to be other people's bashas. We went for a swim and kind of just cooled out. Quite chilled, not feeling too tired, not too fussed about a day's rest tomorrow.

There are rumours going around that we're going to be building rafts, so I hope, after this day off, we're going to get physical again. Because I really need to. We've been doing a lot of exercise, and to stop doing it now, would be a real shame.

JULIE

Oh god, it was another awful day. It rained last night. After the gruelling day before, there was no way I was going to get out of my *basha*, and start collecting water. I don't feel too bad about not getting up in the night to collect water, because Ken didn't either. I just lay in my hammock and had a cigarette, and promptly went back to sleep again. Anyway, it wasn't too early a start, but we were only allowed a drink and a dry biscuit, which sounds like prison rations, doesn't it. But we were all rather cheery anyway. And we all got loaded up and had our pep talk. Alex read us a poem.

I've got a shoulder injury at the moment, it comes and goes, but obviously its worse at the end of the day when we're tired. Claire's ankle is playing her up, and we set off at the back, only to realise that when we'd gone a hundred metres down this track that we'd gone in the wrong direction. You know, bit of a thing really, lots of grumbling going on, but you can't really blame anyone, because I certainly wouldn't want to be at the pointy end and in charge of the whole shooting match. Anyway, we trundled up this incline again, to our starting point, which was the camp,

IF YOU DON'T VISIT, YOU DON'T KNOW WHAT IS IT

COME; AS YOU ARE AS YOU WISH

How to find us

AVIAVA

POST

KOÇBANK

MAMBO Café

ATATÜRK STR.

DOLMUŞ STATION

BAZAAR

Burger King

MÜFTÜLER STR.

PAMUKBANK

HÜKÜMET STR.

İŞBANK

AKBANK

MURPHYS
PUB & DANCING

ATATÜRK STATUE

McDonald's

HARBOUR

Sea

MURPHYS Says; BEER, MUSIC, PARTY, SEXY PEOPLE " Have I Missed Something? "

MURPHYS
PUB & DANCING

Come and enjoy your drink with us in a such a good and lovely atmosphere.

We like to play all THE GREAT TUNES from all around the world...

We would like to serve you all quality drinks and all our special cocktails with friendly service & fair price then set off properly on our walk. Three and a half kilometres, we were told we would have to do today, not an arduous walk, not compared to what we'd already done, but just long. And having very little food and hardly any water, bearing in mind what we all consume on a daily basis – on an average walk of two kilometres, maybe four litres at least.

Sally really isn't well, and looks absolutely dreadful. So I took some of her stuff out of her pack to lighten her load. I don't know whether it did any good, but anyway, we struggled on a little more. We'd been going for about an hour with no communication between the front lot and the back lot, and I was convinced at one point that the batteries in my hearing aid had gone down, because the next thing I know, is this sort of sign language going on. And. "Ssh, ssh. Get down, get down!" Like bloody tactical manoeuvres in the army, we all got down into this crouch, and ten minutes passed and we still didn't know what was going on.

Another ten minutes passed, and we were all, "Ssh, ssh," and then we finally realised that Susanna had spotted a monkey. The last time I saw her, she was storming up to the top of the hill, like a blasted snail, with a camera in her hand. She looked like she was leading a boy scout party.

We all stayed there for about half an hour, and I was getting slightly brassed off. Everyone was tired and the longer we left it the more water we consumed, and we just didn't have any. Eventually after some comments, "Are we looking for monkeys or are we walking?" it was finally decided by Susanna, very disgruntled at this point because she thought it would be nice to look for monkeys, that we should just start walking again, back to 230alpha.

SALLY

This is a day that I'd rather forget, because it seemed a very long, arduous day. All I could really think about was that it was the last day of the trek. And whilst I've enjoyed most of it, it was as though I was impatient to get to the end of the day, it seemed within sight, and yet just out of reach. There was a bit of a navigation problem when we set off along the ridge, and I felt a bit cross about that. And what was heartbreaking about having had a mistake, was having to actually return to the harbour before setting off again. So it was as though we had just simply wasted the first hour of the day, which I could have spent in bed. Anyway, the day just went on, trudging up and down, it wasn't physically hard going, but it was gruelling just because it was the end of fourteen days, and I think the tiredness had been mounting each day. It seemed harder to put one foot in front of the other. But we got there. And it was all really exciting to arrive at 230alpha. There is a little grassy bit, just before the landing strip, and it's the only grass you ever see, or that I've seen, so it was very exciting to come upon that bit, because you knew then that the landing strip was there, and it was just a short twenty metres or so to the campsite. I felt more elation than I had expected, because the night before, and maybe a few nights before that, I hadn't really felt any sense of achievement. Because you set your own goals, it's hard to know when you've actually reached them. It's not like a chemistry test at school, where you get ten out of twenty or twenty out of twenty. There's no sort of set achievement. So I was pleased that I felt some sort of satisfaction that I'd returned.

WENDY

Thought for the Day:

Remember that a good example is the best sermon.

Today I decided that I should stay at the back. We did about three and a half kilometres which was the furthest we've ever done in one day and in quite a good time. Catherine was navigating today and did an excellent job (I think with the help of Patsy) and we got back to 230alpha early so we just had quite a relaxing afternoon – I nominated myself to be group leader – I thought I'd give it a go and taking over from Susanna for the next three days. I don't think it will be stressful. It feels like the expedition has ended but it hasn't really. There's the rafting section to do, but at least the hard trek is over and that's the bit we most feared.

SUSANNA

I've got a feeling that I said last night, that it was our longest day. It wasn't. Today has been, mainly because it followed on from yesterday, and the combination has brought most people to their limits. Unfortunately it didn't quite break Catherine or Dicky; they were the ones keen to be pushed to their limits and possibly beyond, to see how they'd react.

But for most of us, today was quite sufficient, thank you. I found today very difficult from the leadership point of view. It seemed that it was nigh on impossible to please everybody. And I was getting some quite sharp comments from certain quarters, which I felt were a little uncalled for. They probably weren't meant in the way that they came out, but one thing I have learned from this trip, is that it's all in the way things are said. Content can be exactly the same, but the way things are dressed can make all the difference. Asking somebody whether they'd thought of possibly doing it like this, or would they like a bit of help, as opposed to saying, "Here, give it here, I'll do it," can make all the difference. And the same can be said for criticism, I suppose. I think it would have been very hard to get today right.

We had very different strengths, physically, and the shortage

255

of water forced us to push some people beyond their capabilities, and sadly, but sensibly, we ended up dividing into three groups for the last five hundred metres. I felt that it was a failure on my part that I wasn't able to bring the team back to the end of the expedition together. But the whole essence of the last few days has been compromise. And in many ways, that's what teamwork has to be about. And the compromise we reached today was to let the strong ones go on ahead, in order to get things established and get water ready for the arrival of the less strong – I would hesitate to say weak, because nobody on this trip, has been weak; they just have different thresholds.

My general policy was to try and lead from the back, and as far as possible to let other people make their own decisions. And on the whole, I think it worked yesterday, even though once or twice I probably should have been more dynamic. And I feel that we've had lots of different leadership styles, suitable for different phases in the trip, but when the going gets tough, to be over girded can be as damaging as not to be girded at all.

I thought I would feel more than I do, but right now, I've reached my physical limits. I was perfectly happy to be one of the strong party who came back and got on with fire and water and all that, and as leader I felt that I should come back in order to get things set up for the next group, and so that was fine. But we did do it astonishingly fast.

We covered that last five hundred or so metres in about twenty minutes, which having done as much as we had in the last forty-eight hours, was a bit of a feat.

It was only when it came to putting up my *basha*, that I began to find I had reached my limit. I couldn't get a stake in where I needed to. And that very nearly broke the camel's back. Or the mule's back, having plodded along with these great loads, ever more stubbornly.

I have sworn rather a lot in the last couple of hours, particularly at the insects which are rife in the site I've chosen for my *basha*. I think I've picked a bit of bum site.

We deserve to feel triumphant about how we've conducted ourselves over the last fortnight. For that's how long it's been. I've rather lost track of the days, and how they fit together. But we have got everybody through. We haven't had any major illness. We haven't had a major upset within the twelve. There has been a little more upset outside the twelve. But in my book, it's the twelve that matter, and we've all hung together. Yes, there have been tensions, but never really major ones – not nearly as major as I think many of us dreaded at the outset. We can be very proud of what we've achieved on that score alone, which, however much we may not have admitted it, was one of most people's major fears. And physically we've all made it. It was never going to be easy, and at times it hasn't been, but we are all here in one piece. Which is more than I think Ken expected us to be.

I give top marks overall to Sally, who has just surpassed any of us, by carrying such a proportion of weight to her own size. She's been cheerful throughout and very reluctant to give in, or hand over things for anybody else to carry.

I think on the whole I've managed to retain my sense of humour, which was one of the things I was anxious about before the trip. I don't think I necessarily brought it to the fore the whole time, but we had our fair share of clowns amongst the participants. And it's quite nice for me not to have to play up to the crowd. I have to play up to the crowd in my job quite a lot. And singers do tend to throw their weight around a lot in order to prove themselves to one another, and to show people around them that they do work.

I've enjoyed the break from having to do that. I think Alex and Julie and Fi are all quite happy to entertain the crowd, and it's been very nice for me to take a back seat. I was very interested that Alex, whom I've known for four or five years or so, said to somebody that I was very different out here. I was intrigued to hear that, and before I asked her directly what she thought was different about me, I thought about it myself and I decided that one thing would be that I was much quieter. And indeed it was. She said, yes, I was much quieter, but then normally when she sees me, it's on social occasions and either I'm the organiser running a dinner party or entertaining, or I'm trying to be a lively and interesting guest. I don't feel that I have to do either on this trip.

The other things that she said about me was that she thinks that I'm much more organised out here. I'm considerably amused, because back home, I think I'm very organised and I feel that I've been very disorganised out here. In the first few days when I was so tired and wasn't sleeping, I was permanently unable to find the crucial thing. And I had comparatively so little to organise, that I was horrified that I was finding it so difficult to begin with.

People are beginning now to talk to each other along these sorts of lines and it's very interesting. It's a joy to be in my *basha* now. It's a joy to have those horrendous socks off again. They've been getting pretty foul over the last two days. In fact, I went down to the river today and I gave them to the jungle.

GWENDA

We started off this morning and went completely wrong. We'd been over a hundred metres and had to come all the way back. This worried Patsy, as she was concerned about the shortage of water, and we'd finished all the water at breakfast.

She also knew we were low on our supplies and that we had a good five hour trek ahead of us.

For lunch, as there was no water, we just had beef jerky, and biscuits and stuff like that. But we trekked on, and it was a pretty long way.

About six hundred metres from our base, we decided to split the group in two. Some of the women had injuries which were slowing them down, so the first group, which included me, went on ahead so that we could get water back here, and also make the fire. We set a cracking pace, just stopping to get our breath back at the top of a hill, and I really enjoyed it. The sweat was pouring off me, so I really felt we were working hard

I also felt much better than I have for the whole of the expedition. I don't know if it was because it was the end, but I had loads of energy. We got back to find our camp very derelict and yucky. Everywhere was very dry, but when we left, it had been very wet.

Later, everybody else turned up, so we'd completed the expedition bit, and everybody came through it very well. We had photos and a celebration.

We made a new *basha* site, and went for a swim, which was fantastic after two days without water.

I'm chuffed to bits that I've finished it. Always at the back of my mind, was my knee and whether it would hold up, so well done Dr Robinson you did a cracking job on it. It's been brilliant. Touch wood. I hope nothing happens to it now.

I'm mightily pleased with myself, as I thought I would struggle a lot. Sometimes I did, and at times when I thought I would, I didn't, so my body is very cock-a-hoop.

I can't believe that we've been out here three weeks, the time has just whizzed by, and it only seems like yesterday I was thinking, "My God, three weeks in the jungle, how am I going to survive?" But I did. I don't think I'll ever do it again, but I'm bloody glad that I had a chance to do it. And well done Ken. I know I'm married to you, but thank you for getting us here safe and sound.

KEN'S LOG

Day eighteen was the last walking day of this expedition. It was really the sting in the tail.

We had camped on a nice knoll on a fifteen hundred foot ridge. In the morning, we were greeted by Alex with her poetry book, bursting forth with *If*, by Rudyard Kipling, which was fine, but probably inappropriate. The last line is, 'You'll be a man, my son!'

I'd told the ladies last night that they were going to do all their own navigating today. But this morning, I noticed straight away that, having got themselves packed up, they hadn't checked where they were, neither had they checked any of the spurs off this knoll. They've been told often that they must do this before they leave in the morning, to make sure the expedition gets off on the right step.

I thought as soon as we left that we were too far to the left. But they hurtled off at quite a rate. I was talking to one of the Gurkhas and by the time we caught up they were more than a hundred metres down. I looked to my right and I could see higher ground and almost immediately, I realised that they'd gone the wrong way.

When I shouted down to them to tell them their mistake, they were quite tempted to cross-grain to the spur they should have been on.

I told them to return to a point that they knew, and try again. I arrived back at the knoll first and waited for them to get there.

I was then confronted by Patsy, who told me she thought it was wrong that they should be allowed to get lost, and that it was a safety issue because we didn't have much water.

I rather took umbrage at this because in my opinion there was no safety error. They'd only gone around one hundred metres the wrong way, so they weren't going to immediately burn up a couple of gallons of water.

On top of that, it was rather a challenge to my judgement.

The last fifteen days have been fine and if anybody on this expedition has had to sit down and think very hard about water and distance, it's been me.

I very much carried that responsibility, not overtly, because at no time did I want to worry anybody. But there's never been a moment when I haven't been thinking about safety. To cap all that, I would never put anybody in a position of danger, even if I had to go down the ridge myself a thousand feet to get water while they sat there and waited for me.

I saw this discussion as rather confrontational. I didn't get irate at the time but I certainly said to Patsy, "Look, I know what I'm doing. There isn't a safety issue here. The women must take responsibility for their own mistakes; it's their expedition. They wished collectively to have control over it and I've tried to give them as much control as I possibly can. But if they make a mistake first thing in the morning, although I'm responsible overall, I'm not responsible for that short amount of time they lost by going down the wrong spur."

Eventually they all got back up to the top and there was a kerfuffle and a lot of uncertainty. Izzy then turned round and said to one of the Gurkhas, "Will you please tell us when we're going the wrong."

In my view, this was completely the wrong thing to say at the time. She should have said, "Right, we got it wrong. Let's now get it right."

In fact, it took them about thirty seconds to look in front of them and see a track going off down the hill, heading in the right direction. And we set off at quite a good pace.

I could sense that Patsy was burrowing her eyes into me from behind. I forget how the conversation started but we had quite an argument. It wasn't the first time in my life that my leadership has been questioned. It's a tough position being expedition leader - people will question your judgement and often in quite a confrontational and unhelpful way.

Patsy and I had a few sharp words with each other, and it was at that time that I said, "You know, if needs must and we did get lost, I would give you all my water, we would pool it, dish it out and then either I or one of the back-up would go down to find more."

We were not in such a dire situation as perhaps Patsy liked to imagine.

I took her to one side and explained that I have a lot to think about. I'd given her the chance to fulfil her role as the expedition doctor and to look after medical aspects and hygiene.

But she seemed to have an underlying need to assert herself, and that was the last thing I wanted. It was the last day, everybody was getting very tired and I really needed to concentrate hard on what was happening there and then.

But this confrontation did knock me off track for a while and took my eye off the cue ball. I still believe it was a flash in the pan, not really something to get excited about, and, eventually, it did all blow over.

So, having made our first navigational blunder of the day, we set off on what was the right ridge and got along pretty well. They started getting a bit short on water, but not critical. There was a long way – about two and a half kilometres – to go, but most of it was downhill on a route that they had previously trodden on a training march. And, although shortage of water can be quite worrying, it would have been more worrying if they hadn't been going down a pretty obvious ridge towards a big river.

I was certainly feeling the effects of the last fifteen days and I got extremely tired over the last couple of miles – a bit like getting to the end of a marathon when your legs go all wobbly and you feel a bit sick.

To sum up that particular leg of the journey, I was very surprised by the women's powers of endurance – particularly carrying heavy loads they weren't used to, up steep inclines – and it did surprise me that they managed so well.

It never ceases to amaze me that some people, despite lack of training, being slightly overweight, perhaps, or heavy smokers – are able to pull it out of the bag when they've got like-minded people around them. It was certainly team strength that pulled the ladies through this quite remarkable journey through the Ulu Tutong.

KH 21-07-00

chapter twenty-one

Home Sweet Home

DAY 19 - Saturday July22nd

From 230alpha to the coast

After the rigours and ructions of the last two days' march from Shangri-la, Ken gave the Jungle Janes a day off.

Susanna became wistful:

I didn't sleep very well last night because my *basha* was a bit loose and my mosquito net collapsed on my face which is the most irritating thing you can imagine in the middle of the night. You suddenly feel like you're being massacred by a net. But we've had a very peaceful time down by the river this morning. I sat on a log, writing my diary and just enjoying the peace and quiet. There were some others down there as well, so it wasn't total solitude but it was lovely to listen to the birds and watch the butterflies and every so often there'd be a tiny gust of breeze and leaves came tumbling very slowly down from the trees.

One of the nicest things was going up to the landing site on my own this evening and being totally quiet with the jungle around me. I was wondering whether I would despair if I was told that the rest of the world had disappeared and I had to spend the remainder of my life in the jungle – I think the answer would have to be that I would despair. Having said that, I've thoroughly enjoyed the month and it's been a terrific break. I would recommend it to anybody because it's going back to the basics of human life: water, fire, shelter, companionship, and virtually everything else becomes irrelevant. It's very rare in modern life to go back to what you might call the primitive human roots of existence, and I've enjoyed that hugely.

Alex meanwhile reflected on her fellow Janes:

We all decided to relocate our *bashas* from where they were last time. Partly because it had rained a lot, and it was very muddy and slippery walking up and down the slope to the campfire. And partly because we love it when we're all together, all intermingled in a 'Brookside' type close, in a big circle, head to head, snoring and snoring. We were all happy as Larry, with washing lines everywhere. We've done our Mrs Tiggywinkle bit. Now the peace here is fantastic. So, on this lovely day, I'm going to tell you about all the girls.

First we have Claire. The beautiful Claire.

Air hostess, very efficient. How on earth she's managed to stay so clean and tidy throughout this trek, is beyond me. She has her hair tied up in this exquisite scarf. She never sweats. She has creases in her shirt and trousers. Her bra is still white. She's as cool as a cucumber, she never moans, and she's had a twisted ankle. I hope British Airways are very proud of her.

Then we have Wendy.

Wendy is our lecturer. She is our team leader at the moment. She's a good navigator. She's into teams, far more than I am. She likes everything to go just the way it should go. She's also got a very handsome boyfriend. He sends her little messages and little presents. She's sensible, and funny, and I think she's learned quite a lot of the lessons that I've had to learn too.

We've got Sal.

Sal who is amazingly strong mentally. Slim as a pin, she's lost quite a bit of weight here and has found it a hell of a struggle, like I have. Thank God there were two of us, and not just me on my own. But her mental determination is amazing. And she's hilariously funny. She's got this marvellous dry wit and makes me laugh. You never know quite what she's going to say next. I suppose that's something to do with being a solicitor, having a quick wit. She's got these beautiful blue eyes and she wears a blue sash around her head, that makes her eyes sparkle even more.

Then we have Catherine.

Sally's great buddy. Catherine is a Colonel's wife. She's used to this sort of army atmosphere, I reckon – grown up in it. She's very clued up, and a very strong woman. I can't get over how strong she is. She's got this marvellous auburn hairdo that's always in place. My hair is always dripping wet, while hers is always immaculate, like Claire's. Yesterday she was in her element, because she was one of the navigators, and heaven knows where she got all this strength from, but she was running up and down those hills doing reccies while we were all having a rest, like heaps of dead ducks. I suppose she's got a bit of army blood in her, somewhere. She's quite a tough cookie, very funny, loves poetry and singing.

Then we have the indomitable Fi.

Gordon Bennet, what would we do without her, this girl is so strong! Mind you, she has got ten years on most of us. She's fit and she loves all this. She's got amazing team spirit. She swears her head off, and never even notices. She's always in there to help, she's the one who starts the fires and carries the water. She's got a great big red rope in her sack, which everyone's forgotten about. But she never moans, never complains. My God, she's been a real strength to this trek. She's funny, witty – I just can't say enough. She's a good egg.

And then we come to little Peter Pan, Izzy, who is tiny.

And yet, that body is so strong. She wears her hair in a little tiny scarf. She's had some eye trouble, so she's been wearing her glasses and she has the sweetest little face that you've ever seen. She carries a far heavier pack than I do, though she's so tiny. She's a very good navigator. And she says, "How are you my darling," to everybody, and it makes you feel better. She's marvellous in the way she just gets stuck in, like Fi, even when we're absolutely exhausted. When we arrived back yesterday at alpha, that little spirit pulled down all our backpacks from the top to the bottom, I just couldn't believe it, one after another, after another. Fi and Izzy are very good friends, and they look out for each other. And here they've had to look out for us as well, and they've been marvellous. We're all very close. It's almost like we can't bear to be without each other now.

Then Gwenda.

Big chief's wife. It's amazing how she's coped with being a wife here, as well as a Jane. She's very clever in the way she's kept the two separate. She's been a marvellous help to me. She's very good at sorting everything out and getting ready, and just when you want to flop and do nothing, when you get to a *basha*, Gwenda's in there, with her *parang*, sorting out and chopping. "Right Alex, this is where you're going to go and I'm going to go here." Oh, thank God for Gwenda! She always knows where everything is in her pack. She can put her finger on it, if she needs to. And she always looks immaculate as well. She's lost a lot of weight, I think we all have. She looks like an athlete now. Wonderful strong figure she's got. In fact, we're all beginning to look trimmer, and our skins are looking better. It just goes to show you don't need to spend a fortune on Clarins, just come and live in the jungle for a bit. Gwenda's a very peaceful person, but she does call a spade a spade.

Dicky.

Dicky, Dicky. Ever starving Dicky, who is looking very, very thin, but who has a huge metabolic rate inside her. She needs to eat continually. That's all she talks about, well, not all she talks about, but food is her number one priority. She's always in high spirits. But then she is in real life as well. I say real life, you know what I mean. Dicky stated in one conversation that she wanted to reach the ultimate in total mental and physical despair. I wonder why. I don't ever want to feel that. It would be awful if you did, and you couldn't get out of it. Anyway, she's full of beans, very amusing. Douglas hasn't half had a bit of stick on this tour. I hope we all get to meet him properly so we can stand in his corner and hear his side of things, though we know she's only joking. Dicky always puts up her *basha* and has sticks to hang her rosary, her gloves, her cup, her penknife, her fags and her flannel. She is the queen of knick-knacks and she has them all lined up around her, so when she's lying in her hammock, she just has to stretch out a hand to grab whatever she needs.

Susanna. Susanna was team leader during the most stressful three days that we've had - the last three - and she was very good indeed. We all knew where we were, we all knew what we had to do next. It was like having a scout leader in charge, and I respect her enormously for her precision and her time keeping, because it really kept us on the straight and narrow when we were getting very tired and exhausted. How on earth she pulled out the energy at the end, I don't know, but she did. She's a brilliant photographer, too, and even when we were absolutely at our wits end, she would still find time to get out her camera, sort it out and snap the tail end of a butterfly, if she was lucky. She's quite a deep thinker, and I think she likes her own space, although she told a very naughty joke the other night which made us all collapse in fits and giggles. I can't tell you the joke, because it was one, too naughty, and two, too visual!

Then we have Patsy.

Our doctor. She's the one with all the plaits in her hair. My goodness me, she's been a hardworking beaver out here. Whenever we get to our campsite, the first thing Patsy does is bag herself the flat bit at the top, *basha* straight up, gets stuck in, collects the wood, lights the fire, digs the latrine. You can tell she's a Kiwi in spirit. She's had to keep an eye on us all medically, and she's been fantastic. I think she's been worried because she'd have had to make the decision to airlift us out if anything serious had happened. So far, so good. We've all taken our pills, all done as we are told. We have to do three pees at night, and two in the morning and check it's the colour of champagne, which we do. And because we've all been fastidious with our water, and our cups and our spoons, so far so good. We've had to have a bit of anti-histamine here and there, and the only anti-biotics that have been taken were for Patsy herself. So I think really, we've got a lot to thank her for. She's looked after us extremely well. She's checked on us when we've had the slightest complaint, like my feet were a bit sore one night, and she checked on me the next day. She didn't think I was doing enough pees, so she checked on that the next day. She filled me up with three litres of water the night before so I was up all night doing pees, so there's nothing wrong with my kidneys. Of course, lack of water and dehydration is a major problem here, and she has taken it very seriously. She's been a marvellous doctor, and an incredible worker here. She heaved herself up this ghastly stony cliff bit, on day seventeen, the steep day. How on earth she got up is beyond me, because we had our backpacks taken off, and got them up later. But Patsy said, "No, I will take my own," and she had water in it as well. She walked up this complete, slippery cliff edge with her backpack on. Now if that isn't determination I don't know what is. Patsy has tunnel vision out here, and the tunnel vision is, "I will get there, a.s.a.p."

And Jules.

Last but very not least, Jules. Jules is our hairdresser. What would we do without her. She's always hilariously funny and we all love her to bits. She's called Auntie Number One, and that is the greatest honour an auntie can have. She is very naughty as well. She has wonderful stories to tell, and loads of lovely jokes which just make us laugh and laugh and laugh. She's very strong though she's lost a lot of weight. Her legs have become like chicken legs, she says, and that little frame of hers can carry a backpack, fifty five pounds, with water in it. That girl is amazing. Well, she's got eleven new clients now, because when we get back to base, and we have a party, we're all having our hair done. She's got this marvellous husky voice. And you can always hear her coming, and when you can hear Jules coming, it puts a smile on your face. She's been a complete asset to the whole trip. In fact, when this is over, I'm going to be a bit of a lost soul without them all.

Julie has been relaxing, too....

It's been a very, very restful day today. I sorted out the *basha* space a bit more. It looks quite nice around here, a touch oriental. Fi's got what amounts to a Japanese garden, except we haven't got any gravel. It's very nice, with a little rock and a tree, and little terraces all over the place.

Everyone keeps talking about this "administration" stuff that we all do. Actually, it's just a posh word for housekeeping, really, washing and sort of doing your bits. I've done all my laundry, and managed to get most of it dry today, because it hasn't actually rained.

I'm really looking forward to tomorrow, though, because we've got three days to build the 'Hawaii Five O' raft to take us down the river to be picked up. We've got to build these rafts with rubber tyres and I don't know, bits of wood and string, so that's going to be fun!

chapter twenty-two

So Near Yet So Far

DAY 20 - Sunday 23rd July

Not all the Jungle Janes were enthusiastic about the raft building exercise. They didn't see why it was necessary, or why the choppers couldn't come in and collect them from 230alpha, but Ken insisted that they could only be picked up further downstream, at landing site 230, where a junction of rivers broadened the slender flood plain of the Tutong River.

The nearest suitable place for raft construction was about half a kilometre upstream from their camp, and the best way to get there was by wading. The only non-natural aid to building their craft was a supply of large inner tubes, which they lugged up river with them.

Ken was realistic.

I knew that today was going to be a slow day and that it was going to be very difficult to motivate the ladies into building their rafts, ready for their trip downstream. But there seemed to be a mood almost of apathy and a reluctance to move and get on with it. Once we got down to the site on the river, everybody split up to do various tasks, but there still seemed to be a lack of purpose in the air.

Meanwhile Patsy and Susanna were at the forefront of trying to come up with ideas and put together a plan to gather all the materials required to make the first raft. I was encouraged and full of admiration for the way they got stuck into it. Wendy was the leader for the day and a very diplomatic person. She managed to get everybody away doing the different things – gathering *rattan*, cutting logs, blowing up the rubber inner tubes – but it was all happening at a very slow pace.

Even **Dicky** was less than her normal energetic self.

We all found it very difficult to get going. The half kilometre walk to the river nearly finished me. I felt very lethargic and light-headed and I kept stumbling. But I started chopping down trees, which later turned out to be a type of wood that was so heavy it sank! So that was a bit if a waste of time! The raft was supposed to be around nine feet by twelve feet', to hold six of us, and in our case, Paul and Lulu, his sound assistant, as well as all their camera equipment, all our *bergens* and kit.

Susanna found the day brought some compensation.

It's been a funny day of ups and downs. We were assigned our task of raft building, which was met with mixed feelings. I think the fact that we're not going out until Thursday and today is only Sunday made us feel that we'd got to jump through hoops for the sake of jumping through hoops and it didn't seem to be what most of us wanted to do at the time. My personal feeling about it was that it made a change from walking but I could sympathise with those who thought the whole thing was a bit unnecessary. Once we got down to the river, though, we did our usual bit of knuckling under and got on with it.

I had fun talking with Sally while we were splitting *rattan*. This is not the easiest job in the world and we'd started off with some rather old stuff which was very reluctant to split into the spaghetti type material that's required to lash together the logs of the rafts. We were glad when we got on to some newer stuff after lunch. But it was rather peaceful sitting there, nattering, a bit like I imagine a knitting circle would be – not that I've ever attended a knitting circle or am ever likely to – but it's sort of females being companionable with an activity to keep them from mischief.

Alex found the work less satisfying.

We learned how to do *rattan*, which is this vine that you have to split up and take out this inner strand and twiddle it round. And oh, God, it was so bloody tedious! Because all of us were winding down mentally and we had to wade through porridge to try and wind ourselves up again, it was a slightly tense day. It was hot; we were very tired, and we hadn't a blooming clue how to build a raft.

But luckily Patsy took charge, motivating us all, and it was a blooming hard day.

I was very glad when four o'clock came. We'd got three quarters of one raft made and thought, "Oh fiddle, we've got to come back tomorrow, and do another one!"

If this thing is going to sail down the river, it'll be an absolute laugh.

Susanna was still in a thoughtful mood.

In the afternoon, we walked back to our campsite down the river, which was also a pleasant change from cross-graining and battling up slithery banks.

It's been a different day of different moods. This morning I felt ready for the end. I began to think, "Yep, it's time to go home."

I've come to the end of this experience and I'm becoming less tolerant. People are getting on my nerves more and just the slightest remark can irritate me.

But by the end of the day I feel more relaxed again, I don't want to go home! So it's swings and roundabouts at the moment and I think it probably will be now for the next three days. It's a strange way to do it and in many ways perhaps we should have done the rafting earlier or built them before we left, so that we just came back from the expedition and went straight down.

One lovely thing, though; I had a little private moment this morning when I went up to the landing site before breakfast. I had it to myself and spent some time with the wildlife, which is almost as elusive as ever, but I did see three squirrels and a flight of hornbills and a single hornbill which I identified from my bird book as a black hornbill. In fact it has a white beak and a white forehead, but is called the black hornbill, as these things so often are!

Ken, sensing the mood of the Jungle Janes, called them together in the evening for one of his chats.

You'll probably never ever come back here again but the jungle will be here for a long, long time to come and you can reflect, almost to the point of being sentimental if you like, on those places that you trod where no other woman, or man for that matter, has ever been before, and all the little camps that you made which were the scene of great activity and laughter and happiness, only to be deserted when you left. I want you to try and remember those good times - those peaks, as I'm sure you'll remember some of the low times - when you were completely exhausted and wishing you'd never come in the first place.

So, we still have a little mountain to climb in the end, because it's always good to finish on a high. It's very easy to let things trail off and everybody sort of bumble down to the landing site and be whisked off back to civilization. It's better to finish things with a bit of a crack and something that's enjoyable. So that's your aim now - to finish it with a bit of style, and do something different that you've never done before.

Alex had other preoccupations.

I felt very sick in the evening. I opened my silver bag, and found some blooming awful sausages! Sausages were usually delicious, but these ones were sort of frankfurters with faint herbs in, and made me feel sick. So I slipped them into Dicky's cup and she gobbled them down in no time. She needs them far more than I do anyway. And then I went and lay down, because I did feel a bit rough.

I felt much better after ten minutes of just doing nothing, and we ran up to the Ghurkha camp. They gave us beef jerky, cooked in garlic; it was delicious!

We had a good old laugh, and we were all back in bed at about a quarter to nine.

I slept, and slept and slept. According to Gwenda,I snored.

I was dreaming about Rudolph Hess. I don't know how he crept into my dreams but it was quite frightening. I was in prison, and all these funny things were happening to me. I must have been in a really deep sleep. I had endless pees in the night, but luckily I went to sleep again. I've never drunk so much water as I have out here, constantly peeing all through the night, but I don't get spooked anymore. If there's a civet cat underneath me, or a wild boar, I don't give a damn, I say hello to them most nights!

chapter twenty-three

Too Near By Far

DAY 21 - Monday 24th July

The Janes, feeling better after a good night's sleep, and knowing that the first raft had at least been partially launched the day before, came down to the river to complete both craft with more confidence and enthusiasm than the day before.

Susanna.

We achieved a lot more, a lot quicker, which was better for morale. We went down to the river in the knowledge that we had a lot of experience from yesterday to help us speed things along today and the wood gathering was much quicker. We knew exactly what sort of dimensions we needed and, more to the point, what thickness. We knew the style of raft, the measurements – slightly smaller than prototype one. So we achieved a lot really in the morning and had the second craft almost completed by lunchtime.

This turned out to be a good thing because Ken arrived with the news that in fact we've got to leave at six am on Wednesday, thirty-six hours sooner than we were expecting.

The news was met with astonishing neutrality. Personally, I'm rather regretful because the fact that we were building the raft so fast meant that I thought we were going to have two more days here with comparatively little to do and I was looking forward to spending more time where everybody else wasn't, with just me and the jungle – which I have rather enjoyed the last few days.

But now we've got to set off on the rafts tomorrow before midday and make camp down river where the helicopters will land. This means packing up the campsite in the morning, so nostalgia is beginning to kick in.

As **Alex** saw it:

We had the happiest day, because there were no men about, bossing us around and telling us what to do. No-one frowning at us, and grimacing, and telling us that you've got to do this, and you've got to do that, and you don't do this and you don't do that.

Phew. Do you know what? We built a spectacular raft in about three hours. In fact when Ken did turn up, he looked quite surprised at what we'd achieved. We worked together extremely well as a team. And that is the secret of the success of this trek. Partly because we all laugh all the time, as you'll have gathered. We never have a cross moment, and those who are tired, sit down and don't feel guilty, because everybody else understands, and then, somebody else has a sit down. There's no animosity, no hierarchy, there is just complete selflessness between us. So, we've built a raft in half the time, it floats perfectly and we can even stand on it!

Fiona perked up, too, although she's sad at the prospect of leaving the jungle.

I started off this morning a bit a bit fed up. I spoke to Wendy and a few others about the fact that I wasn't personally that keen on having two big rafts; I would rather go for three smaller ones. But it was decided in the end to use two because of all the work that had already been done.

I was thinking that the day was going to be like yesterday,

but as it turned out we were left alone – no film crew, no men, just us. It was brilliant, we knew what we were doing, and the second raft took shape very quickly. There was a lot of laughter, a lot of chatting, a lot of constructive and productive work done. It was great, it was really easy. We just kicked in and got on with it. It was remarkable that after this time together, we are very much a unit, and we work well as a unit.

There aren't two teams any more. That's all gone now. It changed when we set up this new camp, where everybody is just all over the place. For ease at lunch we stay in the two groups which we had, but in the evenings and during the day, everyone just mixes and chats away.

So, the second raft was built and tested. In fact, all twelve of us all stood on it at one point, and it was a great success. It was good fun. I felt much happier with the second one.

I'd quite happily stay here, to be honest, if there was something to do. If someone said to me, you can stay here, with the Ghurkhas, and redo the whole trek again, learning how to fish and trap, how to track; learning properly how to navigate, I'd happily spend another month or so. I don't miss anything from outside. I think the reason that people might be happy to go is that we're all intelligent women, we all need to be busy. We've built the rafts, they'll be ready tomorrow. And nice as it is to sit down and read books, and do nothing, we women need to be productive.

All the women were pleased with the way they'd worked. Most were pleased that they were going, but they were all experiencing mixed emotions, especially Gwenda, who, as Ken's wife had been in the most difficult position of them all, not least because she and Ken had both been away from their young children for so long.

Gwenda talked to Claire.

Walking back along the river with Claire, she said that, now we had a firm departure time, she felt quite sad about it. And it made me reflect that I felt quite sad about it, too; we'd had a fantastic time. I never thought I'd actually say that, because right at the beginning, I said to Ken, I hate being here. But now I've really enjoyed the trip. It was incredibly hard, but I think because the girls were so great, and we worked so well together without any major rows or niggly hassles. I felt my time here was very personal in that I had to think about myself, instead of worrying about my family and the running of the business, and it was a good time for me to reflect on life in general, on what I've done in the past, and what I want to do in the future.

It's also been very strange being here with Ken, but not really being here with Ken, in the married sense of the word. At the beginning it was much harder, because I wanted to argue back when he said things I didn't agree with. And I did say a few horrible things to him at times, though I apologised to him later. It must be jolly hard for him, in that he's had to look after all twelve of us, as well as the crew. And I shouldn't have made his life any harder than it already was.

It was quite difficult at times, when I wanted to ask him to come and help me do things, and of course, I couldn't because it wouldn't be fair on the other girls. But we have managed to get away on our own, and chat about home, and what the children were doing, and how they were getting on. I think he misses them as much as I do, but probably doesn't show it as much. I think he feels very proud of me, and what I've actually achieved. I know at home I was never the first person to say, "Let's go for a big walk today." And certainly not camp. I've never camped with him, ever. This was a real first. Instead of doing it gently, we went right in at the deep end.

But I think he's really pleased with how I've coped. I've been much quieter on this trip than I would have been say fifteen years ago. I think that comes with maturity; you tend to think more before you open your mouth. But no, I must say, well done Ken, and thank you for bringing me here.

chapter twenty-four

The Bloated Leech

DAY 22 - Tuesday 25ᵗʰ July

After a quiet evening, the Janes settled down in their *bashas* at 230alpha, knowing that the next night, which they would spend close to the landing site by the river, would be their last in the jungle.

They had named the rafts *The Bloated Leech*, and *The Happy Dung Beetle*. Sally was skipper of the *Leech,* and Dicky skippered the *Beetle,* and flew a blue spotted neck scarf from the bow.

Once the women had taken down their *bashas* at 230alpha for the last time, they left all their *bergens* on the beach by the camp and went up to the launch point where they'd made the rafts. Feeling very end of term and full of hilarity at the thought of going home, they pushed off, with those women at each corner fending off and punting.

The *Beetle* burst one of its inner tubes in the first ten minutes, before they had arrived back at the beach to pick up the *bergens*. They limped into shore, and wrapped all the rucksacks in their tarpaulins and used four of them as a float to replace the burst tyre. They turned out to give very good buoyancy. Ken sailed on the *Leech,* and Paul, Lulu and their kit on the *Beetle*, with Izzy, Fi, Alex and Claire poling.

The sound of their lusty voices singing 'Row, row, row your boat,' and 'Eternal Father,' echoed across the narrow river valley above the sound of the water and the jungle noises to which they had become so accustomed.

It was a tricky journey. The river was littered with obstacles in the form of deadfall, rocks and rapids, and they all wore life jackets. In some parts, the river was over six feet deep where they couldn't feel the bottom with their poles.

At about half past one, they were stopped by a massive blockage of shallows and unmoveable deadfall. They had to lift both craft out of the water and over the deceased tree. Ken reckoned each raft weighed about three-quarters of a ton, fully loaded. Dicky's skinny arms looked very sinewy as she heaved and lifted. There may not have been much flesh on them, but soon after that, a tiny green fly settled on her little finger and stung it very sharply. Within minutes the finger had swollen like a sausage and felt very tight and hot. Izzy served up some antihistamines, but, though the pain diminished a little, the swelling spread all over Dicky's hand.

After two and half hours very slow passage, they finally reached LS230 (not alpha), where they disembarked, not before time. By now, the *Dung Beetle* was very low in the water and slowly sinking.

They dismantled the rafts, released what air was left in the tubes, and found that all their kit – hammocks and everything – was completely soaking. All the same, *bashas* had to be up for the last night before the helicopters came.

Then, at 5.30, it started raining, and it didn't stop. Within seconds everything was soaked and dripping, and several of the Janes suffered temporary lapses of plot with a lot of obscenities flying around the jungle. For one thing, they were all very hungry; they had had no breakfast and no lunch.

Dicky got a fire going under someone else's sarong and managed to warm up some silver bags, but soon they gave up and sat around gloomily under dripping tarpaulins.

After discarding their wet clothes, everyone climbed into wet sleeping bags and hammocks.

Dicky crouched under Sally's *basha* for ten minutes and they shared the last bite of a peanut brittle. They couldn't light their *hexi-stove* because the lighters were damp, and the *hexi-blocks* were wet.

Only some of the Janes slept that night.

DAY 23 - Wednesday 26th July.
PATSY

We get up in the dark. It's been drizzling all night, but the girls sing 'Happy Birthday' to me from the steep valley and the Gurkhas let off flares and smoke. It is an unforgettable and very beautiful moment.

I have a pile of birthday presents. Someone has carried a little gardening book called 'Old Roses' for me, the whole trip. I've also been given a walking pole, and somebody's last Lancashire hot-pot, and some wrinkled and damp birthday cards.

Somebody has even kept a new pressed dry handkerchief, which only finally got damp yesterday.

To get to the landing site, we have to wade across a stream so we're soon wet through, again, but none of us are bothered by this stage.

The helicopter arrives at 6.30 but the pilot can't land, because it's just not safe due to low-lying mist – the only mist we've seen on the trip – and it leaves.

I find my trousers starting to steam in the heat.

An hour and a half later, the helicopter comes back.

As we fly back over the jungle, we can see the undulating ridge lines which we've traversed so frustratingly. I imagine what it must be like to be lost in there. It looks truly vast. We've had a ball, some of it was hell, but I won't ever forget it.

Our clothes are a mass of damp stained, foetid awfulness. The helicopter pilot suggests that we burn them.

Back at Sittang camp, Julie spends an hour getting the knotted plaits out of my hair.

At last I can really relax for the first time. I no longer have to be focused on my job, or the trek.

I've been into Tutong village and bought some scales. There's much gloom when people find that they haven't lost as much weight as they thought, probably due to conversion of fat to muscle.

But this despondency is short-lived and soon dissolves into general hilarity.

DICKY

I woke at 4.50 and called the others, but they were all awake anyway.

I had one dry biscuit for breakfast, issued by Patsy, then an extra half, on compassionate grounds (my hand was very swollen and Patsy said I've lost a lot of weight)!

We crossed the river, only up to our knees, to wait for the helicopter on the shingle bank on the other side. When the heli couldn't land, we had to sit and wait and wait and I was very, very hungry!

As we flew out and I saw the canopy below, it suddenly hit me how I would miss the womb-like existence of the last three weeks – total seclusion and lack of hustle and bustle. I had no idea what had been happening in the world. There could have been a war and we wouldn't have known, and suddenly one was faced with plunging back into a different life, like a new girl at school or a single person taking a deep breath before entering a raving party in a crowded room. Suddenly, I wanted to be back in there. If Ken had said, "Another two weeks, ladies?" I might have gone for it.

Back at Sittang Jungle Training Camp there was coffee, which never tasted so good, then, in the Naafi dining room, a late breakfast – sausage, mushroom and fried egg! I took a plateful but couldn't eat it! It was all too much, so I ate a biscuit.

I showered and washed my hair for half an hour. I think it will be weeks before I get my fingernails clean.

At three o'clock we had a de-briefing from Ken, and advice on how to deal with the press who would be arriving tomorrow. Ken said he was very proud of us …. and he never expected us all to finish!

ALEX

Today is the day that we leave the jungle.

We'd had a bit of a rotten old night really. We'd had so many good nights together laughing round the campfire – just having hoots all the time and keeping our spirits going – but last night it was pouring with rain, we were in a ghastly *basha* site, I was on a cliff edge again and couldn't get out of my hammock. Incidentally now we seem to get our *bashas* up in no time – we're real little experts at the job. We were soaking wet – everything was wet because we'd been floating our *bergens* in the water the day before and it had rained all night.

We were up at ten to five in the pitch dark. We packed away as quickly as possible to get onto the river bed by six. It was pretty treacherous in the dark trying to get down on these pebbles all slimy and slippery but as instructed we found our way up to the landing site and were there on time.

When the helicopter arrived and it couldn't land, it didn't matter; we only had an hour to wait and that's nothing in the jungle. We played games and we threw stones in the river and we laughed and thought, "God – today's the day we leave the jungle" – and it began to dawn on us. Today's the day we leave the place that we have lived in for twenty three days, and become part of and begun to love and to respect.

It's Patsy's birthday today, too. We all sang 'Happy Birthday' to her at five o'clock in the morning through the trees. She's been quite remarkable really, keeping us all fit and healthy.

Eventually, in the distance, we heard the blades of the helicopter coming towards us – three girls on one side, three girls on the other side. It lands, such a dramatic moment when it comes in. We do as we're told, whip into our seats – in go the *bergens*, doors slam and we start to move upwards and upwards.

When we arrived at the Sittang camp landing strip, it was a very exciting moment because we knew we'd actually completed this great adventure. We all jumped out and waved to the pilots and smiled our little heads off and hugged each other until we squeezed every ounce of blood out of each other. But we went back and did our chores – unloading the *bergens*, putting back everything we'd borrowed from the British Army. Wrapped up tidily - immaculate I might add, on the lawn, drying everything, sorting it out.

On the lawn there was a cup of fresh coffee in a china cup that was clean. We chat to the Gurkhas who are here at the moment and the cleaning ladies – so pleased to see their faces again. We were the first lot waiting for the others, almost like we're not a team until we're all together again. And then suddenly you could hear the helicopter blades thumping their way through the sky above us and our immediate reaction was to drop everything and go back to the landing strip across the main road and meet our other half – it never once dawned on us to go and make our beds and get ourselves unpacked and sorted in the showers - all we wanted was to be together again – so immediately we heard the blades we ran onto the landing strip - hailed them in full glory and the helicopter landed and out came the other six girls. What a joy it was; we were all together hugging each other – weeping with each other – none of us really knew the emotions the others were feeling, but we were together again, and we were safe!

CATHERINE

A real moment of revelation came to me once we were in the helicopter and above the canopy. For the first time in the whole expedition, I began to get an inkling of what we had done, and I will use the word 'achieved', although it's not a word I use lightly. To look at that vast great expanse and to realise that we had been somewhere like tiny pinpricks in the middle of it, made me feel very small but at the same time I felt proud – again, not a word I use lightly. I felt I'd achieved something – there's no doubt about that – it's an enormous place but I didn't really get a sense of it until I was high above it.

FIONA

There's a part of me not many people get to see that I've left behind in the jungle. I felt I was in my element there – I loved it. And in the helicopter – flying over the canopy and just seeing its vastness and its untouchability – I wanted to go back. Some people might say that's escapism. There are very few places where you feel at home, but, in a weird sort of way, I felt at home there.

I'll probably never go back but in a way I'm glad. I guess it's like going on holiday, if you've spent time somewhere and you go back, it's never the same – and it could never be the same. I'd never have that same group of people with me – and we're the only people who can ever share those experiences.

I can honestly say I don't want to go home. I don't know what's in store for me, but to be part of something like this – it's something that doesn't come up once in a lifetime for some people and it's come up for me – my God, I'll never ever forget it!

GWENDA

I'm sitting in Sittang Camp in a chair. I can lean against something and I can have a cigarette, some wine – a mug of wine I should say, not a glass – left over from when I bought it at the airport coming out.

I thought of Harry and the broccoli as I flew over the jungle.

I didn't feel any loss at leaving the jungle I felt quite mellow, and happy that we'd all got out safely. We got back to Sittang, got out and started hugging and kissing each other. That's when I started to feel really sad that it was at an end and that I would never do that again or be with this extraordinary group of people again. I found that really sad because without them I wouldn't have managed at all. I think it was a huge team effort and every single one of them in their own way helped me get through the expedition. We unloaded some kit and then eventually the others arrived and we did more hugging and kissing and there were even more tears then, but it was brilliant to see everybody.

As I stood under a shower with cold water I thought, Gosh, three weeks ago we stood under these showers and thought eugh, yucky, but in fact they're really nice now – after the jungle. So yet again, we just adapt to our surroundings and anything after the jungle is pure luxury.

So all I can say now is I've had a fantastic month – I've been with a great bunch of people – really pleased that Ken was there and I think we both did really well, at not being husband and wife, and I know he had added pressure with having me there and being away from the children. I think we've done incredibly well and I can't say that enough.

SALLY

I hadn't anticipated it but when I came back in the helicopter, I was in the second group – it was very exciting to find that the others had actually waited for us. I hadn't expected that they would, and it was lovely because it was very hard when the group split up. We'd actually had to decide who was going to go first and who was going to go second, so it had been a bit of a parting of the ways. We'd been together for four weeks and suddenly we were split, so it was wonderful to see them. I thought they'd be back at camp, already washing and cleaning themselves and the kit.

I've enjoyed the experience enormously, although walking with the heavy weight was the hardest bit for me. I haven't got the sort of frame to cope with carrying fifity pounds but I've enjoyed the community spirit and the being in a group – actually working in a group, and I've enjoyed the jungle and I can't imagine not being in it. It's been a wonderful time and I feel very privileged that I was on the trip. Very privileged and very lucky.

WENDY

Most of the girls had a really soggy, wet night – their kit had got really wet coming over on the rafts. I don't know whether it was luck or good packing but my kit and Claire's was perfectly dry. We kept pretty quiet about that because I don't think it goes down very well when you're snuggled in your sleeping bag and everyone else is freezing. The bottom half of my body was fine but I'd lent my T-shirt to Sally so I hadn't got anything on my top and I was really cold, so when five o'clock came I was wide-awake thinking, I don't really want to get up.

Six of the girls went ahead in the first helicopter flight, and when we landed at Sittang, I jumped out and helped with the sacks and baggage. By the time I turned round everybody was hugging each other. And that was the first acknowledgement in a sense that the expedition was over and we'd come through it. So I joined the crowd and I genuinely wanted to go round and hug everybody to make sure I hadn't missed anyone out. It was such an amazing feeling that we were back together and looking forward to the next few days of constant chatter, it hasn't stopped really.

CLAIRE

Today – gosh we woke up so early – 5.30 in the morning. We had to be ready to catch our helicopter at six o'clock. But hang on a second, guess what? half past six,, seven, eight …. The helicopter came, didn't land and went away again!

So, we sit and wait. My goodness! Such apprehension; one minute we're going, next minute we're staying, one minute we're going.

But here it comes again, finally, yes, the clouds have broken. There's a blue, blue sky and beautiful sunshine. And here comes the helicopter. What a welcome sight!

It takes the first group of girls away and a few of us are left behind because it can only do six or seven at a time.

Now it's our turn. My goodness – helicopter lands, really exciting, then up, up away.

Oh my gosh! Look down. It was our home; the Tutong was my home and now I look at it and I am feeling so sad – really very sad. I look at the river that we used to run through gloriously, and swim. We used to look forward to finding the river – any part of it, running water or still. It was our saviour and now I look at it from high, high above the clouds as we leave and say goodbye to the Tutong. My goodness what an empty feeling I have – I didn't expect it – ever. We were excited by the helicopter and its pilots before, now I'm excited looking back down at the Tutong – looking at the high ridges, looking at the different rivers, streams and bends and I remember it was so friendly. I remember it, too, being fierce and wild and rugged and steep for us; I also remember it being quite ruthless – the palms, the wait-a-whiles, all the ants and the mosquito bites.

I remember it being very gentle to us at nights. And so I leave it finally – will we ever see it again? Such a strange feeling, as if I'm being wrenched away from it. And finally, my gosh, I can see in the distance the ocean and Sittang Camp. And as we land, my goodness what a beautiful sight – we circle around over the ocean and back in swiftly and then we're lower, we land and we jump out of the helicopter to greet the other girls.

Everyone's come to meet us – how lovely – and we run into each other's arms and we laugh, but we cry, we say my goodness we've done it – it's been a success. But we all have tears. Somebody told us – a little birdy told us that we would cry when we left Tutong and they were right. It's been a wonderful time – a wonderful end and it makes me wonder when did it start and has it actually finished? Goodbye Tutong – for now anyway.

chapter twenty-five

Out of the Jungle But Still a Jane?

One of the more surprising aspects of the Jungle Janes' journey through the Ulu Tutong was the internal harmony with which it was achieved.

If the whole trek had been devised from the start as a piece of television entertainment, it seems likely that the women would have been recruited and selected on the grounds of lack of compatibility. But this group was selected by casual word of mouth, by osmosis, as Patsy put it, and they all came to it with broadly similar motives.

Here were twelve women who have all had careers, mostly professional, very often dealing with people – as lawyers, teachers, airline pursers, doctors. Seven were mothers of two or more children. Their average age was about forty (Claire reserved the right not to reveal hers).

They were all bright, competent women who had plenty of practical experience of how the world works, and an understanding of the dynamics of human relations. In other words, they knew the value of self-control. This, more than anything, was what in the end held them altogether and sustained the strong sense of loyalty which they developed towards one another.

Although they shared some obvious common characteristics, in as much as there is a limited number of women who would have put themselves forward in the first place for an expedition like this, with all the effort, discomfort and sheer inconvenience involved, they were a fairly disparate group. It seems that a strong bond is created by the sharing of an experience that is in some way life-changing, or that makes a contribution to an individual's 'personal myth'. In much the same way that people stay attached, against all the odds, to those with whom they were, say, at school, or in the forces with.

In assessing whether the expedition achieved what it set out to, it's worth looking more closely at the basis on which the women went. They all had to move heaven and earth to go, as the level of commitment was so high. They had to find the money, about fifteen hundred pounds each (another factor in self-selection), most of them had to come to terms with partners or husbands, and make arrangements for children as the trip ran over into the start of the summer holidays. It required, according to Ken Hames, a great leap of faith.

They were also women who either weren't, or weren't prepared to be seen as, in thrall to the fame-generating power of television, and that additional element to the trip was not an incentive. In fact, it did not arise until after most of the women had confirmed that they wanted to take part.

Paul Berriff, who filmed and directed Channel Four's Jungle Janes was happy to be dealing with a group who had not chosen to be on television or responded to a casting advertisement. This would give him a truer perspective of the realities of the journey. But it surprised him, as much as it did the other people involved in the expedition, that there was such harmony, and that not one woman had to be taken out of the jungle for illness or injury – statistically very much at odds with military training operations in the same jungle. The Gurkha back-up predicted at the start of the trek in Sittang that at least half the women would have to come out.

That they all came through without any major injury or illness was a remarkable testament both to their determination to reach the end, and to Patsy Spicer's indefatigable relief of preventative medicine.

Sally is still suffering a little, but she's well on the mend and has no regrets.

It was fun; there was so much laughter, though not during the day when we were carrying our packs. I found I was able to abandon my concerns about everything else, and when I did think, it was about the big issues. I found that when I came back everything seemed small and cluttered, and I was less concerned about trivial problems. My husband says I have a distant look from time to time, but I think that may simply be pain.

I got on fine with the rest of the women. It wasn't an issue. I knew Catherine, of course, and I'd met Gwenda. But whomever they had been, I took the view that a month of self-restraint was manageable, though maybe it wouldn't have worked if I had gone with twelve existing friends. I got irritated sometimes, but I was always prepared to back off. It wasn't hard. Ken had said the jungle is a great leveller, and I think he's right. We were all learning new things, new skills, and perhaps that made us more diffident. I would say that all the women had fairly strong characters; they had a lot of self-confidence, each had some particular contribution to make, and there weren't noticeably any odd ones out. I certainly stayed on good terms with Catherine, whom I've known for over twenty years.

I think, when people were upset, they would find someone else to talk to, and sort it out privately. Then they sometimes found that other people were having the same problem, which made it easier to deal with. Generally, I found I tended to hold back negative, irrelevant thoughts, which wasn't that difficult.

The trip hasn't really left me with any great sense of achievement. I certainly enjoyed learning new skills, and it was in many ways a wonderful experience, but it hasn't been utterly life-changing. I didn't like the TV camera being there, especially if I'd just crawled to the top of a bank, scrabbling and sweating. I felt thoroughly humiliated by it. But I think the biggest problem I had was simply my size. I was carrying over half my body weight, and I lost a lot of weight anyway, which is only now coming back. The last few days' walking, when I got my hernia, were very tough, but I was determined not to be Cas-evacced. Patsy was very encouraging, and I'm very glad I finished it.

Whether or not it was important to me in the long term, I don't know yet. I hope it has been a natural break, a punctuation mark in my life. It's left me with a more positive approach, and I'm simply not prepared now to go on doing things I don't want to. I may not, for instance, go back to the practice because of the law. I think it's changed a lot over the last twenty years. I would very much like to do something else completely, perhaps even to write.

Catherine, along with Dicky and Gwenda, was one of the three Catholic women on the trek. Was there a spiritual dimension to her sojourn in the wilderness?

No, not really. I was too busy just surviving. But I felt great contentment there, away from all the problems of the modern world. And it was a liberating experience to be living at such a basic level, so simply and close to the earth. On Sundays, I was conscious that I would normally have been at mass, and one Sunday, we did all say 'The Lord's Prayer'. I've certainly found in broad terms that the experience has clarified my view of things; it's reawakened some interests and I very much enjoyed the whole business of going into the unknown.

Although it was hard, I loved doing it, and I especially enjoyed learning new things like tracking and navigation. I wasn't particularly uncomfortable with the camera, I found I was rather conscious of my own family's reaction and I did have some sympathy with those who were reluctant to appear in front of it. It was interesting, though - some blossomed in front of it; others were prepared to put their animosity on hold.

As a professional oratorio and concert mezzo-soprano, **Susanna** is not short of self-confidence. What did she derive from the Jungle Janes' trek?

I suppose, more self-belief, because I discovered I really could cope. It's the sort of thing one simply doesn't know until one's tried. I loved the jungle, and I'd love to go back, as it were, on my own terms. I would have liked to have seen more wildlife, and had a more specific aim to the trek beyond a simple circular journey.

It wasn't as life-changing for me as, say, the four months I spent working with Mother Teresa in Calcutta, where at least at the end of each day, you know you have specifically helped someone who couldn't help themselves. Of course, on the trek, we were all helping each other, but that was mutual. I did feel that it was a shame we women didn't do more to help Alex, though. I'm not sure how she would have coped if she hadn't had Bhuwani to help her; having said that, all he did was pace her; she was carrying her own kit, but we didn't expect her to carry extra water.

I found the walking hard but perhaps not as hard as I expected, especially after Cader Idris in Wales. Once I'd started, I knew I'd be fine. I did my share of water carrying, but I didn't do so much slashing up front. Some of the others - Claire and Gwenda - were particularly keen on that. I got on well with the other women, and I was quite happy to socialise, but I'm used to spending quite a lot of time on my own and I do need space. If there were those who irritated me at times, on the whole I was able to handle it myself. It was only for a month, after all. It was a matter of being pragmatic, I suppose. Patsy's been a friend for a long time, of course, but I was also particularly glad to get to know Sally, Claire, Catherine and Dicky.

Looking back now, I'm very glad I did it. There were some magical scenes, and experiences. I found what wildlife I saw absolutely fascinating – extraordinary insects, and the dung beetles whose activities were riveting, they worked so hard and efficiently. Above all, I enjoyed the complete freedom from the normal hassle and anxieties of my every day life in England.

Three months after her return, rolling a fresh, slender cigarette, **Julie** leans back in her chair.

I'm very glad I went. I found it very tough, though, specially

296

on the last night after we'd rafted to the final camp. I nearly switched off then. Our raft was sinking, and it had all the cameras and stuff on it! So that was a bit of a nightmare. Then Ken made us dismantle the rafts and we found that *everything* was wet. I was looking forward to a party – for our last night in the jungle, but it started absolutely pissing down and soaked everything, and I was still hacking for an hour to get my *basha* up. That's when I lost it. I went totally mad.

I only calmed down when Paul appeared with his camera. I liked Paul, actually. You'd think he was a bit of a dour Yorkshireman, but he was very funny when he wasn't working. Anyway, I calmed down, and had a fag. I took my roller with me to the jungle, and I was surprised how many of the girls smoked. That can create a bit of a bond.

I didn't get that close to all the girls, though. Claire, for instance, spent a lot of time in her hammock, and she would go off on her own. I found her once, sitting on a rock by the river, reading her bible, which I thought was really nice. Susanna, although she was a bit inclined to behave like a scout leader, did have a surprisingly dry wit.

I think some of the most memorable moments were the hardest – like climbing the sheer banks on the second from last day. The Gurkhas were great, though, encouraging me - They'd say 'Come on, Auntie!'

Julie breaks into a long peel of husky laughter.

The trees, the views, were brilliant. I felt very privileged to have been to a place where so few others have been. In the end, I'd say it was the most fantastic holiday I ever had in my life, and I don't suppose anyone will ask me to do anything like it again.

For **Claire**, the Jungle Janes' trek demonstrated that she could do anything she had set her mind to doing.

Being there, having made the choice, there was no point in not just getting on with it. Like now, back in England. I might get back from a fourteen hour flight, and have an evening class for my psychology degree. Even if I'm totally knackered, I'll say to myself that I've chosen to do this, so I'm doing it. And off I go.

There was a diversity of people in the group, and in my team. I was interested in them but I also wanted time to myself. I mean, how much do we need other people around us? Our team was much quieter than the other was. We spent time reading and doing our diaries, which gave me more solo time, which believe me, I needed. But the fact is, most of the women on the trek were already too self-contained, they were old enough to be that. So, though I will probably remember all their names in thirty years' time, I didn't get as close to some of them as I might have liked. If there were a follow up expedition, it might be different.

The trip did give me at least as much as I expected, and a few things I hadn't – mostly the weight, the filth, and the sweat!

"Claire is a very private person," **Wendy** says. But, as buddies, we got on very well, worked well together and were very supportive of each other. She's extremely self-sufficient and had a great sense of humour.

There were very few confrontations between any of the women, I think because we were mature enough to know the dangers. Most of them were educated and articulate, and that must help. There was certainly a lot of diplomacy going on.

There were some very tender moments in our group, for instance, one night we had a candle-lit poetry reading, which was wonderful. There was no doubt that life in England became irrelevant. Even Alan, my partner became irrelevant, not that I didn't still love him, it's just that he had nothing to do with where I was then.

Before I went on the trek, I'd lost a certain amount of confidence in myself, and the trek did replace this. Now, I look at other women and say to myself – I'm different from her. She's never done anything like I've just done.

The theme of diplomacy recurs in the Jungle Janes' appraisals of the trek. It seems that they had firmly taken on board Churchill's foreign policy maxim in the early stages of the Cold War that to 'Jaw-jaw is better than to war-war.'

Izzy also thinks that, as they got to know each other better, they understood each other's traits and accommodated them. Group loyalty helped and the fact that the women were able to express a problem and discuss it. She was impressed, too, by the way in which people would help each other, especially her buddy, Fiona.

When Alex was at the back, really struggling up the sheer sides of a gully two days from home, Fi got back down there, and was doing everything to encourage her. For most of us, it was all we could do to get ourselves up. But losing Alex, having her drop out, would have seriously damaged the morale of the whole group.

Dicky agreed that an important factor in helping Alex was the sense that they must stay together as a team of twelve, or the whole expedition would be invalidated in some way.

What does Dicky feel about it now?

I very much live life for the moment. As far as I'm concerned, I've done it, and I'm back. I'll see some of the Janes again, those that live near. I'd be glad to see any of them, but I don't suppose I'd go too far out of my way. I didn't have a huge amount in common with some of them, apart from having chosen to do it. I'd hope that in twenty years time I might still be seeing something of Patsy and Susanna, who's no lightweight, and Sally.

I did find in a curious sort of way that the trek deepened my faith – just seeing the jungle, the sheer vastness of it, knowing that it was all there without any help from Man. A bit like Lough Derg in Ireland, it opened a window in life that confirms your faith, humbles you and makes you more aware of the presence of a greater being.

I don't regret having done it. It was the hardest thing I've ever done, but it hasn't changed me. I wouldn't do it again, though I would do a different one. I got on all right with everybody. I boarded at my convent, and I think you learn to live alongside other people, to understand that you have to wait your turn. At boarding school and in a big family, there's no such thing as 'your own space'. You can't be very private and that must make it easier to cope with this sort of expedition. But having said that, in the jungle, you can still find your own space - in your head.

Fiona, despite being probably the most practical woman on the trek, found the same.

When you're lying in the jungle, surrounded by it, listening to the sound of it, it's easy to think it's never going to end. So, once you've sorted out the business of survival, you find your mind opens and everything becomes much clearer.

But I also liked the real hard physical challenges. I loved the hard day on July the twentieth when we were really up against it. It gave me such a sense of achievement to get there.

Another aspect of the trip that pleased me was not being one of the organisers, which I usually am. It gave me a different perspective on it, a greater insight and stronger sense of direction.

Being the youngest woman on the trek wasn't really an issue. I did have the odd grump, and blow my top, but it never lasts. Once, when Catherine told me to do something, I turned to her and yelled, 'You're not my bloody mother!' A few minutes later, I was hugging her and saying, 'Sorry.'

For **Gwenda**, there were loads of tough moments, few of them enjoyable. Although she was one of the fitter women, she found carrying sixty pounds very daunting and didn't get used to it.

But before I went, I honestly didn't think I could do it. I didn't enjoy myself at all for the first few days at 230alpha. I missed the children like hell, I couldn't sleep properly and I kept thinking, 'Why the hell am I here?' But as the trek went on, I got better, and overcame my tendency to give up. Ken never doubted I'd make it, but the real incentive to keep going was the team. If I gave up, I wouldn't just be letting myself down, but all the others too. And that makes a big difference. Now, of course, I'm really glad I did it. It was the biggest challenge I've ever undertaken and it gave me a real sense of achievement. I also found the whole experience very liberating, so by the end of it, I was feeling like a confident, carefree twenty year old.

Patsy, as the official doctor in the group, had a substantially different role from the rest of the Janes. As far as she was concerned, this was a professional assignment. Inevitably this coloured her whole approach to the trip. There were other factors, too.

I've always thought the way to tackle any challenge was with sheer Kiwi grit and determination. But if I learned one thing from this expedition, it was the value of laughter, and the part it has to play in physical recovery.

Certainly, it's clear from all the Janes' accounts that a lot of laughter filled the jungle each night. They were all struck by how quickly they recovered after a gruelling day's trek, especially Alex, who would be on her knees one minute and performing at full volume ten minutes later. **Pasty** had some reservations about the way the laughter was generated.

I really couldn't be bothered to get drawn into totally trivial, silly conversations; I simply had no interest, and I preferred to take myself off to bed, even if I wasn't going to go to sleep. Having said that, I quite enjoyed the silliness from afar. I couldn't believe how many of them smoked, even on the move, and of course, that was anathema to me as a doctor. I did get rather irritated by Alex' struggles and histrionics because the problem was her own – she simply hadn't trained enough. If people thought I was punishing myself in some way by eating my silver bags cold, they were quite wrong. I'd decided from the start that I would have them cold, because it would save time waiting for water to boil; to some extent, it would save water, and anyway, they were designed to be eaten cold as well as hot, and I thought they were delicious like that. It is true though, that I wasn't happy about the presence of the cameras. But for no other reason than simply not wanting my private emotions filmed, edited and exposed for several million people to examine.

For me, one of the most striking aspects of the trip was the way that the women didn't try to compete. They were mature enough to help each other selflessly and showed consideration you wouldn't have expected. Before I went, I thought that the 'women are better team players' myth was overplayed. I'm not so sure now.

There is no doubt that Alex was the weak link in the Jungle Janes' chain. She demanded more than her share of attention and help, yet it was given freely by the team with very little display of resentment. In return, she did a lot to revive the spirits of the others when they were recovering at the end of each day.

In a sense, she really didn't deserve to finish the trek, but with the encouragement and agreement of the others, in return for her own special contribution, she did.

And, in celebration of this triumph of co-operation, **Alex** has the last word.

Why was it that this trek worked so well? It's a very difficult question to answer and I think if you asked some of the girls, they wouldn't be able to answer it either. I'd say it's due to a combination of a thousand different personal qualities, all coming together. We were very lucky that, although we were twelve strongly different personalities, we all had enormous respect for each other and each other's talents. Nor was there ever any competition between us. We weren't twenty five year olds or glamorous sort of ex-models; nobody tried to look better than anybody else; nobody ever tried to get up to the top of the hill before anybody else; nobody ever complained that they'd built the fire more than anybody else; or dug the latrine more than anybody else. We all just got stuck in together. We all learned how each other worked, so that we knew when people needed a bit of space. We knew when people were on the verge of tears that perhaps they didn't want to be hugged because it would make things even worse.

Having been in the acting world for many years, my whole life is geared around people's personalities and trying to understand them and I really feel that I have understood these girls and they have understood me. All our professional lives have been stripped away from us and we've become completely equal, in that we're just ordinary women who had a huge fight on their hands, but who, together as a team, coped extraordinarily well.

Why didn't we fight? Women are renowned for fighting, but we never fought once. I think that was because we were in an environment that didn't belong to us - where we were guests and we knew we had to live by a new set of rules. We were all on equal pegging.

If ever anybody was in any difficulty at all, which generally was me, I could feel the warmth and strength of the arms of all the other women pulling me up those hills, willing me to get there at the end. I don't know if there are many people in the world who could have created that amazing feeling of togetherness, but it's true to say that we were one heck of a team of women. And I'm proud to be part of this team; I'm proud to be a Jungle Jane and I wonder if I could have done it with anybody else. I wonder if I could have got up those hills without those faces looking down at me, willing me to get there with them. I wonder if I could have laughed so much with anyone else.

It must have been fate that we were all brought together. Some of us knew about this trek long before the others; some of us inspired other people to join it because we knew they were the right sort of girls to be on it.

What was it that made us all special enough to complete this mammoth odyssey?Why was it that we carried on and on until the bitter end? But it wasn't bitter at all – it was happy – it was so happy! It was a sort of miracle really.

Gosh, I'm proud to be a woman!

Speech made at the party at Sittang Camp at the end of the expedition: A Vote Of Thanks For Ken.

I would like to say a few words on behalf of The Janes... ... a task far more terrifying than anything I faced in the jungle.

I believe many people were fairly sceptical about our chances of surviving in the rainforests of Brunei for a month without something traumatic happening to at least one of us. A bunch of women over a certain age with very little experience of physical hardship seem unlikely candidates for such a venture. It was a triumphant moment therefore, to arrive back at Sittang to the news that there had been a sweep amongst the troops as to just how many would survive, and to be told a lot of money was owing.

There are some very good reasons why we proved the sceptics wrong. It shows what can be accomplished when a group of people have one common aim (ours was to go in together and come out together), a willingness to learn, a gutsy determination, and above all a sense of humour. Oh, and the ability to talk non-stop.

We also had a superb leader in Ken, whose idea this was in the first place for challenging himself to accompany twelve women into the jungle for a month without being forced to abandon them. He was, and is, our inspiration. And even at the end of a gruelling day summoned up the energy to check our well-being and even at times, became a one-man entertainment show.

Thank you Ken

Thank-you Letter from Dicky

Thursday August 10th

Dear Ken,

It has taken all this time to put pen to paper and I still don't know what to say! Thank you doesn't begin to cover it but it will have to do and I'm quite sure you understand. Our jungle month was without doubt the highlight of my whole life so far, the biggest adventure, the greatest challenge, (mental and physical), the best and the worst, the agony and and the ecstasy(?!), and all the extremes that one is capable of experiencing and I do thank you for letting me be a part of it all. Nothing will ever happen again quite like that and I feel really proud of myself and everyone else and you, to have been a member a unique team for one month in my life.

Needless to say, life has been pretty ghastly since, with everything going wrong!! New clutch in the car, washing machine broken, hoover blown up, Douglas moaning, dogs needing constant walks, children needing taxi service. I phoned Sally in desperation yesterday and she promptly burst into tears! She has sciatica… Please get our next trip organised quickly so we have something to look forward to!!!

You are an absolute star and seriously have my lifelong loyalty, admiration and love. Am off to dig a latrine in the orchard.

Lots of love,
Dicky

Ken's Final Word

The Ladies
Wherever you are!

August 2000

Just a quick note from me to say congratulations a huge 'well done' on the expedition. I hope it was what you thought it would be at the end of the day and I hope you feel a sense of fulfilment and peace. These trips are always far from easy and they bring peculiar pressures that are often unforeseen. Do not underestimate your achievement - you will be marvelled at for some time to come and in particular when the programme is televised. It was an amazing effort for both individual and team and you can take enormous pride in your endeavours and the fact that you trod paths that no other women (or men in some areas) have ever trod before. I am exceptionally proud of you all and to have had the privilege of leading you.

From my own point of view I found it bloody hard - no excuses here but just to let you know how I felt. As you well know I had the aspirations of three groups to cope with not just one and that took its toll. By the end of the march I was done for and maybe I didn't pace myself properly but I was utterly drained and it took me all my effort to make you blow up the rubber tubes (and deflate them!!) Behind the scenes there was perhaps the greatest pressure of all and that was to get you back to your loved ones in one piece with all your vital organs in place and not totally deranged. You were, in my opinion just about at the end of your tethers by the time we got the rafts downstream.

At that last camp I prayed hard that we would continue with our good fortune and that all branches would stay attached to resident trees and that all rotor blades would stay attached to helicopters! We were blessed with good luck. If at times I came across as abrupt or cross or both it was never anything personal, just the responsibility that comes with duty of care. You were in danger at all times and it was my responsibility to alleviate that threat, however I could without detracting from your ownership and leadership of the trip. Certain items may appear on TV that you don't like – I know Paul will make a good film but at times our frailty as humans will become evident. Try and take these things in your stride – any expedition has its pressure points and arguments and we all makes chumps of ourselves from time to time. Above all don't take things personally – it will be a reflection on what actually happened and how we coped with a massive undertaking into unknown territory both geographically and mentally.

Thank-you for all your kind letters and messages and I apologise for not writing sooner. Gwenda and I miss you all and in particular those campsite rituals that became such an important part of our lives – I feel our journey together is not over and there is another JJs to come – I am sure when you read this that even if it is only a trip to Centre Parks you will want to be there. My love and respect to you all – I leave you with one last quote.

The adventure – and it is the test of a good adventure – goes on, the same for every generation. It can lose nothing by time or repetition. The first sight of the sea, of the desert, of the jungle, or of a mountain, remains the first sight for each new child, and evokes afresh the same response. The passion for discovery, for the mastery of unknown difficulty, stays always the same.

Other Titles from TravellersEye

Desert Governess

Author: Phyllis Ellis

Editor: Gordon Medcalf

ISBN: 1903070015

R.R.P: £7.99

In 1997 badly in need of a new start in life, Phyllis answered an advertisement: *English Governess wanted for Prince and Princesses of Saudi Arabian Royal Family.* She soon found herself whisked off to the desert to look after the children of HRH Prince Muqrin bin Abdul Aziz al Saud, the King's brother. In this frank personal memoir Phyllis describes her sometimes risky reactions to her secluded, alien lifestyle in a heavily guarded marble palace, allowed out only when chaperoned, veiled and clad from head to foot in black.

Both as a Governess and as a modern western woman she constantly ran up against frustrating prohibitions and unexpected moral codes, only a few of which she could work her way around – usually in the interests of her young royal charges.

Discovery Road

Authors: Tim Garratt & Andy Brown

Editor: Dan Hiscocks

ISBN: 0953057534

R.R.P: £7.99

Their mission and dream was to cycle around the southern hemisphere of the planet, with just two conditions. Firstly the journey must be completed within 12 months, and secondly, the cycling duo would have no support team or backup vehicle, just their determination, friendship and pedal power.

"Readers will surely find themselves reassessing their lives and be inspired to reach out and follow their own dreams."

Sir Ranulph Fiennes, Explorer

Fever Trees of Borneo

Author: Mark Eveleigh

Editor: Gordon Medcalf

ISBN: 095357569

R.R.P: £7.99

This is the story of how two Englishmen crossed the remotest heights of central Borneo, using trails no western eye had seen before, in search of the legendary 'Wild Men of Borneo'. On the way they encounter shipwreck, malaria, amoebic dysentery, near starvation, leeches, exhaustion, enforced alcohol abuse and barbecued mouse-deer foetus.

"Mark has the kind of itchy feet which will take more than a bucket of Johnson's baby talc to cure… he has not only stared death in the face, he has poked him in the ribs and insulted his mother."

Observer

Frigid Women

Authors: Sue & Victoria Riches

Editor: Gordon Medcalf

ISBN:0953057526

R.R.P:£7.99

In 1997 a group of twenty women set out to become the world's first all female expedition to the North Pole. Mother and daughter, Sue and Victoria Riches were amongst them. Follow the expedition's adventures in this true life epic of their struggle to reach one of Earth's most inhospitable places, suffering both physical and mental hardships in order to reach their goal, to make their dream come true.

"This story is a fantastic celebration of adventure, friendship, courage and love. Enjoy it all you would be adventurers and dream on."

Dawn French

Riding with Ghosts

Author: Gwen Maka

Editor: Gordon Medcalf

ISBN: 1903070007

R.R.P: £7.99

This is the frank, often outrageous account of a forty-something Englishwoman's epic 4,000 mile cycle ride from Seattle to Mexico, via the snow covered Rocky Mountains. She travels the length and breadth of the American West, mostly alone and camping in the wild. She runs appalling risks and copes in a gutsy, hilarious way with exhaustion, climatic extremes, dangerous animals, eccentrics, lechers and a permanently saddle-sore bum.

We share too her deep involvement with the West's pioneering past, and with the strong, often tragic traces history has left lingering on the land.

Slow Winter

Author: Alex Hickman

Editor: Gordon Medcalf

ISBN: 0953057585

R.R.P: £7.99

Haunted by his late father's thirst for adventure Alex persuaded his local paper that it needed a Balkan correspondent. Talking his way into besieged Sarajevo, he watched as the city's fragile cease fire fell apart. A series of chance encounters took him to Albania and a bizarre appointment to the government. Thrown into an alliance with the country's colourful dissident leader, he found himself occupying a ringside seat as corruption and scandal spilled the country into chaos.

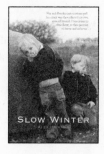

This is a moving story of one man's search for his father's legacy among the mountains and ruin of Europe's oldest, and most mysterious corner.

The Jungle Beat – fighting terrorists in Malaya
Author: Roy Follows
Editor: Dan Hiscocks

ISBN: 0953057577
R.R.P: £7.99

This book describes, in his own words, the experiences of a British officer in the Malayan Police during the extended Emergency of the 1950's. It is the story of a ruthless battle for survival against an environment and an enemy which were equally deadly. It ranks with the toughest and grimmest of the latter-day SAS adventures.

" It tells the story with no holds barred: war as war is. A compelling reminder of deep jungle operations."

General Sir Peter de la Billière

Touching Tibet
Author: Niema Ash
Editor: Dan Hiscocks

ISBN:0953057550
R.R.P:£7.99

After the Chinese invasion of 1950, Tibet remained closed to travellers until 1984. When the borders were briefly re-opened, Niema Ash was one of the few people fortunate enough to visit the country before the Chinese re-imposed their restrictions in 1987. *Touching Tibet* is a vivid, compassionate, poignant but often amusing account of a little known ancient civilisation and a unique and threatened culture.

"Excellent - Niema Ash really understands the situation facing Tibet and conveys it with remarkable perception."

Tenzin Choegyal (brother of The Dalai Lama)

Heaven & Hell

An eclectic collection of anecdotal travel stories – the best from thousands of entries to an annual competition. See website for details.

"…an inspirational experience. I couldn't wait to leave the country and encounter the next inevitable disaster." *The Independent*

Travellers' Tales from Heaven & Hell

Author: Various
Editor: Dan Hiscocks

ISBN: 0953057518
R.R.P: £6.99

More Travellers' Tales from Heaven & Hell

Author: Various
Editor: Dan Hiscocks

ISBN: 1903070023
R.R.P: £6.99

A Trail of Visions

Guide books tell you where to go, what to do and how to do it. A Trail of Visions shows and tells you how it feels.

"A Trail of Visions tells with clarity what it is like to follow a trail, both the places you see and the people you meet."

Independent on Sunday

"The illustrated guide."   The Times

Route 1: India, Sri Lanka, Thailand, Sumatra

Photographer / Author: Vicki Couchman
Editor: Dan Hiscocks   ISBN: 1871349338
                         R.R.P: £14.99

Route 2: Peru, Bolivia, Ecuador, Columbia

Photographer / Author: Vicki Couchman
Editor: Dan Hiscocks   ISBN: 093505750X
                         R.R.P: £16.99

TravellersEye Club Membership

Each month we receive hundreds of enquiries from people who've read our books or entered our competitions. All of these people have one thing in common: an aching to achieve something extraordinary, outside the bounds of our everyday lives. Not everyone can undertake the more extreme challenges, but we all value learning about other people's experiences.

Membership is free because we want to unite people of similar interests. Via our website, members will be able to liase with each other about everything from the kit they've taken, to the places they've been to and the things they've done. Our authors will also be available to answer any of your questions if you're planning a trip or if you simply have a question about their books.

As well as regularly up-dating members with news about our forthcoming titles, we will also offer you the following benefits:

Free entry to author talks / signings
Direct author correspondence
Discounts off new and past titles
Free entry to TravellersEye events
Discounts on a variety of travel products and services

To register your membership, simply write or email us telling us your name and address (postal and email). See address at the front of this book.

About TravellersEye

I believe the more you put into life, the more you get out of it. However, at times I have been disillusioned and felt like giving up on a goal because I have been made to feel that an ordinary person like me could never achieve my dreams.

The world is absolutely huge and out there for the taking. There has never been more opportunity for people like you and me to have dreams and fulfil them.

I have met many people who have achieved extraordinary things and these people have helped inspire and motivate me to try and live my life to the fullest.

TravellersEye publishes books about people who have done just this and we hope that their stories will encourage other people to live their dream.

When setting up TravellersEye I was given two pieces of advice. The first was that there are only two things I ever need to know: You are never going to know everything and neither is anyone else. The second was that there are only two things I ever need to do in life: Never give up and don't forget rule one.

Nelson Mandela said in his presidential acceptance speech:
"Our deepest fear is not that we are inadequate. Our deepest fear is that we are powerful beyond our measure... as we let our own light shine, we unconsciously give other people permission to do the same."

We want people to shine their light and share it with others in the hope that it may encourage them to do the same.

Dan Hiscocks

Managing Director of TravellersEye